GHOSTHUNTING
MARYLAND

AMERICA'S
HAUNTED ROAD TRIP

Titles in the *America's Haunted Road Trip* Series:

GHOSTHUNTING
MARYLAND

MICHAEL J. VARHOLA
AND
MICHAEL H. VARHOLA

CLERISY PRESS

Ghosthunting Maryland

Published by Clerisy Press
Distributed by Publishers Group West
Printed in the United States of America
First edition, second printing 2011

Library of Congress Cataloging-in-Publication Data

   Varhola, Michael J., 1966–
      Ghosthunting Maryland / by Michael J. Varhola and Michael H.
   Varhola; foreword by John Kachuba. -- 1st ed.
      p. cm. — (America's haunted road trip series)
   ISBN-13: 978-1-57860-351-0
   ISBN-10: 1-57860-351-X
   1. Ghosts—Maryland. I. Varhola, Michael H. II. Title.
   BF1472.U6V36 2009
   133.109752--dc22
                                 2009028969

Editor: John Kachuba
Cover design: Scott McGrew
All photos are courtesy of the authors, except the photos on pages 116, 136, 217, and 220, which are in the public domain.

Clerisy Press
PO Box 8874
Cincinnati, OH 45208-0874
www.clerisypress.com

TABLE OF CONTENTS

BALTIMORE CITY

Ghosts are believed to haunt several of the historic vessels berthed in Baltimore's Inner Harbor, including the wooden warship USS *Constellation*, the Coast Guard cutter USCGC *Taney*, the submarine USS *Torsk*, and the schooner *Pride of Baltimore II*. This chapter also takes a look at nearby Fort McHenry.

Many spirits, including that of Edgar Allan Poe, are believed to haunt the former bars, boarding houses, and bordellos of this once-rowdy seaport area that is now famed for its 120 bars and active nightlife.

Built in 1828, this 238-foot-tall ammunition manufacturing structure was the tallest building in the United States until the construction of the Washington Monument. Passersby frequently hear strange sounds coming from within the tower when no one is inside and it is widely reputed to be haunted.

Edgar Allan Poe is among the one thousand prominent Baltimoreans buried at this site, which dates to the eighteenth century, and his unquiet shade is among those that people have reported seeing walking its grounds on moonlit nights. This chapter also looks at the nearby house where the tormented author lived and worked.

CENTRAL 47

NATIONAL CAPITAL 79

SOUTHERN 189

His embittered ghost is believed to still dwell within the farmhouse where he and his family lived during the Civil War, and where he died fourteen years after President Andrew Johnson pardoned him in 1869.

The ghost of John Wilkes has Booth has, ironically, been spotted at nearly as many places as that of President Abraham Lincoln, most of them places he visited during the last few weeks of his life or those where his body lay following his death.

WESTERN

Site of the single bloodiest day of America's bloodiest conflict, during which more than twenty-two thousand casualties were inflicted, the shades of Civil War soldiers have long been seen marching across the fields where they were violently slain.

Home of "Blair Witch," Elly Kedward, who was banished in 1785 for witchcraft, this town has been the site of numerous ghost sightings over the years, particularly of Civil War soldiers killed in the nearby woods and hills.

For more than 140 years, people in the local area have held that this old Catholic church has been haunted by the shade of a Civil War soldier who was executed for killing his commanding officer.

Many ghosts are believed to haunt the homes and other buildings of one of Maryland's oldest cities, including Civil War patriot Barbara Fritchie and a German pacifist who was one of the only people ever to have been drawn and quartered in the United States.

Welcome to America's Haunted Road Trip

DO YOU BELIEVE IN GHOSTS?

If you are like 52 percent of Americans (according to a recent Harris Poll), you *do* believe that ghosts walk among us. Perhaps you have heard your name called in a dark and empty house. It could be that you have awoken to the sound of footsteps outside your bedroom door, only to find no one there. It is possible that you saw your grandmother sitting in her favorite rocker chair, the same grandmother who had passed away several years before. Maybe you took a photo of a crumbling, deserted farmhouse and discovered strange mists and orbs in the photo, anomalies that were not visible to your naked eye.

If you have experienced similar paranormal events, then you know that ghosts exist. Even if you have not yet experienced these things, you are curious about the paranormal world, the spirit realm. If you weren't, you would not now be reading this preface to the latest book in the *America's Haunted Road Trip* series from Clerisy Press.

Over the last several years, I have investigated haunted locations across the country, and with each new site, I found myself becoming more fascinated with ghosts. What are they? How do they manifest themselves? Why are they here? These are just a few of the questions I have been asking. No doubt, you have been asking the same questions.

The books in the *America's Haunted Road Trip* series can help you find the answers to your questions about ghosts. We've gathered together some of America's top ghost writers (no pun intended) and researchers and asked them to write about their states' favorite haunts. Each location that they write about is open to the public so that you can visit them for yourself and try out your ghosthunting skills. In addition to telling you about their often hair-raising adventures, the writers have included maps and travel directions so that you can take your own haunted road trip.

Mike Varhola's new book *Ghosthunting Maryland* proves that the "Old Line State" contains a lot of old ghosts. The book is a spine-tingling trip through Maryland's small towns, cities, and historic sites, from the shores of Chesapeake Bay to the Allegheny Mountains. Ride shotgun with Mike as he seeks out Civil War ghosts at the Antietam and Monocacy battlefields. Travel with him to Edgar Allan Poe's house in Baltimore where a ghost—perhaps that of the macabre writer himself—taps visitors on the shoulder. Come aboard as he stalks the spirits of long-dead seamen on the eighteenth-century warship USS *Constellation*. And who belongs to the disembodied voice that whispers "I'm sitting right here" in Gabriel's Inn? Hang on tight; *Ghosthunting Maryland* is a scary ride.

But once you've finished reading this book, don't unbuckle your seatbelt. There are still forty-nine states left for your haunted road trip! See you on the road!

John Kachuba
Editor, America's Haunted Road Trip

GHOSTHUNTING
MARYLAND

AMERICA'S
HAUNTED ROAD TRIP

Introduction

"THERE ARE MORE THINGS IN HEAVEN and earth," Shakespeare wrote in his play *Hamlet*, "than are dreamt of in your philosophy." One of my guiding principles has long been that incisive phrase spoken by Hamlet to his friend Horatio (while holding a skull, no less). In short, there are countless things in this world that cannot be adequately explained by any single conventional system of beliefs. This book, and the America's Haunted Road Trip series of travel guides in general, are devoted to exploring sites where inexplicable things of a haunted nature are believed to occur, and to helping people who are so inclined to visit them.

Ghosthunting Maryland is, in fact, a travel guide and the primary criterion for inclusion in it is whether or not a place is publicly accessible. This book is a collaboration between me and my father, Michael H. Varhola, who wrote five of the chapters—those about Ellicott City, Fells Point, Gabriel's Inn, Historic Frederick, and the Schifferstadt—and contributed to a number of other sections in it.

While visiting the sites described in this book we conducted varying degrees of paranormal investigation, sometimes in conjunction with individual ghosthunters or groups of them and sometimes on our own. At no point, however, did we personally endeavor to perform a "full investigation" conforming to the standards of any particular organization. After all, the point of this book is to tell people about promising sites to visit, give them the information they need to do so, and then let them enjoy the sites as they see fit.

GHOSTHUNTING IN MARYLAND

Maryland is home to an absolutely amazing number of reputedly haunted places and, suffice it to say, is fertile ground for ghosthunters and contains no shortage of potential venues for investigation. To say that this book could have a hundred chapters devoted to publicly accessible haunted sites would be a marked understatement, and to say that it could have a thousand if private venues were also included would not be inaccurate. Distilling all of the possible choices into a mere thirty chapters was not the smallest challenge associated with this project. That was, of course, one of the incentives for including an appendix of Additional Haunted Sites for anyone who is interested.

Maryland is divided into six regions for purposes of this book: Baltimore, Central, D.C. Metro, Eastern Shore, Southern, and Western. Geographically, Maryland is not a large state. It is, however, among the oldest in the country, and has a rich, varied, and turbulent history that has contributed to an exceptionally high number of haunted sites. It also contains a variety of communities and landscapes, from some of the busiest metropolitan areas in the country to sparsely populated rural locales, and from mountainous terrain in the west to extensive areas of shoreline in the east and south.

Because it is relatively compact, Maryland is in many ways an ideal state for a haunted road trip—especially in an era of historically high gasoline prices—and many haunted sites within the same area can easily be reached on a single weekend-long trip by people visiting from other areas. For those living almost anywhere in Maryland itself, a great many sites, even more than one at a time, can be visited on day trips.

As with my previous book, *Ghosthunting Virginia*, my earliest research revealed a striking number of sites reputed by various sources to be haunted. With space in this volume for only a limited number of these, my co-author and I have carefully attempted to identify a representative selection that both emphasized variety and a struck a balance between "must include" sites—such as the graveyard where Edgar Allan Poe is buried—as well as lesser-known ones that do not appear in any other books.

Several people, places, and themes peculiar to Maryland and its history emerged while we were working on the various chapters in this book. These include the state's Colonial era, the War of 1812, the Civil War, the B&O Railroad, Edgar Allan Poe, and Francis Scott Key, among others, all significant elements in the state's normal and haunted histories. Ghosthunters can plan itineraries based on one or more of these themes (e.g., visiting sites along the route of the B&O Railroad, visiting sites associated with the war of 1812).

My own connection to Maryland goes back nearly four decades, to when my family moved to the Old Line State when I was three, and I have both lived there and visited sites throughout the state off and on since then. This, combined with the degree in journalism I earned at the University of Maryland in College Park, has played a large part in inspiring me to write this book. My father and co-author has, likewise, spent much of his life in the state, and has resided in it for many years.

PARANORMAL PHENOMENA

Prospective ghosthunters who visit enough sites should expect to eventually experience various sorts of paranormal phenomena. These might range from anomalies in photographs or recordings—which I have experienced fairly consistently in my fieldwork—to more profound and much rarer phenomena like apparitions, disembodied sounds such as footsteps and voices, and the like.

Ghosthunting Maryland is my second contribution to the America's Haunted Road trip series and follows my *Ghosthunting Virginia*. When my editors asked me to write that book, they knew me to be an established author of nonfiction books; to have a strong background in history, research, and fieldwork; and to have lived in the Washington, D.C., metropolitan area, with easy access to both Virginia and Maryland. They had no way of knowing that I'd had an abiding interest in the paranormal for some thirty years, nor indeed, that I had been a "ghosthunter" some years before that term would have meant anything to most people.

Ghosthunting as a pursuit has come into its own over the past few years and has been the subject of numerous television shows and movies. In my experience, however, real ghosthunting bears little resemblance to what is depicted even in "reality" shows related on the subject. The real thing is generally much less manic, a lot quieter, and—despite the absence of noise, running back and forth, and jerky camera angles—much more intense. It also does not result in evidence of haunting on every expedition, or even most of them.

Many ghosthunters today use a wide variety of electronic equipment, and there can certainly be some value associated with this approach. One of the main purposes of using such devices, however, is for purposes of "proving" the existence of various paranormal phenomena to other people. While there is certainly nothing wrong with this, I would encourage prospective ghosthunters to question the premise that substantiating anything is of primary importance and decide for themselves how ghosthunting best meets their needs; my own belief is that this activity should be much more about personal fulfillment, rather than trying to prove things to people who have probably already made up their minds as to whether or not ghosts are real.

I do not believe anyone should hesitate to engage in ghosthunting based on a lack of equipment, and am myself much more of a "naturalistic" ghosthunter. For various reasons, I use a minimum of equipment in my investigations and not much more than I have ever used as a writer and reporter: a micro-cassette recorder and/or an MP3 player, a digital camera, a pen and notepad, and a flashlight. I have also found a full tank of gas and some food and water to be useful when heading into isolated areas.

I also think a ghosthunter's innate senses are just as critical to an investigation as any sort of equipment. While I make no claims here to be a "psychic investigator," I do believe that most people have access to certain paranormal senses that they can draw upon if they choose to and are aware of them. People who can use such abilities reliably, of course, have generally spent many years honing them and learning to differentiate exterior phenomena from internal thoughts and other sensations. People without such experience should probably err on the side of caution and, in the absence of corroborating evidence, acknowledge that whatever they are "sensing" could very well be nothing but the products of their imaginations.

All other things aside, a good attitude is crucial in ghost-hunting. While the following chapters include a lot of information that can be useful when visiting the specific sites, there is one bit of general advice I would like to offer to ghosthunters: show respect for both the rights of any relevant living people (i.e., property owners) and for the dignity of any spirits that might be lingering at a particular site.

In any event, ghosthunting is an endeavor fraught with its own potential hazards, and my sense is that anyone who acts inappropriately for too long is ultimately going to suffer some unhappy consequences—whether legal, spiritual, or otherwise. And while the capacity of ghosts to visit various misfortunes upon people is limited, but if it is at all possible to call them down on oneself, this sort of behavior is probably the way to do it. A "ghosthunter's code of conduct" that provides guidelines about what sorts of behavior people should or should not engage in while conducting investigations is long overdue and has increasingly become a subject of interest to me.

Determining exactly what ghosts are is beyond the scope of this book, and throughout it terms like "ghost," "phantasm," "specter," and "spirit" are used fairly synonymously and are not intended as technical terms indicating manifestations with specific and differing characteristics. This is, after all, primarily a travel guide, not a tome devoted to the classification of earthbound spirits, which would be of little practical use to most readers.

That said, the term "ghosts" runs the gamut from nonsentient residues of spiritual energy—residual haunting—that can be detected by various means or even seen by some people under certain conditions, to intelligent manifestations that can make their presences felt in various ways. My sense is that the vast majority of hauntings are of the lower order and that it is quite possible to have subtly haunted sites that are never identified as such due to a lack of investigation.

One thing I have encountered while investigating potentially haunted places is the phenomena commonly known as "orbs," which are sometimes captured in digital photographs. No one can be involved with ghosthunting for too long without stumbling across the ongoing debate over these spherical objects and what they might be. Some people believe orbs are manifestations of spiritual energy. Others—including many veteran ghosthunters—dismiss these phenomena for various reasons (e.g., because they are trying to adhere to standards of particular groups or television shows).

I am definitely of the former school of thought. In short, in the years since I have been using a digital camera, I have taken tens of thousands of pictures under all sorts of conditions. Of all those pictures, the only ones that have displayed orbs are ones I have taken at just a dozen or so locations, all of them reputed to be haunted. To me, these phenomena are compelling evidence of what I believe to be some sort of spiritual energy and a hallmark of haunted sites.

That said, all of the sites covered in this book are reputed to be haunted, I am willing to go on the record as saying that I believe any of them could be, and am firmly convinced that several of them definitely are. But the point of this book is not for me to convince anybody of anything. It is, rather, to provide a tool ghosthunters can use to help them find haunted sites, conduct their own investigations, and draw their own conclusions. I wish you the best of luck and look forward to hearing from you as you conduct your own visits to the sites listed in this book!

Michael J. Varhola
Silver Spring, Maryland

Baltimore City

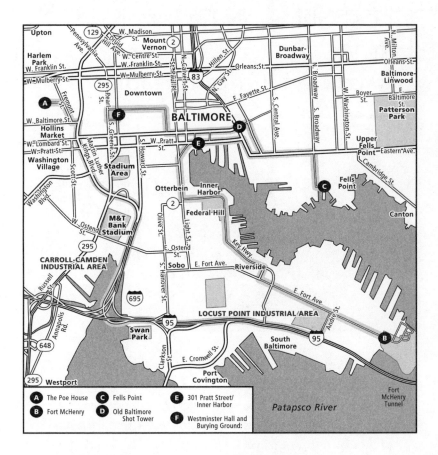

Baltimore/Inner Harbor
Ghost Ships of the Inner Harbor

Baltimore/Jonestown Neighborhood
Old Baltimore Shot Tower

Fells Point (Southeast Baltimore)
Edgar Allan Poe & Guests

West Baltimore
Westminster Hall Burying Ground

CHAPTER 1

Ghost Ships of the Inner Harbor

BALTIMORE/INNER HARBOR

USS *Torsk* is believed by some to be haunted by the ghost of a sailor drowned while trying to get back into the submarine before it submerged.

... these sites are usually inhabited by the spirits of those who died tragically aboard the vessel. Generally, the ghosts aboard follow many of the same rules of their haunted house cousins, although they usually haunt much smaller venues and must restrict their activities considerably. In addition, [they] seem to possess a uniform sadness.

—W. Haden Blackman, *The Field Guide to North American Hauntings*

INNUMERABLE VESSELS have passed through Baltimore harbor over the more than three centuries that the city has served as one of the most important ports in North America. Some of these have come to stay for good and, like historic buildings, have been restored and can today be visited at Baltimore's Inner Harbor. Also like historic buildings, a great many of them—all storied vessels and in several cases veterans of combat in foreign seas or other harrowing action—have ghost stories associated with them. And many of them, even those that are not "officially" occupied by ghosts, participate in "haunted ship" events around Halloween.

I most recently visited the Inner Harbor and its haunted vessels in June 2009, with my friend Brendan Cass and his mother Susan Cass. That was by no means my first time, however, and ever since I first visited Baltimore as a child nearly four decades ago, and as the various ships have come and gone, I have increasingly come to know them and the ghosts that haunt them.

USS CONSTELLATION

Perhaps the most haunted ship in the Inner Harbor—also, probably not coincidentally, the oldest—is USS *Constellation*. Just how old is not entirely clear, however, and a passionate debate has raged for years over whether the ship actually dates to the late eighteenth century or the mid-nineteenth century. Some explanation is in order.

In 1797, the U.S. Navy launched USS *Constellation*—its first ship with that name—a 1,265-ton frigate built in Baltimore that was 164 feet long, 41 feet wide, with a draft of 13 feet, 6 inches, a crew of 340, and armament consisting of thirty-eight twenty-four-pound long guns. For more than five decades, this vessel served the United States around the world, participating in missions throughout the waters of Africa, South America, the West Indies, the East Indies, Hawaii, and the Mediterranean. USS *Constellation* was, in fact, one of the ships that carried U.S. Marines "to the shores of Tripoli" in North Africa in 1805. It was active in several wars, defeating a number of powerful warships in the 1798–1800 Quasi-War with France and participating in the Barbary Wars, the Seminole Wars, and the War of 1812. By 1853, it had reached the end of its useful service, and it was dismantled at the Navy Yard in Norfolk, Virginia. Its name, however, was never stricken from Navy records.

That year, the Navy began construction of a slightly larger sloop-of-war that apparently incorporated elements of USS *Constellation* and was underwritten in part with funds allocated to rebuild the earlier vessel. Commissioned as USS *Constellation* in 1854, this fourteen-hundred-ton ship was 179 feet long, 41 feet wide, had a draft of 21 feet, and carried a crew of 240 and armaments consisting of sixteen eight-inch shell guns and four thirty-two-pound pivot guns. It served in actions off the coasts of Spain, Cuba, the Congo, and Turkey, and fought in the Civil War, against Confederate commerce raiders in the Mediterra-

USS *Constellation* is haunted by the spirits of several former members of its crew.

nean and blockade runners in the West Indies and along the Atlantic coast of the southern United States. Used in various training and ceremonial roles in the decades following the Civil War, USS *Constellation* was finally decommissioned in 1933—but was briefly and incredibly returned to service as an admiral's relief flagship during World War II!

Decommissioned for the final time in 1955, USS *Constellation* was moved to Baltimore. Over the following decade, it was restored to . . . the appearance of the original 1797 vessel. This, perhaps more than anything, has contributed to the controversy over the provenance of the ship. Thereafter, it served as an off-and-on historic attraction, but lack of funding meant that it was frequently too decrepit to be on public display or for people to board. Since 1999, the ship has been berthed at the Inner Harbor and is now seaworthy, being periodically sailed to nearby ports like Annapolis, Maryland—where it has served as a floating museum.

In the years following its decommissioning, USS *Constellation* has increasingly gained a public reputation for being strongly haunted, especially following a famous investigation by ghosthunter Hans Holzer. Ghosts from both incarnations of the vessel have been identified in these endeavors.

But the haunted history of USS *Constellation* actually begins much earlier, and starts no later than June 20, 1863, during the Civil War, as indicated by an entry in the diary of Moses Safford, the ranking staff petty officer on board at that time.

According to Safford, cook's mate Ike Simmons had begun telling people that two sailors who had recently died on board the ship had appeared before him and begun dancing and singing. This had a disturbing effect upon many of the other crewmen and the captain had Simmons locked up in the ship's brig. But other sailors had similar experiences.

"Twice on stormy nights last fall, Campbell, the captain of

the forecastle, whom we lost in the Atlantic, was supposed to have been seen standing near the lee cathead," Safford wrote in his journal. "Whatever may be the explanation of these phenomena, the sentences which Simmons has received will tend to discourage the men from giving undue publicity to their supernatural observations."

Since this early account—and especially since the vessel was put on public display—many more episodes of paranormal phenomena have been reported on board USS *Constellation* and a number of specific ghosts identified.

One of these is Commodore Thomas Truxtun, a career naval officer who was the first commander of USS *Constellation* and who led it to glory in the Quasi-War with France. That was the pinnacle of his more-than-thirty years of service, and soon thereafter he retired under less than desirable circumstances. And so, while conventional accounts suggest his spirit haunts the vessel as the result of his brutal nature, it seems much more likely that he spent his best and happiest years upon USS *Constellation* and has thus simply been unwilling to leave it.

It may be that the first sighting of Truxtun occurred in 1955, by U.S. Navy personnel assigned to a vessel berthed alongside USS *Constellation*. One night at 11:59, an officer on board that vessel took a blurry picture of an apparition that looks like it may be Truxtun and the *Baltimore Sun* ran it soon thereafter. The haunting was now a matter of public record.

Over the years, what appears to be Truxtun's shade has been seen numerous times by many people, one of the most famous episodes occurring in 1964 and involving a Catholic priest who reported interacting with it.

Another ghost who has been identified on board by paranormal investigators is that of Neil Harvey, a sailor who is believed to have fallen asleep while on watch and been summarily sentenced to death by his captain—Commodore Truxtun. The means of Harvey's death varies from story to story, but in the most widespread one he was tied across the muzzle of a cannon and blown to bits.

Yet another ghost who has been identified on USS *Constellation* is that of a young ship's boy, who some investigators claim was stabbed to death by two sailors for unknown reasons.

A number of other named ghosts have been identified on board USS *Constellation* over the years. Beyond full and partial apparitions of various sorts, just about every other sort of paranormal phenomena has also been reported on board the historic vessel over the years, including orbs and phantasmal sounds.

With little doubt, USS *Constellation* is the most haunted vessel at Baltimore's Inner Harbor. It is by no means, however, the only one to have paranormal phenomena associated with it, and several others have gained similar reputations.

USCGC *TANEY*

Launched in 1936, U.S. Coast Guard Cutter *Taney* is notable as being the last ship afloat that fought at Pearl Harbor during the surprise Japanese attack on Hawaii in 1941. That alone would warrant it having a few ghosts aboard, but its period of active service continued for many more years and the vessel was not decommissioned until 1986. USCGC *Taney* also served as command ship at the Battle of Okinawa and as a fleet escort in the Atlantic and Mediterranean during World War II, interdicted enemy supplies during the Vietnam War, patrolled in support of drug interdiction and fisheries protection, and joined in the search for lost aviator Amelia Earhart.

In chatting with people who work around the Inner Harbor, we learned that after USS *Constellation*, USCGC *Taney* is the local vessel with the greatest reputation for being haunted. Many staff of the vessel and visitors alike—especially those participating in overnight programs—have reported constantly

USCGC *Taney*, the last ship afloat that fought at Pearl Harbor, is believed to be one of the most haunted vessels at the Inner Harbor.

catching movement out of the corners of their eyes when aboard and seeing spectral forms gliding across its decks and past its open hatchways.

USS TORSK

This submarine had a phantasmal reputation long before any ghosts were seen onboard and was known during World War II as the "Galloping Ghost of the Japanese Coast," where it preyed on enemy vessels. Commissioned in 1944, USS *Torsk* was active during the last year of the war and holds the distinction of destroying with its torpedoes the last Japanese warship sunk in World War II. It served thereafter primarily as a training vessel until 1971 and was brought to Baltimore and turned into a museum ship in 1972. During its career, USS *Torsk* set an all-time record for dives, a total of 11,884.

That record did not come without a price, however, and one of the tragedies associated with *Torsk's* service involved a sailor who was left on deck when the submarine was forced to submerge. He reportedly drowned while trying to get back into the diving vessel and, since then, there have been people who believe his desperate spirit haunts the top deck of USS *Torsk*, forever trying to get back into it.

PRIDE OF BALTIMORE II

Another ship in the Inner Harbor that has a reputation for being haunted is *Pride of Baltimore II*, an authentic reproduction of a nineteenth-century clipper topsail schooner that sails around the world as a goodwill ambassador for the city of Baltimore. Its predecessor, the *Pride of Baltimore*, was sunk in 1986 in a legendary white squall in the waters north of Puerto Rico, claiming the lives of four crew members, including Captain Armin Elsaesser.

Today, a monument at the Inner Harbor memorializes these four, who also include Engineer Vincent Lazarro, Carpenter Barry Duckworth, and Seaman Nina Schack. Some people also claim that the spirits of these four former crew members of the Pride of Baltimore now haunt the decks and cabins of *Pride of Baltimore II*, possibly with the benign intent of helping those who have followed in their footsteps.

There are numerous other historic vessels operating in the water in and around the Inner Harbor, including lightships, tugboats, and the unique local vessels known as skipjacks, and many of them also have fascinating stories associated with them—and reputations for being haunted by the ghosts of former crewmen.

Spotlight on Ghosts: Fort McHenry

Just across the Inner Harbor is Fort McHenry, the object of the battle immortalized in Francis Scott Key's *The Star-Spangled Banner*, America's national anthem. A symbol of freedom when it prevented British invasion during the War of 1812, the fort came to represent oppression to many pro-Southern Marylanders when the Federal government occupied it and used it to help maintain its grip over the local area during the Civil War.

With such history and passions associated with Fort McHenry, it should not be too surprising that it has also long had a reputation for being one of the most haunted sites in a very haunted city. Over the years, all sorts of paranormal activity have been reported at Fort McHenry, including sightings of spectral figures on its earthen ramparts, disembodied voices, footsteps in empty areas, spots of unnatural cold, and furniture that levitates and otherwise moves around. Some investigators have even postulated that the fort's shape—that of a five-pointed star—has some occult significance and might play a role in the preponderance of supernatural events that have occurred at the site.

A number of specific ghost stories have also been associated with the site and recounted in numerous articles, television shows, and Internet postings.

One of these involves the ghost of U.S. Army Lieutenant Levi Clagett, who, along with some of his men, was killed when a bomb burst not in the air but in their gun emplacement. Numerous people have seen walking along the top of the star point sometimes known as "Clagett's Bastion" both a spectral figure and a man dressed in a uniform appropriate to the period at times when no costumed people were present in the fort.

Another named ghost associated with the site is that of Private John Drew, a soldier who was reportedly confined in one of the fort's cells after he was caught sleeping while on guard duty and who, in shame, killed himself. His specter has been seen both in his cell and on the ramparts where he walked his last post, forever trying to correct the mistake that ended his military career and his life.

Some of the most dramatic paranormal events at the fort involve attacks on people by what has been variously described as a woman, a white figure, and an invisible entity that has reportedly done such things as push some people down stairs and knock others unconscious. Some believe this spirit is that of the wife of a noncommissioned officer assigned to the fort whose children died during an epidemic in the 1820s.

One ghosthunting group that recently visited the site and experienced things there is Maryland Tri-State Paranormal. Founder Ana Bruder told me that while they were there, her friend Laura suddenly said, "I feel like I am being watched." Ana, who is sensitive to the presence of spirits, turned and saw the ghost of a uniformed soldier staring at her friend, just one of several spirits she detected while at the site.

Numerous other ghost stories and episodes of paranormal activity have also been associated with the site.

Many of the accounts of ghostly activity at Fort McHenry were originally reported by park rangers assigned to the site, and that remained the case up until a couple of decades ago. Today, however, in what they say is an effort to keep the site from being regarded as a "haunted fort" and to instead emphasize the nonsupernatural history of the National Monument and Historic Shrine, the managers of Fort McHenry decline to directly comment on phenomena that are still regularly reported by visitors.

Potential ghosthunters should also expect to have anything they ask to do at the site be curtailed by red tape. A favored tactic at Fort McHenry is to require application of a "special use permit" for anything its managers don't really want people to do—the major exception to this being, it would seem, historic reenactment, for which the site has become a virtual playground. The important thing to remember is that the site is public property and that very little of what is involved in most investigations should actually require any sort of permission anyway.

CHAPTER 2

Fells Point

Southeast Baltimore

The Horse You Came in On, a historic saloon frequented by Edgar Allan Poe, is one of many reputed to be haunted in the Fells Point neighborhood of Baltimore.

We have lots of different sorts of hauntings. Some people we think we know. Some we've no idea. And some we've raised glasses with ourselves. People we know have come back and haunted the pubs we saw them in when they were alive.

—Leanna Foglia, Baltimore Ghost Tours

BARS, BORDELLOS, AND BOARDING HOUSES. Those were the three "Bs" that were the hallmark of Maryland's rowdiest seaport in the eighteenth century. That is where the action was and, not surprisingly, that is where ghosts are today, in the buildings that once housed those establishments. Many of those bars are now cozy pubs but they still harbor spirits, some dating back to Fells Point's earliest days and others quite recent. Whether old or new, however, the spirits all have one thing in common: their attachment to this unique area was such that they were reluctant to move on and cross over.

Today, Fells Point is a neighborhood of Baltimore, but once it was a notorious town in its own right. Thanks to its charming waterfront location, its well-preserved Colonial-era row houses, and its narrow cobblestone streets, the once unruly seaport has been "discovered" and is well along in the process of gentrification.

Fells Point was founded in 1730 by its namesake, William Fell, who was drawn to the location by its deep water and proximity to agriculture and thick forests. It soon became a shipbuilding and commercial center. About 1763, William's son Edward Fell laid out streets and began selling plots for homes. The town grew quickly and in 1797 incorporated with Baltimore Town and Jones Town to form the City of Baltimore. The area grew wealthy on the tobacco, flour, and coffee trades through the eighteenth and nineteenth centuries.

The history of Fells Point is intertwined with some of the most significant events in America's history and some of the first vessels commissioned for the U.S. Navy were built in Fells Point shipyards. They included the USS *Constellation*, built in 1797 and now moored nearby at Baltimore's Inner Harbor. (See the separate chapter in this book on this haunted and historic vessel.) Ultimately, however, the town became best known for producing topsail schooners—known incorrectly as Baltimore clippers—which were justly renowned for their great speed and maneuverability. During the War of 1812, they were frequently used as privateer vessels to prey upon British shipping. They had a deadly effect on the British, but ultimately brought retribution and a unique humiliation to the young United States.

Armed with Letters of Marque and Reprisal issued by Congress, these privateers—many sailing out of Fells Point—captured or sank some seventeen hundred British merchant vessels during the three-year conflict. For the American skippers and their crews, this was both a patriotic contribution to the war effort and a lucrative financial venture. Each ship taken was a prize to be sold. For the British, this became intolerable.

Finally, in retaliation, the British launched the Chesapeake Campaign in 1814 with the expressed purpose of "cleaning out that nest of pirates in Baltimore." Their goal was to shut down the shipyards at Fells Point and halt the production of the deadly "Baltimore clippers." Unfortunately for our new nation, the British, on their way up the Chesapeake Bay, managed to capture and sack Washington, D.C.—and in the process burn both the Capitol and the White House.

The vengeful redcoats then continued up the Bay, with the goal of capturing Baltimore and Fells Point by way of a combined land and naval attack. They failed on both fronts. Their ground forces were decimated by the Maryland militia at North Point, while the guns at Fort McHenry, strategically placed at the mouth of Baltimore harbor, prevented the British fleet from entering it. (See the separate chapter in this book on this historic redoubt and the ghosts that haunt it.)

Fort McHenry withstood a ferocious twenty-five-hour naval bombardment on September 12 and 13, 1814. It was during this bombardment that Maryland lawyer and poet, Francis Scott Key, was able to see "by the dawn's early light" the huge "star-spangled banner" still flying over the fort. It's well known that his poem became our national anthem. What is less well known is the role that Fells Point played in prodding the British to attack Fort McHenry in the first place. Quite simply, without Fells Point and its deadly clippers, there would have been no attack on Fort McHenry and there would thus have been no "Star-Spangled Banner."

One can sense that history in the Fells Point of today—and, indeed, it should not be surprising that such a feisty population would produce more than its share of ghosts. Nor should it be surprising that a disproportionate number of these ghosts would be found in the places that sailors and shipbuilders frequented, namely bars and pubs, of which Fells Point still has a remarkable number—about 120. Many of these have their roots in the eighteenth century.

Some, like the Wharf Rat and the Horse You Came In On, were frequented by none other than Edgar Allan Poe. The poet is interred at the nearby Westminster Burying Ground but, many locals maintain, his spirit is not there, but can instead sometimes be seen in the wee hours swaying unsteadily down Thames Street, making his way from the Wharf Rat to the Horse. (See, however, the chapter in this book on the fascinating Westminster Hall and Burying Ground.) In fact, some believe, Poe haunts the Horse in particular. It is the custom there at closing to appease his spirit by setting out for him a glass of cognac, his favorite drink. In the morning the glass is found empty, washed and put away. So if you have a cognac there, you may be drinking out of the very glass that Poe sipped from the night before.

Fells Point today, as in Poe's day, has an active nightlife. With plenty of live music, walkable streets, and friendly locals, it is easy to see why some spirits became so attached to their local "haunts" that they have not been willing to move on. Some pubs, like the venerable Bertha's, famous for its mussels, have dozens of ghosts—or so we were told by our guide, Leanna Foglio.

Indeed, the best introduction to Fells Point ghost life is the ghost tour. Actually, there are two run by Baltimore Ghost Tours— the Ghost Walk and the Pub Walk. We did the Ghost Walk and were so impressed that we will definitely go back for the other.

The tours are the brain children of Amy Lynwander and Melissa "Missy" Rowell. It was, in fact, Missy's personal encounter with a ghost soon after moving to Fells Point that stimulated the interest that led these friends to do the research that ultimately resulted in the tour.

Missy had dropped into the Cat's Eye Pub on Thames Street to buy a souvenir T-shirt for her father, who had visited the pub some years earlier and had asked her to pick one up for him. The bartender at the Cat's Eye was a tall, thin man, who bore a striking resemblance to Abraham Lincoln, and turned out to be a font of knowledge about Fells Point. He had been there for years, and he knew where to go and who to know. There were few customers, so Missy ordered a drink and listened attentively as he filled her in on what made her new neighborhood interesting and unique. After about half an hour, the conversation died. Missy picked out a shirt, paid, got her change, and left, feeling really good as she exited the building and stepped back into the sunlight. Directly across the street she could see the old immigration building, which she now knew was where the TV series *Homicide: Life on the Street* had been filmed.

"Wow!" she thought to herself. "My neighborhood is so cool."

In the two years after that, Missy encountered so many ghosts in her little house on Bethel Street that she decided to ask other people if they had experienced similar things.

"Do you have a ghost? Do you have a ghost?" she went around asking. "Because I have a ghost," she explained. Well, everybody had ghosts. That's when she got together with her friend, Amy, and they decided to do the research that resulted in the tour. In the process, she went back to the Cat's Eye Pub, both because they had heard about the "junkie" ghosts there and because she had a contact there, the bartender who seemed to know everything and everybody in Fells Point. This time, however, there was a woman behind the bar. Missy asked her about the tall, thin bartender she had met there two years earlier, the one who looked like Abe Lincoln.

"You mean him?" the woman replied, pointing at a picture on the wall.

Missy nodded.

"That's Jeff," the woman replied. "He died about eight years ago."

"But I talked to him," Missy protested.

"He's dead," she insisted. "Now what would you like to drink?"

The spookiest thing, Missy explained later, was not that she had actually talked to a ghost, but that he had given her change. Who would think? A ghost that not only converses but also gives change!

Leanna recounted many such stories as she led our group from one haunted site to another. She threw herself into her role, and breathed life, so to speak, into the local ghosts. At Duda's Tavern she told us about "Doc," the polka-loving tenant, who, although long dead, still expects the jukebox to carry his favorite songs— and has caused it to play them even if they are not loaded into it! And at the Wharf Rat, we heard the sad story of John Rakowsky, its proud immigrant owner, who had been senselessly murdered on July 20, 1907, by an enraged patron. Even today, Rakowsky returns to his beloved pub to wipe the tables and watch over the establishment he loved so much in life.

She also took us to the site of William Fells' grave. William had a grandson, also named William, whose life had been cut short in its prime, at the age of twenty-seven. Locals report that late at night the younger William, well-dressed and handsome, can still be seen walking along Shakespeare Street apparently coming from Market Street, where his favorite pub was located. As he approaches the grave site, he turns, walks through the cast iron fence, approaches the grave marker, and suddenly disappears.

Leanna also advised us on what may be an effective tactic for dealing with troublesome ghosts. At Leadbetter's Tavern, there once lived a man who was quite abusive to his wife and teenage son—so abusive, in fact, that his son was ultimately driven to shoot him. His angry and confused spirit still haunts the apartment above Leadbetter's, terrorizing the bartenders and their girlfriends who have lived there.

Interestingly, it was a witch who provided the solution to the situation. She explained to them that there is nothing that ghosts like better than presents, and that the present they like the most is, of all things, Brach's peppermint candy, the red-and-white-striped confection often found in bowls at the checkout counters of family restaurants. Why this particular type of candy would be so desired by ghosts is unclear, but it worked. The bartenders set out several pieces in a small bowl where the ghost was sure to find it. After a few days, they found a piece that was pink, as if somebody had licked it. That somebody had to have been the ghost—because the candy was still in its cellophane wrapper!

The tour ended in the square in front of Bertha's Restaurant & Bar. Beneath this plaza, we learned, there was once a mass grave, dug for the victims of the yellow fever outbreak that had devastated Baltimore some two hundred years earlier. While the remains of the victims have been mostly removed, Leanna said the square is still a source of psychic activity.

Bertha's, in any event, is one of the most psychically active places in Fells Point. It is actually composed of three buildings, each with its own unique history. Leanna pointed out the spot of the greatest spiritual activity, in the second building going back from Market Street. On the landing going up to the second floor, patrons sometimes encounter the lady in the gray cloak. She is mostly a skeleton with two eyeballs but, according to legend, is clad in a lovely gray cloak. She is reputed to follow patrons up the stairs and then suddenly disappear.

The ladies' restroom on that floor is also filled with psychic energy, possibly emanating from the storeroom across the hall. There is so much ghostly activity associated with that storeroom, Leanna said, that employees are required to sign an agreement as a condition of employment that they will not enter it alone. Inevitably, of course, one did, Leanna said, and was promptly terrified by a ghost—and was then fired for having violated the prohibition against going into the problem area by himself.

The tour being over, we decided to have a beer in Bertha's bar. Leanna was already there, seated at the bar and enjoying a plate of Bertha's famous mussels. She introduced us to her husband, who plays the base fiddle there with a local group— and he was pretty darn good. My purpose, though, for going to Bertha's was not music, or mussels, or even beer. What I wanted was to induce my wife into visiting the ladies' room on the second floor. It took some convincing, ostensibly because there was one much closer on the first floor, but she finally did. She observed that there was also an upstairs restaurant, and it was full of patrons, but no lady in a gray cloak. Evidently, there was just too much activity for the spirit to make an appearance.

I hope to return to Fells Point this winter and visit Bertha's again. Maybe on some gray winter evening, there will be fewer patrons. Of course, I want to try the mussels—but also, I hope, if conditions are right, the lady in the gray cloak will make her appearance as my wife makes her way up the back stairway en route to the ladies' room on the second floor.

CHAPTER 3

Old Baltimore Shot Tower
BALTIMORE/JONESTOWN
NEIGHBORHOOD

For many years, the Old Baltimore Shot Tower was the tallest structure in the United States.

On this site purchased in 1773 . . . The first permanent meeting house, a dwelling for the pastor and a school house were erected and a cemetery established for the First Baptist Church of Baltimore . . .

—Inscription on a plaque affixed to the Old Baltimore Shot Tower

IT IS NOT SURPRISING that many people who see the Old Baltimore Shot Tower from a distance and know nothing about it assume it is some sort of a monument, or perhaps even a lookout tower built as part of Baltimore's early harbor defenses. It is, in actuality, the last remaining element of an innovative nineteenth-century factory that used the natural energy of gravity to fashion its products—ammunition.

Whether because of its unique architecture, events that happened within or around it, or whatever occupied its site prior to its construction—or all of these things—people have long reported all sorts of strange phenomena in the vicinity of the tower. The most prevalent incidents, which have scared unsuspecting passersby on numerous occasions, have involved voices and other sounds emanating from within the sealed tower.

Known first as the Phoenix Shot Tower, and then as the Merchant's Shot Tower for the company that had originally owned it, the Merchant's Shot Tower Company, the 234-foot-tall red brick structure was the tallest building in the United States and the tallest free-standing masonry structure in the world when it was built in 1828 by architect Jacob Wolfe (it held those records until 1846 and 1884, respectively).

The fourteen-story Old Baltimore Shot Tower—one of four shot towers that once graced the local skyline—is an impressive structure; the massive circular tower incorporates an estimated 1.1 million bricks, manufactured locally by the Burns and Russell Company. Its walls are about four-and-a-half feet thick up to a height of around fifty feet, after which they periodically narrow in increments of four inches, for a final thickness at the top of twenty-one inches. It has a diameter of forty feet at its base and of twenty feet at its top. Its foundation extends seventeen feet below the surface of the ground, and its interior areas reportedly contain a cast-iron spiral staircase, steel floors, and an elevator. This huge industrial edifice was, incredibly, built in just six months and without recourse to exterior scaffolding. The site also once contained a number of other affiliated factory buildings, hinted at today by the presence of an iron entryway about twenty feet off the ground that once corresponded with the upper level of an adjacent structure.

Charles Carroll, a signer of the Declaration of Independence whose mansion was located just a few blocks to the south and who at that point was about ninety-one, laid the cornerstone for the Old Baltimore Shot Tower.

Ammunition was produced at this tower and others like it through a process that involved pouring molten lead into a colander-like device at the top of the tower. These measured blobs of liquid metal would then drop toward the base of the tower like fiendish raindrops, forming into perfect spheres as they went, and then harden upon impact with the cold water in the vat at the bottom. This process was used to produce both "drop shot" for small arms like rifles and pistols and "molded shot" for larger weapons like cannons. The Old Baltimore Shot Tower typically produced 2.5 million pounds of drop shot a year, which was then dried, polished, and sorted into 25-pound bags. Its capacity could be doubled in time of war or other periods of high demand.

By 1892, a new method for producing shot had effectively made the tower obsolete and, after more than six decades, it ceased operations. It was reopened briefly a few years later but, in 1898, the Merchant's Shot Tower Company shut down for good.

In 1921, the Union Oil Company purchased the tower with the intention of tearing it down and building a gas station on it location. Outcry from the community forestalled these plans, and by 1928 activists had raised enough money to buy the tower themselves, which they then turned over to the city of Baltimore. It was designated a National Historic Landmark in 1972, then was restored and opened as a historic site in 1976.

I visited the Old Baltimore Shot Tower on a Saturday in June 2009, with my friend Brendan Cass and his mother, Susan Cass. We parked in one of the many public garages located on the streets running parallel to the Inner Harbor and then walked up Lombard Street, on which the tower is located, a few blocks north of the harbor and a bit west of the city's Little Italy. As we approached the tower, it became apparent to us that, despite its proximity to downtown and numerous tourist attractions, it was located in a somewhat marginal area. Four or five middle-aged men who appeared to live at least part of the time in Shot Tower Plaza, the little park that surrounds the structure, sat, slept, or shambled around the area.

Ghostly lore we had heard about the Shot Tower included reports by passersby of strange noises coming from within the

Ghosthunter Susan Cass investigates claims that people have heard strange sounds coming from within the Old Baltimore Shot Tower.

structure. So, the first thing Brendan and I did upon approaching it was to put our ears to one of the iron doors. We immediately heard a sharp "clang" from within the sealed-up building
and jumped back! That was much more than we had expected.

Cautiously, we pressed our ears to the door again and listened. We could feel a low quivering in the door itself and, beyond
it, hear all sorts of ominous groaning and rumbling noises. As
far as we could tell, the vast interior of the tower was amplifying
the sounds of nearby traffic, which was in turn causing the iron
portals of the building to vibrate faintly. That did not, however,
do anything to explain the metallic clang we had heard.

I decided to ask some of the local denizens if they had ever
noticed anything odd and, approaching a pair sitting nearby,
asked if they had ever heard any strange noises coming from
within the tower.

"Yup," one of them said to me very matter-of-factly.
"Screamin', and hollerin', and someone yellin' orders." And, he
added, pointing to a nearby historical building, "If you knock on
that door, a man with a key will let you inside."

The last we had heard, the tower was no longer ever open to
the public, so I was both pleased and a bit surprised to hear this
latest bit of information. I thanked our confidant and headed
over to the house he had indicated. It bore a placard identifying
it as "9 North Front Street," an eighteenth-century home that
had once been typical of the surrounding Jonestown neighborhood and in which had dwelled a number of professional types,
including Thorowgood Smith, the second mayor of Baltimore.
In later years, it had been used as a hotel, a restaurant, and an
auto parts store, but now seemed to be run as a historical attraction. No one, however, answered the door for us.

Moving on to nearby Carroll Mansion, which together with
the tower is managed by the same historical organization, we
chatted with the docent, Matt. He told us that the tower really

could be accessed by appointment on Sunday mornings at 10:30, and implied that we probably could have visited that day if he had not been the only on duty. Even better, he said, it was sometimes possible to ascend to the parapet of the tower, more than two hundred feet above the streets of the city.

Matt also mentioned an industrial accident that had occurred in one of the buildings affiliated with the Old Baltimore Shot Tower when it was operational, and said that one of the workers had been mangled to death in some machinery. He also mentioned that a number of injuries had occurred in or around the tower.

Why the place might be haunted was becoming increasingly clear, and some additional discussion and research revealed a few other interesting facts. One was that a military armory had once been near the site, perhaps accounting for the spectral shouted orders we had been told about (although it was not inconceivable orders might be shouted in a factory as well). Another was that the site had, in fact, prior to the construction of the tower been the site of a church and its cemetery!

The presence of an archaic, abandoned cemetery could, of course, go a long way toward explaining paranormal phenomena at the site—especially when one considers that unmarked graves were as common as marked ones in early cemeteries, and that any attempt to relocate the interred would thus necessarily be incomplete. And the voices of their spirits, amplified by the unique construction of the tower, might be those that people can still hear calling out from within the massive structure.

CHAPTER 4

Westminster Hall and Burying Ground
BALTIMORE

Westminster Burying Ground contains the remains of more than a thousand prominent Baltimoreans, including author Edgar Allan Poe.

Thy soul shall find itself alone
'Mid dark thoughts of the gray tombstone
Not one, of all the crowd, to pry
Into thine hour of secrecy.

Be silent in that solitude,
Which is not loneliness—for then
The spirits of the dead who stood
In life before thee are again
In death around thee—and their will
Shall overshadow thee: be still. . . .

—Edgar Allan Poe, "Spirits of the Dead"

MORE THAN ONE THOUSAND SOULS, many of them
luminaries from Baltimore's storied past, lie buried within the
brick walls of Westminster Burying Ground, and there is reason
to think that the spirits of many of them haunt its grounds. For
most people, however, the place is significant as the final resting place of writer Edgar Allan Poe—who, to his innumerable
other distinctions, can add being buried three times and having his final resting place marked at two different spots in the
eighteenth-century graveyard.

When it was established in 1786 by a prominent local Presbyterian congregation, the burying ground lay to the west of
the Baltimore city limits and was located there due to fears of
contagion that were not completely unfounded.

"Four of the city's earliest mayors, including the first, James
Calhoun, are buried here, as are a number of generals of the
American Revolution and the War of 1812, eighty lesser officers,
and more than two hundred other veterans," a pamphlet published by the Westminster Preservation Trust says. "Hollins,
Gilmore, Stricker, Ramsay, Stirling, McDonogh, Calhoun, Ben-
talou, Sterrett . . . all share the distinction of having Baltimore
streets named in their honor."

A church was not originally built on the site and was not
added until six decades after the first bodies were laid to rest
there, both to meet the needs of the growing congregation and
to help protect and maintain the burial ground. Completed in
1852, Westminster Presbyterian Church was a Gothic Revival
structure that had a number of interesting architectural characteristics that make it exceptional if not unique.

Foremost among these is that the church was constructed on
brick piers over many of the tombs, giving the impression that
they are located in underground catacombs. Numerous large
family sepulchers and individual grave markers, many of them
crumbling, darkened with age, and ivy-covered, fill the walled

yard surrounding the building as well, creating a compact and somewhat confined little necropolis. While "Gothic Revival" will undoubtedly spring to mind for a small proportion of visitors, "Gothic Novel" will resonate for many more, and those are by no means the most interesting or eerie attributes of the place.

When Edgar Allan Poe died in 1849 at the age of just forty— under mysterious and somewhat suspicious circumstances that are disputed to this day—he was buried in an unmarked grave in the Poe family plot near the back of the Westminster Burying Ground. Today, a gravestone near a number of other Poe

Baltimore school children raised the money needed to erect this prominent monument to Edgar Allan Poe near the entrance to Westminster Burying Ground.

graves—including that of his grandfather, General David Poe Sr. and his brother, Henry Leonard Poe—bears his name and is thought by many to be where he was buried prior to being relocated to the ground beneath the more impressive marker near the front of the graveyard.

"That is not his original burial place. He was actually moved twice," Luann Marshall, tour director for the site, explained to me. Poe's fame and the affection admirers of his work felt for him grew posthumously, and when these sentiments were matched with sufficient funds, a large monument to him was purchased. It was too large, however, to fit on the plot in which he was buried, and the author had to be disinterred and was reburied elsewhere in the family plot in April 1875.

"People would come in to pay their respects and would search for his gravesite but couldn't find it, even after his fans went to all the trouble to put the monument on his grave," Marshall told me. "So, in November of 1875, they purchased the plot just inside the cemetery gates from the family that owned it and moved him there so that people would be able to see him as they went by." This monument, which cost six hundred dollars at the time, was paid for by Baltimore schoolchildren collecting "pennies for Poe," and today it is customary for visitors to leave one-cent coins on the white stone marker. Another interesting fact associated with this monument is that the inset bronze medallion bearing Poe's likeness is a replacement for a marble original, which was stolen and eventually turned up in a flea market in Charleston, West Virginia, and was subsequently donated to the Poe House in Baltimore, where it is periodically on display. (See the separate chapter in this book on the Poe House.)

A much smaller gravestone—bearing the image of a raven, which has become both the symbol of Poe and the city of his death—now marks the second spot where he was buried. One can only imagine that Poe would probably have profoundly appreciated not just the fame his work eventually enjoyed but also the morbid details, so reminiscent of scenes from his own stories, associated with the disposition of his remains.

In the decades following the reburial of the churchyard's most famous celebrity, the Westminster Presbyterian Church struggled to remain viable and, by the centennial of the new marker had, sadly, dwindled to almost nothing. In 1977, it was turned over to the Westminster Preservation Trust, a private, nonprofit group established under the leadership of the University of Maryland School of Law, and its days as a house of worship came to an end. Today, the place is known as Westminster Hall, which has been fully restored by the trust and is now used for secular purposes that include tours of the "catacombs" and graveyard.

The most visited spots in the graveyard are, of course, the ones dedicated to Poe, which have virtually risen to the status

The above-ground sepulchers of this eighteenth-century burying ground make it feel very reminiscent of many old European graveyards.

of pilgrimage sites. Associated observances include an annual birthday celebration at the hall hosted by the nearby Edgar Allan Poe House and Museum each January on the weekend closest to his birthday (an event that, in 2009, observed the two-hundredth anniversary of the author's birth). And, every year on January 19 since 1949, a mysterious individual has come to Poe's grave, left three roses and a half-filled bottle of Martell cognac—believed to have been the author's favorite drink—and made a toast to him (there is evidence that the original toaster died in 1998 and that the role was subsequently bestowed upon a successor). The roses are generally believed to represent Poe; his wife, Virginia; and his mother-in-law, Maria Clemm—all three of whom are buried in the churchyard. The toaster has sometimes also left notes, many of them cryptic and, in recent years, sometimes even controversial (e.g., an apparent dig at the French in 2004).

I visited Westminster Hall and Burying Ground for the first time in May 2009 with a dozen members of the Inspired Ghost Tracking paranormal group. The first thing that struck me upon entering the graveyard that damp, drizzly Saturday evening was how reminiscent it was of some of the above-ground cemeteries I had visited in Europe, notably Père Lachaise in Paris. True, it was not nearly as large as the Old World burial grounds of that ilk that I had visited (although it was, overall, much better maintained). But the dark, moldering stone sepulchers and markers, all jammed together into a tiny, mazelike microcosm, created a minuscule world of the dead within a city of the living which, it seemed to me, could not help but be haunted.

We were not, suffice it to say, disappointed.

Almost immediately upon arriving at Westminster Hall, Inspired Ghost Tracking group-organizer, Margaret Ehrlich, and two of her friends, Ross and Amy Twigg, heard organ music coming from the former church, which is the home of a fully restored 1882 pipe organ. Upon revealing this, however, to Luann Marshall, the Westminster Hall representative overseeing our tour, they learned that the building was completely locked up and that no one was in it! This particular phenomena is, it turns out, one that is regularly reported at the site.

Over the next couple of hours, we collectively experienced a number of other phenomena of an apparently paranormal nature while exploring the site. These included detection of the presence of spirits by some of the sensitives in the group, the capturing of several very profound orbs by several members of the group, and one of Margaret's assistants, Maria Blume, becoming overwhelmed by the spiritual energy in the catacombs and having to leave them.

I myself took a picture of one member, Wendy Super, and was stunned to see a large, substantial green orb appear in the image beside her! When I somewhat excitedly told her about this, she very calmly explained that she is a Reiki master who specializes in helping earthbound spirits cross over to the afterlife and that it is common for them to gravitate to her as someone who is able to help them.

A number of other members of the group reported similar experiences.

"I kept feeling activity in that area; that is why we asked Ross to come over as well," said Brenda, an Inspired Ghost Tracking member, of a particular section of the tombs beneath the former church and the photographs she and some of the others took there. "It looks like Ross and I were having an orb meeting."

Luann Marshall, who has worked at the site for nearly three decades, told me a number of other incidents people have experienced at it over the years. She herself has on more than one occasion suddenly felt the hair on the back of her neck stand up and experienced a feeling akin to panic while in the covered crypt and dispelled it merely by stepping outside. And, she said, during the filming of some footage at the site, the cameraman told her that he had felt someone touch him on the shoulder and whisper in his ear, "Go away!" There was, of course, no one visible around him, and he was understandably shaken by the experience.

We also learned a number of nonparanormal facts about the place that contributed to the macabre aura that surrounds it. One of the strangest involves the local water table, which rises dramatically during heavy rain. Historically, this would cause interred bodies—which in the past were frequently buried just two or three feet below ground—to rise to the surface and sometimes be carried by the flowing waters through the streets and into the nearby residential and commercial areas of the city.

This problem was addressed by placing heavy stone slabs on the ground over areas where bodies were buried. It could not remediate the situation in a crypt beneath the main part of the "catacombs," however, where until even a few years ago the rising waters would lift a coffin that has since finally disintegrated. On one occasion during a tour of the place, Luann Marshall told me, the floating casket kept banging against the walls of the crypt, much to the horrified delight of the middle-school students witnessing it. Talk about a scene straight out of a Poe story! And just an hour before we had been irritated that it was raining at all, and now some of us were disappointed that it was not a significant enough downpour to create any similarly ghoulish effects.

The lack of such melodrama did not dampen our enthusiasm, however. Westminster Hall and its graveyard are, in short, incredibly fertile ground for paranormal investigators, history buffs, and fans of horror literature alike, and are much more accessible than many sites of similar age and significance. Their atmosphere and history alone are enough to ensure a fruitful and enjoyable visit, and it is hard to envision a group

Several orbs can be seen converging around paranormal investigator Wendy Super in the Westminster Hall Burying Ground, including an especially profound one just to her left.

of ghosthunters who would not find the experience incredibly worthwhile. But it is an open question whether any spirits they encounter would include that of Poe or merely those of prominent Baltimoreans whose fame has been eclipsed by that of the city's most renowned poet.

Spotlight on Ghosts:
Edgar Allan Poe House and Museum

Located just eight blocks from where Edgar Allan Poe is buried at Westminster Hall and Burying Ground is, ironically, one of the many houses the author lived in over the course of his life. It was not, however, his home at the time he died in Baltimore in 1849 at the age of forty, as many people assume—possibly because of all the paranormal phenomena that have occurred at the site.

The author dwelled in this small, unassuming brick townhouse for just a couple of years, from March 1831 to October 1833, with his aunt, Maria Clemm, and her children, Henry and Virginia (whom he married in 1835, when she was thirteen and he was twenty-seven). His stay there followed his discharge from the United States Military Academy at West Point and preceded his move to Richmond, Virginia, to work as a staff writer and critic for the *Southern Literary Messenger,* a periodical devoted largely to fiction, nonfiction, poetry, and reviews. While living in the Baltimore home, the author lived and wrote—possibly creating as many as a dozen published stories and poems—in a little top-floor room with a pitched ceiling.

In the early 1930s, the city of Baltimore planned to demolish the house as part of an urban clear-cutting campaign and to extend the almost tastelessly named "Poe Homes" housing project onto the site. The Edgar Allan Poe Society managed to obtain the property and opened it to the public in 1949.

Exhibits at the little museum include a lock of Poe's hair; some china that once belonged to his guardian, John Allan; a reproduction of the portrait Poe painted of Virginia after she died in 1847; a reprint of the 1849 obituary from the October 24, 1849 edition of the *Philadelphia Dollar Newspaper;* and Poe's original announcement

Spotlight on Ghosts:
Edgar Allan Poe House and
Museum (continued)

about the creation of *The Stylus*, a literary magazine that never got off the ground.

Strange phenomena people have reported at the site include the sensation of someone tapping them on the shoulders, mysterious muttering voices, lights moving around in the house when no one was in it, inexplicable cold spots, windows flying open or slamming shut—and, in at least one case, a window falling out of its frame and smashing onto the floor.

Some people have, predictably, also claimed to see the ghost of Poe in this house—and perhaps part of his spirit does remain behind there residually, or visits periodically during its rounds to the many other sites where people have seen it. What even more people have claimed to see or otherwise sense, however, is a specter that many have described as a heavyset, middle-aged woman. Who she might be, however—and whether or not she has any connection to Poe—remains unclear, and further investigation would seem to be in order.

Spotlight on Ghosts
Inspired Ghost Tracking

Inspired Ghost Tracking is a meetup group of like-minded people who visit haunted sites, share paranormal experiences, and arrange for experts in the field to come to their monthly meetings and speak about subjects like ghosthunting techniques. The group is headquartered in Odenton, Maryland, about halfway between Baltimore and Washington, D.C., and was founded by Margaret Ehrlich in October 2008. The group has visited Westminster Hall and Churchyard in Baltimore, the Fells Point neighborhood in the same city, and the haunted Ramblewood House in Darlington, Maryland.

"I've always been interested in the paranormal," Margaret told me, noting that she once lived in a haunted house. She never really delved into it, however, until after becoming single in 2008 and having the opportunity to pursue some of her own interests, particularly energy healing (e.g., Reiki). She was also interested in joining some sort of a ghosthunting group, but could not find one in or around Anne Arundel County, the part of Maryland in which she lived.

After her friend Christy Puglisi suggested the name Inspired Ghost Tracking for the group she was thinking of starting, Margaret was inspired to move ahead with doing so right before Halloween of 2008. Six people showed up for her first event, as compared to around fifty at a recent one, and the group now has about eighty registered members. And the organizational needs of the group have increased so much that Margaret has had to recruit a number of assistants—who have included Julie Leese, Maria Blume, Amy Twigg, Ed, Darla, and Wendy Super—to help her coordinate events and activities.

Central

Ellicott City
  Historic Ellicott City

Ilchester
  St. Mary's College

Pikesville
  Druid Ridge Cemetery

CHAPTER 5

Druid Ridge Cemetery
PIKESVILLE

The Blackshere monument at Druid Ridge Cemetery is one of the spots at the site around which people have reported paranormal phenomena.

Almost as soon as the sculpture was in place, it acquired a reputation as something supernatural. Groundskeepers would apprehend two or three teenagers a week trying to test their nerve. The cemetery became a popular site for midnight fraternity initiations, where an anxious pledge might be required to sit on the lap of "Black Aggie" to see whether it was true that her arms would reach out and embrace you. It was said that her eyes turned red after midnight, and that anyone returning her earthly stare would go blind. Just as the clock struck twelve, it was claimed, she would let out a blood-curdling shriek, over a background of clanking chains.

—Mary Ellen Thomsen, *Druid Ridge Cemetery*

ANY SEARCH FOR INFORMATION about paranormal activity at Druid Ridge Cemetery will turn up innumerable references to the legend of "Black Aggie," a statue with which there is associated a strange story replete with peculiar details both mundane and preternatural. This is somewhat unfortunate, in that on the one hand it draws attention away from more worthy and genuine stories associated with the beautiful site—and on the other that the statue has not actually resided on the site for more than forty years, despite references in sources published since then that implies it still does.

In 1925, Felix Agnus, a U.S. Army brevet general during the Civil War who thereafter became a prominent publisher, placed over the grave of his wife the bronze statue of an androgynous robed figure by sculptor Edward L.A. Pausch. Controversy sprung up almost immediately around the sculpture, which was an unauthorized, some said inferior, reproduction of an allegorical statue by sculptor Augustus Saint-Gaudens erected at the Adams Memorial in Rock Creek Cemetery, in Washington, D.C. (ironically, the name Black Aggie has subsequently been applied by many to the original). Agnus successfully sued the party who sold him the imitation statue but thereafter refused to remove it from the gravesite.

Perhaps it would have been better if he had. Almost immediately, the statue became a magnet for young vandals whose criminal depredations were dismissed by those whose property was not being destroyed as "rites of passage." For four decades, people performed inane rituals at the site, scrawled obscenities on the statue and the marble pedestal upon which it rested, and in one case, actually chopped off part of the statue with a hacksaw.

Eventually, the despairing Agnus family decided to have the statue removed from the site to a place where it might be appreciated. The Maryland Institute of Art expressed interest in the statue but refused to pay for a base to support it. The Smithsonian Institution accepted it in 1967 and promptly put it into apparently permanent deep storage, despite the family's belief that it would be given a prominent place. It was eventually moved to the rear courtyard of the Dolly Madison House, now part of the Federal Courts building in Washington, D.C. (although legends persist in some circles that the statue was never actually removed from Druid Ridge Cemetery and is actually buried beneath the Agnus family gravesite or hidden elsewhere on the burial grounds).

While removal of the statue ended the history of pranks and vandalism associated specifically with it and the Agnus plot, it did not end the incidence of apparently genuine paranormal phenomena reported by visitors to the site, and it remains a popular venue for investigators.

Psychic Beverly Litsinger of the Maryland Ghosts and Spirits Association, for example, has detected spiritual presences at Druid Ridge Cemetery. She also told me about the apparition of a dark, shadowy figure that appears in the middle of the cemetery and can be seen walking toward one of the graves. Other people have reported a wide variety of other phenomena at specific areas around the cemetery—especially around the Gail, Marburg, and Blackshere family burial plots—to include orbs, mists, EVPs, and apparitions.

Much of such activity, to include phenomena similar to what was traditionally associated with Black Aggie, has been reported around the striking green bronze Gail monument, a distinctly female figure that, despite the fact that it looks very little like Black Aggie, is often erroneously identified with the more famous statue. It is worth noting, however, that many of the stories about Black Aggie mention physical characteristics that it does not have (e.g., an arm that could be sawed off), but which the Gail statue does. This statue is located just a few hundred feet away from where Black Aggie formerly sat.

My mother and I visited Druid Ridge Cemetery in early June 2009 and were immediately struck with the magnificence and size of the place, a sprawling, 208-acre site that is truly a city of the dead. The cemetery includes numerous above-ground family and community mausoleums, columbaria for cremated remains, raised and sunken gravestones, bronze and marble statuary of every sort, and a staggering variety of sculpture that includes everything from obelisks to Celtic crosses and a significant number of monumental benches where people can sit to meditate upon life and death. It is, in short, an essay in stone, earth, and landscaping on the American funerary tradition over the past twelve decades.

The cemetery was established on January 14, 1896, on the site of a large historic estate called "Annandale" that was being

People have seen and heard any number of strange things around the monument to the Marburgs, a family with a strange and almost gothic history.

operated as a dairy farm. The largest of the more than two dozen sections of the cemetery, where many of the most interesting and impressive monuments can be found today, is named for this historic property.

Druid Ridge itself, a highland area three miles north of Baltimore, had received its name at least in part because of the massive native oaks—a type of tree strongly associated with the Celtic priests known as druids—that graced its beautiful and mysterious slopes. Some writers have implied that the name of the site is somehow derived from the Ancient Order of Druids, a fraternal organization founded in 1781 that migrated from England to the Americas in 1833 and which called its lodges "groves." There is no direct evidence, however, that this secret society ever operated a lodge in or around Baltimore in general or on the misty ridge in particular.

But it would be safe to say that to us the site did indeed feel magical, very possibly haunted, and undeniably—although not surprisingly, it being a cemetery—somewhat melancholy. It rained steadily the entire time we were there, the heavens mourning the nearly forty-thousand departed souls buried in the fields around us.

During our visit to the cemetery we were each drawn to particular memorials about which we knew nothing before our visit—which made it all the more startling when we discovered that of the thousands around us, they were among a handful that have been highlighted in various published works about the cemetery and around which other visitors have reported paranormal phenomena.

One of these was the Marburg family monument, which my mother was undeniably drawn to. It consists of a large private mausoleum, before which is a statue of what I immediately took to be Icarus. The inscription upon it revealed it to be dedicated to Theodore Marburg Jr., an American who had served with the

British Royal Flying Corps during World War I and died four years after the conflict ended, at the age of just twenty-nine. What might have caused his spirit to remain at the site was not immediately obvious, although we wondered if some sort of lingering illness from the Great War might not have contributed to his demise. (Some research after our visit revealed a strangely gothic family history and any number of possible candidates for ghosthood, including a manipulative father and a deranged maiden aunt; see the sidebar to this chapter for more.)

At around the time my mother was occupied with the Marburg monument, I was exploring nearby and kept catching movement out of the corner of my eye, all from the direction of a memorial that I could not make out well from where I was. This happened several times, but each time I looked, there did not seem to be anything there but immobile stone. My eye was consistently drawn, however, to the back of a white stone sculpture a few hundred feet away, which closer examination revealed to be a mourning woman in classical garb standing watch over the Blackshere family sepulcher. The movement in the corner of my eye ceased once I reached it, and was replaced by the odd feeling that there was a presence of some sort centered on the statue, which seemed as if it might animate at any moment. I was not surprised to subsequently learn that other people have, in fact, reported similar experiences around the Blackshere monument and that many consider it to be haunted by the spirits of at least some of the family it memorializes.

Based on our cursory experiences at Druid Ridge Cemetery, we were not surprised that many other people had come away from the place believing it was haunted or having experienced paranormal phenomena there. Black Aggie is no longer there but thousands of souls and innumerable other stories are, and the place certainly warrants continued investigation.

Spotlight on Ghosts:
The Marburg Monument

One of the monuments at Druid Ridge Cemetery at which people have reported experiencing various paranormal phenomena—including sensing a spiritual presence, seeing apparitions, and capturing mists and orbs in photographs—is the Marburg family mausoleum, in front of which is a bronze figure of Icarus.

The base of this statue is fitted with a plaque dedicating it to Theodore Marburg Jr., which mentions his service with the British Royal Flying Corps during World War I and includes some rather strange verbiage about the need for an American presence in Europe. It also indicates that Theodore was born in 1893 and died in 1922, begging the question of how he might have died not during the war but a mere four years after it ended.

Investigation after our return from the site revealed the strange, convoluted, almost gothic history of the Marburg family in general and the macabre events surrounding the death of Theodore in particular. A brief review of Theodore's life during and after the war would certainly suggest he was an almost classically tormented soul, and it was not hard to believe he might haunt the final resting place of his remains.

When the Great War began, Theodore was a student at Oxford, in England, and in the furor to stop the German advance across Europe he joined the British Royal Flying Corps—despite the fact that Americans were prohibited from serving in foreign military organizations and that his father was a career diplomat and a friend of former President William Howard Taft.

In 1916, Theodore's plane crashed while flying a frontline mission and, as a result of the injuries he sustained, he had to have his left leg amputated. During his convalescence, he met and married a Belgian baroness who was also a divorcee and the mother of a three-year-old girl and whose background was, suffice it to say, a bit questionable.

Not much about the couple's life together is known, but two years later, when Theodore became a partner in a cattle ranch in New Mexico, the baroness refused to go with him. In an exception to the norms of the era, he claimed abandonment and they were divorced shortly thereafter.

In early January 1922, Theodore was married again, this time to a woman ten years his junior. She was not with him at his ranch either when he put an automatic pistol to his head seven weeks later and shot himself. It took him a week to die, during which the doctors had to remove his eyes. His wife arrived from Baltimore after he had expired.

There is a lot that is not known about the mounting tragedies that afflicted Theodore in life, but it is not too hard to imagine that

"Black Aggie" no longer sits over the Agnus family plot at Druid Ridge Cemetery, but some say her presence can still be felt there.

Spotlight on Ghosts:
The Marburg Monument
(continued)

his tormented spirit might still linger on our own sphere after his earthly troubles had been brought to an end. But, as it turns out, a number of the other Marburgs have weird stories as well, and it is easy to conceive of any number of them lingering on as ghosts. These include Theodore Marburg Sr., a man who cultivated a reputation as a peacemaker but urged the United States to enter World War I, and his sister, an increasingly desperate spinster who at one point unsuccessfully offered a European tour guide two-hundred-thousand dollars to marry her (he declined, opting for her niece instead). Any of them—maybe all of them—might be among the spirits that continue to linger among the sepulchers and monuments of Druid Ridge Cemetery.

CHAPTER 6

Historic Ellicott City
ELLICOTT CITY

Some paranormal investigators believe that the granite construction prevalent throughout historic Ellicott City has contributed to its extremely high incidence of hauntings.

So rapid was the rise of the water that many persons barely escaped from their houses on the high banks in time to see their dwellings carried away by the rush of waters and the impact of the floating masses of wreck. Children perished in the sight of their parents, and wives before the eyes of their husbands.

—J. Thomas Scharf, *History of Maryland, From the Earliest Period to the Present Day*

SOME MEDIUMS SAY that granite attracts and channels spiritual energy. If so, that might explain why this historic Maryland town may be the most haunted town in Maryland, if not in the entire country, as some people claim. Granite is everywhere. The houses are built of granite blocks hewn from the nearby quarries that line the Patapsco River. The foundations are set in the solid granite bedrock on which the town rests. Moreover, the streets are paved with cobblestones of granite, and granite steps lead up through narrow passageways between the buildings. Most Maryland towns are built of brick or wood. Some still have the sturdy log cabins built by the original settlers. Some have marble court houses and city halls of limestone. None, as far as I know, are built almost entirely of granite; and maybe that is why none seem to have the sheer volume of ghosts that Ellicott City has.

Maryland in general has more than its share of ghosts. Those in Frederick can be largely attributed to its proximity to Civil War battlefields. Fells Point hauntings seem most often to be associated with its bars and those who frequented them. At each location there seems to be an explanation that more often than not is rooted in some dramatic event, a violent death, a murder, a suicide. Ellicott City has had its fair share of those too, but no more than any other historic Maryland town, yet it seems to have disproportionately more ghosts. The answer may lie in the granite.

Many of Ellicott City's ghosts seem to simply be those of ordinary folk who lived out their lives and came to a peaceable end. In other places, most such spirits just move on. But not so in Ellicott City. The "Duchess of Main Street" is a case in point.

The Duchess was the wife of Gramps, who is the owner of Gramps' Attic Books on Main Street. She gained her nickname because Main Street is where she held court, and she could be seen almost every day proceeding up and down the street, engaging friend and stranger alike in conversation. She loved to socialize and would visit the businesses on Main Street just to gossip with the employees. The Duchess also had a peculiar custom: She would blend two or more of her favorite perfumes into a single very distinctive scent. She never shared that recipe with anybody. It was hers alone.

The Duchess died a few years ago in the apartment the couple shared in the back of the bookstore. Nevertheless, customers report that they can still smell her distinctive perfume drifting through the bookstore, and some take that as evidence that her presence persists there. The lawyer whose offices are next door to Gramps can attest to this. He was one of the people the Duchess "haunted" when alive.

The lawyer always knew it was the Duchess who was approaching the glass door of his office by the distinctive shadow that she cast in the hallway. So, he knew it was she when, not long after she died, he looked up from his desk to see that familiar shadow.

"Oh, no, it can't be," he thought. He got up and walked into the hallway, but the shadow was gone. There was no one there. Maybe she had come only to make her last farewell, because he has not seen her shadow since.

There are also, of course, the spirits of people who came to violent and untimely ends, such as those who perished in one of Maryland's greatest floods. On July 24, 1868, there was an exceptional rainfall all over the state, producing widespread flooding. The high-water mark is recorded on a marker located between the train station and the railway overpass over Main Street and is several feet above the level of the overpass. Scarcely a bridge was left standing over any major stream, and many houses, mills, and other buildings were swept away. The Patapsco River rose precipitously and, in about twenty minutes, became a swollen and furious torrent sweeping everything before it. Trees, masses of timber, and other debris were swept downstream with tremendous force. At Ellicott City, the flood was most destructive. Thirty-two buildings were swept away, and forty-three people killed.

Among those who perished were nine children from a single family, and there is some reason to believe their spirits continue to linger in Ellicott City. At least that is the conclusion that some have drawn from the strange experience of L.J., who is one of the tour guides for the Ellicott City Ghost Tour. She had parked her car in the parking lot behind Caplan's Auction Company one evening in October. After conducting the tour, she returned to her car and began to drive home. That is when she noticed an inexplicable whirring sound coming from the engine. The car did not stall, however, and she succeeded in making it home safely. But the strangeness did not stop there.

She exited the car and closed the door but, before she could lock it, she heard a click. It had locked itself. Then, as she walked away from the car toward her house, she could hear it unlock itself. Using her remote control, she locked it again, only to hear it unlock itself again. She then walked back to the car and locked it manually—but, as she walked away, it unlocked itself again.

It was late, and being frustrated by the whole experience, L.J. decided to go to bed and deal with the problem in the morning.

Early the next day, before she could go outside, L.J. heard a knock on her door. It was one of her neighbors.

"I just wanted to let you know that the headlights on your car are going on and off," he said.

L.J. stepped outside, and sure enough they were. She went over to the car and climbed inside. She turned on the dome light. No change. The headlights kept going on and off. She checked the owner's manual. No help. She went back inside, turned on her computer and checked the manufacturer's Web site listing of issues or recalls. Nothing relevant.

This went on for several days, and during that time L.J. tried everything she could think of. She parked her car away from other cars. She changed the battery in the remote locking device. She detached her cell phone from the ring on which she also had the device. Nothing worked.

Reluctantly, she came to the conclusion that she might have brought some ghosts home with her from Ellicott City. She called a friend for advice.

"Why don't you just take you car back to Caplan's in Ellicott

At least two ghosts are believed to inhabit the Judge's Bench Saloon, including one of a young woman who killed herself there.

City?" he suggested, assuming she might have picked up the hitchhiking shades there.

"If they're ghosts from Ellicott City, they should be able to find their own way back," she said, perplexed.

"Not if they are ghosts of children," her friend replied.

L.J. waited until that evening to see if the light show would start again. It did. Her car lights went on, then off, and showed no sign of stopping.

"I've had it," she said to herself. She got in her car and drove to Caplan's parking lot in Ellicott City. She parked the car, opened the door, and, looking in the rearview mirror, said, "We're back in Ellicott City. I hope you enjoyed playing with the gizmos and gadgets in my car, but I've brought you home and it's time to leave."

L.J. then stepped out of her car and walked a short distance and waited. After a few minutes, she got back into her car and drove away. She held her breath, but there was no whirring sound and the lights worked normally.

L.J. never experienced those phenomena again—but she also never again parked in Caplan's parking lot.

Although the Patapsco and its floods have been the source of more than a few ghosts, its swift-flowing waters are also the reason Ellicott City was built to begin with. It was the river that brought the Ellicott brothers, Joseph, Andrew, and John, to this spot in the late eighteenth century. The brothers had searched throughout Maryland and Pennsylvania for a site where they could grow wheat and harness water power for a mill, and in 1771 they purchased many acres along the Patapsco River and built their mills there.

By the early 1800s, these mills had developed a respected reputation.

"Here is one of the largest and most elegant merchant mills in the United States," wrote Joseph Scott in 1807. "It is one hundred feet long and forty feet wide, with four water wheels, which turn three pair of seven-foot stones and one of five feet. She is capable of manufacturing 150 barrels of flour in a day. Here also is a mill, with one water wheel and a pair of burr stones, for the manufacturing of plaster of Paris. Here likewise is a saw mill and an oil mill which is worked with great spirit."

Ellicott City prospered through the 1800s but, unfortunately, began to deteriorate in the middle years of the twentieth century. It never fully recovered from the Great Depression. While the rest of the country prospered during World War II, Ellicott City did not. It began taking on a rough edge. Rowdy bars and pool halls dominated Main Street. Crime was rampant. It became so bad that the commanders of nearby Fort Meade placed the town off limits to soldiers. There seemed to be no end to the downward spiral—but the Patapsco intervened again.

In the early summer of 1972, Hurricane Agnes swept through the area. Ellicott City was ravaged—but that turned out to be a blessing in disguise. The town fathers, disgusted with what the town had degenerated into, decided they would use the federal disaster funds to rebuild Ellicott City into a town they could be proud of. The sleazy bars, the pool halls, and the slumlords were told to clean up their acts or do without any money to rebuild. They got the message.

Today, Ellicott City is a pleasant and vibrant town whose residents are justly proud of what they have accomplished. They are dedicated to the preservation of its historic character and to making it an inviting place to visit, which it most certainly is. Antique shops and other small businesses abound. It also has several good restaurants and many more coffee houses and pubs. The latter includes the Ellicott Mills Brewing Company, which has good beer and food, and which I enjoyed very much during one of our visits to the town. It is also haunted, of course, with the ghost of a young accountant who was let go at the outset of the Great Depression and ultimately hanged himself in desperation. He can still be seen from time to time on the second floor of what was then the Talbot Lumber Company, which had employed him. They say he is dressed for the office, in the stiff collar and cuffs that characterized men's dress in 1929.

Being a Marylander, I had known of Ellicott City, and my wife and I had visited it several times to walk around, enjoy a good meal, and sometimes hike out on the trail that follows the old trolley line toward Baltimore. (The Trolley Stop Restaurant, located at the trail head, serves good meals and has a good nice selection of beer. It is also haunted—ghosts inhabit the second floor and are responsible for inexplicable footsteps and slamming of doors heard by the restaurant staff late at night. Ghosthunters have investigated the second floor and confirmed the ghostly presence.) It was not, however, until I took the ghost tours sponsored by Howard County Tourism that I came to understand the sheer volume of ghosts in Ellicott City, and the role that the local granite rock possibly plays. There are so many ghosts that they have had to offer the tour in two parts: Part One is on Friday night and Part Two on Saturday night.

But there is also another reason to take the ghost tours that many towns offer: the people you meet. Some are casual tourists, some are serious ghosthunters, and some are there for other reasons, like the young girl we met on one of the Ellicott City tours we took. After the tour was over, my son and I lingered to talk to Terry Trembeth, our tour guide. The rest of the group of about twenty had dispersed, but we noticed that a pretty little blonde girl of about ten years and her mother had also stayed behind. The girl seemed shy, but was also strangely intense. It was she who wanted to talk to the tour guide. As it turned out, she was seeking professional advice.

"Why do some spirits not move on?" she asked. "Why do they stay around?"

"Well," Terry explained, "there are lots of reasons. Some just have unfinished business. Others can be so attached to a place or an object that they just don't want to leave."

"Oh," said the little girl, who had clearly been hoping for more.

"You see," her mother said, noting our interest and turning in our direction, "We have a ghost in our basement. Only she can see it—and we took this tour hoping we might learn more about what we're dealing with."

CHAPTER 7

St. Mary's College
ILCHESTER

A flight of sixty-six crumbling steps leads up the hill to the overgrown ruins of St. Mary's College, a former Roman Catholic seminary.

Ilchester is a small station on the Baltimore & Ohio Railroad, and is situated on the right bank of the Patapsco River . . . Ellicott had erected a fine stone house four stories high, intending it as a small hotel for travelers. But few people stopped at Ilchester and his hopes were soon dampened . . . Ellicott abandoned it . . . He offered to sell the hotel and farm, but for many years no one could be found

to buy it and the entire property was neglected and suffered
considerable damage. The hotel remained closed and unin-
habited; the stable and farmhouses were rapidly decaying;
and the orchard and gardens were falling prey to brushwood
and briars. This was the state of things when the place was
purchased by the [Redemptorists].

   —From a 1905 newspaper article

OVER THE YEARS, many people had high hopes for the
spot on the bluffs overlooking the Patapsco River that became
known as Ilchester and were drawn to it first for its suitabil-
ity as a holiday spot and then as a spiritual retreat. It probably
would have been inconceivable to any of them that the place
would eventually be regarded as one of the most frightening
and haunted spots in Howard County or that its most prominent structure would end up becoming known as Hell House.

   In 1886, George Ellicott managed to sell the decaying handful of buildings that constituted the village of Ilchester to the
Congregation of the Most Holy Redeemer—a Roman Catholic
sect founded to minister to the poor, disenfranchised, and alien-
ated that is more commonly known as the Redemptorists—and
the things that had doomed it as a holiday site became assets.

   "The qualities that made it unfit for trade made it fit for the
purposes [they] had in mind—retirement, study, and prayer,"
wrote Paul T. Stroh, a former seminarian at the school, in his
book *Ilchester Memories.*

   For a century, the place served the Redemptorist order as
a seminary, and at its peak hundreds of people dwelled in the
hilltop community. It must have seemed to many of them like
a timeless place, with immense stone buildings that would last
until the end of time, grottoes devoted to Our Lady of Perpetual
Help, and paths passing through wooded clearings and running along cliffs overlooking the river below.

Over the years, the Redemptorist fathers, students, and laity expanded the school into a sprawling complex of dormitories, classrooms, and refectories that included additions to Ellicott's original inn and tavern, among them a small chapel; a huge, five-story brick building that ultimately had a large chapel attached to it; and numerous other structures like garages, greenhouses, and shrines. They turned the rest of their 110-acre campus into a garden, lining pathways with stone from the hill and cultivating roses in its dark earth.

Despite its isolated location atop the hill, the Redemptorist priests and seminarians were not monastic, and ministered to Catholics in the local area, many of whom were too poor to travel to Baltimore every week for services. They were eventually made their own congregation, Our Lady of Perpetual Help, the aspect of the Virgin Mary venerated by the group (which continues to function in the area, albeit not under the Redemptorists, and is headquartered in a new complex about a mile south on Ilchester Road).

In the second half of the twentieth century, St. Mary's College struggled to remain viable, and years before it finally had to shut its doors, people had already begun to remark how forlorn and overgrown the place was starting to look. There were only ten seminarians in its last graduating class, and the congregation shut down the school in 1972. And that is when its real troubles began.

Sometime after the Redemptorists left, the state of Maryland acquired approximately seventy-seven acres of the site and added it to adjacent Patapsco Valley State Park, while a developer named Michael Nibaldi acquired the college itself and the remaining thirty-three acres of land. Nibaldi had, in conjunction with a local architect, hoped to convert the college into apartments but was ultimately foiled by the opposition of county boards and area residents.

During this period, the place remained largely vacant, and it was then that local youths began to vandalize the place. At that time the first rumors of the place being haunted began to circulate, the centerpiece of which was a lurid story about a priest who forced seven nuns to hang themselves and then killed himself in a similar manner. According to the tale—which, by the way, can still be elicited from people in the local area to this very day—their tormented ghosts now haunt the grounds of the ruined college, etc., etc. The weakest point in this wretched fabrication, of course, is that the site was a seminary and not a convent and would thus not likely have had any nuns present to be slaughtered, much less seven.

As is quite often the case, of course, it is possible to have a genuinely haunted site for which the actual origins of its haunting are unknown, and this would seem to be the case with St. Mary's College. Indeed, numerous ghosthunting groups have claimed to have experienced paranormal phenomena at the site over the years. According to material posted on one such organization's Web site, for example, "People from the area that have been able to go there have seen and heard many spirits while visiting."

An extended body of urban legend has included tales of Satanic altars and drug labs hidden within the sprawling main building and the tunnels and chambers beneath the complex. If such things were indeed present in the decaying remains of St. Mary's College, they were, in all likelihood, established by the very people who were going up to the place and wrecking it. Kids would, in any event, challenge each other to see how far they were willing to venture into the place, a foray onto just the second floor of the main building—where all forms of awfulness were rumored to reside—being regarded as a sign of especial bravery by the timorous and unimaginative young bumpkins.

In the early 1980s, the nonprofit Kamakoti & Tirupati Foundation began looking at the site with an eye toward converting it into an International Institute for Religious Studies, a nonsectarian spiritual center that could be used for research, discussion, and retreat. Initially the group rented the site, and between 1986 and 1988—sources vary—it was acquired on its behalf by Sateesh Kumar Singh, who purchased it for about four-hundred thousand dollars through BCS Limited Partnership, a corporation he formed with a number of other people around the country. Funding for the project never really came together, however, and while its organizers struggled to bring their dream to fruition, the property remained largely uninhabited and unmaintained.

In the meantime, the local police could not—or would not bother to—protect the site from the continuing depredations of local teenagers who, not content with merely visiting the place, routinely vandalized and stole from it. Vandals broke windows, ripped phones out of the walls, tore down fences and "No Trespassing" signs, smashed security lights, and even stole copper downspouts.

Nearby neighbors were also victimized as part of these rampages and reported incidents that included having their windows shot out. The almost depraved indifference of the local police to these violent acts was revealed in a contemporary newspaper article.

"Mischief is really the key word here," said Howard County Police spokeswoman Sherry Llewellyn. "We're not concerned that there are any serious crimes being committed." Even when the local authorities caught a kid engaged in such vicious and destructive "mischief," little or nothing came of it. But, as events would eventually demonstrate, considerably more concern was shown when the victims were not property owners with strange foreign names or hermetic groundskeepers, and when the perpetrators were not the scions of local families.

One person struggled to protect the place during this era, a resident caretaker named Allen Rufus Hudson, who came to be feared and resented by the local youth and vilified by them as "the Hillbilly." Over the years he lived in the progressively decrepit site, he paid a heavy price for his efforts.

Between 1992 and 1997, the six foot, three inch, 225-pound Hudson was arrested a half dozen times at the site and charged with offenses that included assault, battery, false imprisonment, intent to injure with a deadly weapon, reckless endangerment, failure to confine a dangerous dog, and various weapons possession charges. In 1992, he was jailed for three weeks following an altercation with a couple of police officers, but the net effect in the other cases was that he was not convicted—often because the prosecutor declined to pursue the case or because mitigating circumstances, such as probable cause, were found to be present. During this time, Hudson was also the defendant in a number of civil lawsuits brought by trespassers who either he or his dogs had attacked and had settlements of up to five-thousand dollars brought against him.

When three young men menaced the forty-five-year-old caretaker with baseball bats one night in 1996 and he shot one, wounding him, Howard County police again arrested Hudson, charging him with assault, battery, and assault with attempt to murder. About seven weeks later, the assistant state's attorney opted to not pursue the case and the charges against him were dropped.

In 1997, a year after Hudson used lethal force to defend himself, arsonists set fire to the main, five-story building and completely destroyed it. A year later on Halloween, a similar blaze claimed part of the original structure built by George Ellicott. Although the local fire authorities declared the acts deliberate, no one was ever charged in connection with them.

A huge pile of rubble is all that remains of the two largest buildings that were once part of the St. Mary's College campus.

And because the fire-damaged site had become unstable and was prone to collapse onto the caretaker's residence, Hudson was forced to move. (In 1998, Hudson was finally convicted of something—of driving a motor vehicle with a revoked license—and sentenced to two years in prison, all but three months of which was ultimately suspended. He was the plaintiff in another case in 2002, but dropped out of public view after that.)

"I'm of the frame of mind that if someone wants to buy it, even at a low price, I'll sell it," said Singh of the property in a newspaper article, his dreams of maintaining the place as a spiritual sanctuary going up in smoke.

In 2006, whoever the owners of the place were at that point brought in heavy equipment and had the fire-damaged structures razed to the ground and their building materials formed into a huge pile of rubble on the site where they had stood. What had been a vibrant ecclesiastic complex three-and-a-half decades before was now nothing but smashed masonry, scorched timbers, and rubbish. Today, the surrounding forest is beginning to overrun the site and, in a matter of years, will likely almost completely eclipse it—if someone does not build something on the hill first.

I visited the ruins of St. Mary's College in May 2009 and discovered the site to be at least as enchanted and mysterious as it is haunted and, simultaneously, both wonderful and ominous. During the hours I spent exploring the site and walking through the shadowy woods at the top of the hill, I constantly felt as if I were being watched, as if someone were behind me, as if something might materialize at any moment. I also felt as much at risk from physical threats as from spiritual ones and had to remain constantly vigilant not just against them but also against the hazards of maneuvering through a crumbling and decrepit ruin.

Knowing the ruined complex was located on the bluffs above the Patapsco River and near where the B&O railway line intersected with Ilchester Road, I parked as close as I could to the black iron railway bridge that crossed over the road. More than a dozen other cars were already there, most of them apparently belonging to kids swimming in the river.

Gathering up my gear, I walked toward the bridge, passed under it, and then turned left and started to walk up toward the tracks, between them and the river, which now lay to my right and, just across it, a sprawling, ruined, paper mill.

As I started up the path, a large red fox appeared ahead of me and, hanging from its clenched jaws, I could see the limp remains of a black snake. The fox glanced over at me and then turned away and continued up the path alongside the bridge, turning left toward the tracks. I followed in the same direction and, when I reached the top of the bridge, looked back across the tracks and could see him sitting by the tree line that obscured the nearby hillside.

I immediately sensed that this was an occult omen of some sort—but, having just enough experience with such things to recognize them, I was unsure of how to interpret it. Not wanting to harass the animal, I opted to head directly away from it and not yet cross the tracks, walking instead alongside them while scanning the overhanging cliffs for any sign of the stairs I knew were there or a place that looked as if it might be ascended without too much difficulty.

I eventually found a spot that looked promising and used it to clamber up the steep, wooded slope, spotting, when I was about halfway up, what appeared to be a stone building near the top.

Reaching this structure, I discovered it to be a stone and concrete platform, projecting out over the edge of the cliff, which once was the basement level of a now nonexistent building. A large rift in its floor led into an area below. Beyond it, I saw a sunlit clearing in which was an immense pile of bricks and rubble, and beyond it in all directions the silent woods.

Crawling down the slope of rubble that led into the aged, former basement, I found and explored two large rooms, one of them chocked with debris but the other relatively clear and open. Windows in the thick walls looked out over the wooded hillside below. Based on its construction, it may well have been the basement to the original building constructed by Ellicott on the site, but I had no way of knowing this for sure.

My subsequent explorations revealed this to be the only structure I could find to enter at the site, almost everything else being reduced completely to rubble. Until just three years before, there would have been at least the ruins of the numerous buildings that had once been comprised by the Redemptorist seminary, but now it was impossible to be sure exactly where many of them had even been located. There were several spots, however, where I could see narrow hints of entrances to an underworld that might yet be present beneath the hill, its obvious approaches choked with debris, and any others that might exist not apparent to the casual explorer.

For the next couple of hours, I cautiously wandered along overgrown paths and through the ruins of the hilltop complex and the forest that surrounds and is increasingly encroaching into it. Many of the online posts I had read about the place had mentioned "No Trespassing" signs, but if any remained, they were obscured by foliage. More likely they had simply rotted away, and no one cares anymore.

Most of the paths through the former campus were stone-lined and led through the shadow of the overhanging forest, but one passed through a large ruin that might have once been the greenhouse and was now a large, overgrown area choked with clingy blackberry bushes. Toward what I took to be the back of the complex, I discovered a sign on a tree beside a mossy path that indicated I had reached the boundary of the Patapsco Valley State Park.

Everywhere I went, the wonders of the place were revealed to me. On a downward slope above the valley, I found a crumbling shrine that had likely once been part of the grotto and, a little ways away from it, a tiny natural spring, bubbling right up from the ground and down the hill. On a high point, rising in almost pagan splendor from the forest, were the remains of a small chapel, its domed roof supported by eight classical columns that turned out to be made of iron. Large quartz boulders jutted up through the grass in numerous little clearings. Crumbling stairways disappeared up or down into the woods. And at the geographical high point of the spot, the remains of whatever had once stood there were piled up in what now looked like a primitive stone altar.

Walking through the eerie, sun-dappled ruins, I realized that the place would have actually been incredible while its gutted

A wrought-iron cupola over an altar is one of the many haunting spots within the complex of ruins once known as St. Mary's College, which overlooks the Patapsco River Valley.

buildings still stood, almost like a lost city on the top of the lonely, wooded hill. But with their barren souls and limited imaginations, the youth of the surrounding area did indeed transform it into a "Hell House," progressively destroying and desecrating it with their vandalism, spray paint, and "partying"—and then, finally, burning it down. Even in the absence of anything but ruins—and the omnipresent graffiti and trash—the place was like a charmed garden, sad, beautiful, magical, but nonetheless somewhat fey and menacing.

Fearing the onset of darkness in this strange place, I eventually and somewhat reluctantly located the paved path that descended the hill, which split and headed in two different directions. To the south, it led to an entrance off Ilchester Road that at some point must have been added as a vehicle approach. To the north, it eventually ended in a long, stone stairway that descended sixty-six steps to a point near the railroad tracks, the original entrance the seminarians and other people coming to St. Mary's would have ascended after disembarking from trains.

Descending the stairs I exited the timberline and recognized where I was; to my right was the parking area by the bridge, and to my left was the route I had taken between the railroad tracks and the cliff before making my ascent—and the fox! He saw me as well, ran back down the direction I had originally come from, and, as he did, I realized that the spot he had stopped at before was exactly the one in which I was now standing and that had I followed his path, it would have led me directly to the main entrance to St. Mary's College. The arcane portent I had recognized but been unable to interpret was now clear to me, and, as I departed the site, I had a sense of having gone full circle, of closure.

Having visited the abandoned and now-ruined seminary once known as St. Mary's College, it is my belief that almost any sort of investigation will confirm the decades-long rumors that it is haunted. One can find, strangely, Internet postings from people who count Hudson and his dogs among the ghosts that haunt the place. So, either they are absolute ninnies who cannot tell a living caretaker and animals from spectral ones, or the now-obscure Hudson has indeed died—albeit at a relatively young age—and begun to haunt in death the site he was desperately unable to protect in life. I am open to both of those possibilities and they are by no means mutually exclusive.

My guess, in any event, is that the ghosts that inhabit the overgrown ruins are the melancholy shades of those who had hopes for the spot on the hill overlooking the river—foiled by circumstance and the malice of those with dreams less lofty.

National Capital

Clinton
 Surratt House Museum

College Park
 University of Maryland

Colmar Manor
 Bladensburg Dueling Grounds

Germantown
 Waters House

Mount Rainier
 Exorcist House

Rockville
 Beall-Dawson House
 St. Mary's Cemetery

Upper Marlboro
 Mount Airy Mansion

CHAPTER 8

Beall-Dawson House
ROCKVILLE

When Upton Beall built his home around 1815, it was the largest and most impressive residence in Rockville.

"I don't like being here in the dark, when there's nobody else here. It's a little spooky. If someone left a light on upstairs and I have to come in here at ten o'clock at night to turn it off, I do sometimes say, 'It's just me, Margaret!'"

—Joanna Church, Curator, Beall-Dawson House

WHEN UPTON BEALL BUILT HIS HOME in Rockville around 1815—having been delayed by the British invasion of the region during the War of 1812, when marauding redcoats burned his supply of construction timber—it was the largest and most impressive residence in Rockville. In those days, a mere three dozen houses and two hundred souls resided within the town, and Beall's home, set on a seventy-acre estate overlooking one of the main roads into the little county seat, would have commanded attention.

As Clerk of the Court for Montgomery County—a significant post in that era—it was important to Beall that he project an impression of substance, elegance, and means, and the three-story, asymmetrical side hall Georgian-style house that he built reveals a mixture of New World American ostentation and Old World Scottish frugality.

The front and most visible façade of this structure, for example—now the oldest and largest of three wings—is constructed of expensive Flemish bond brick, while a cheaper but still relatively costly common bond is used elsewhere. Likewise, while Beall furnished his home with many fine and expensive items—including an eight-day tall-case clock that was the most valuable item on the 1827 household inventory—he eschewed the use of wallpaper, which would have been standard in homes of his era (although it is only a guess that he did so as a way to save money).

Like many such places, Beall's home has over the years acquired a reputation for being haunted and a repertoire of stories has become associated with it, which is ample reason to include it in this book. Beyond that, however, I am descended from the Bealls who emigrated and were exiled to the Americas in the seventeenth and eighteenth centuries and, thereby, a distant relative of Upton Beall. I thus did not want to miss the opportunity of including in this book an appropriate site that once belonged to someone whose bloodline I share.

The Bealls provide an interesting case of the sort of social mobility that was possible for industrious people in the British Colonial era and the decades following it. In 1650, Bells—

without the now-characteristic "a"—were among the fourteen thousand Scottish soldiers who faced an invading English army at the Battle of Dunbar in 1650, during the Third English Civil War. After a back-and-forth conflict that looked as if it would favor the defenders, the Scots were defeated by a more experienced eleven-thousand-man force led by Oliver Cromwell. About three thousand of the Scots were killed and some ten thousand of them were taken prisoner.

About half the prisoners were considered to be too badly injured to constitute a threat to the English forces and they were paroled. To prevent them from being rescued, however, the remaining five thousand were force-marched south toward England and ultimately imprisoned with inadequate food, shelter, or fuel for fires. Only about fourteen hundred survived, and they were transported to English colonies in North America and the Caribbean, where they were used as slave labor. And thus it was that the Bells came to America, many eventually having their sentences commuted upon condition of severing their ties to their old Scottish clans through alteration of their names—the immigrant "Bells" thereafter being transformed into "Bealls."

Once freed from bondage, the energetic Bealls generally did quite well for themselves, acquiring rank in the local militias, receiving land grants in exchange for battling Indians along the frontier, and eventually controlling large estates throughout Maryland and the surrounding areas, including much of Georgetown in what is now the District of Columbia (where Upton Beall himself spent his boyhood, adopting from it some of the most popular architectural conventions for his Montgomery County home).

And, as the case of Upton Beall demonstrates, the scions of the original prisoners of war maintained their standing in the years after the United States of America supplanted the British crown in the region.

Beall married Jane Robb, daughter of a prominent Rockville tavern owner, and with her had three daughters, Jane, Mathilda, and Margaret. None of the girls ever married, although existing correspondence indicates they had suitors, and by 1870 only fifty-seven-year-old Margaret remained. Determining that she could not live alone, she invited her cousin, Amelia Somervell, to come and live with her.

Amelia subsequently married farmer and landowner John Dawson—second namesake of the house—and the couple lived in the house with Margaret and, ultimately, their nine children (eight of whom, five boys and three girls, lived to maturity). When she died, Margaret divided her estate among the surviving children and left the house to her three nieces, Margaret, Mary, and Priscilla. They lived in the house until the last of them died in the 1930s, and then the house passed out of their family and had a variety of owners over the following decades.

Today, the Beall-Dawson House serves as the headquarters of the Montgomery County Historical Society, which maintains a library and exhibit in it. Set in the historic heart of an area that has been inextricably transformed since the middle of the last century, it is also a reminder of the architecture and heritage of an earlier era . . . and, via its ghosts, the people of a previous era as well.

I visited the house for the first time in May 2009 and was guided through it by its curator, Joanna Church, who talked to me about both its mundane and paranormal history. She had worked at the house about ten years and, while she is not convinced that it is haunted, has certainly sensed the kinds of things that indicate it might be.

"I don't like being here in the dark, when there's nobody else here," Joanna said. "It's a little spooky. If someone left a light on upstairs and I have to come in here at ten o'clock at night to turn it off, I do sometimes say, 'It's just me, Margaret!'" She said that she has no reason to think the place is haunted by

Margaret Beall as opposed to anyone else who lived there over the years, but does say it is Margaret's personality to which she feels drawn to respond.

"Docents also say if they're working in the house alone that they sometimes hear footsteps," Joanna said. "And one person has sworn up and down that a platter got moved." Joanna said she has, in fact, heard inexplicable footsteps on the floors above her when she was the only living person in the house (she dismisses out of hand the incident with the platter, however, and maintains her belief that it can likely be explained away by mundane means).

Over the years, people have also reported similar inexplicable thumps and bumps coming from the upper floors and burglar alarms being set off for no apparent reason. Witnesses have also given accounts of incidents that are even stranger and less generic in nature.

Several years ago, for example, one of the site's volunteer docents, Rae Koch, was dipping candles in the kitchen when she caught some movement in her peripheral vision. Turning to look into the adjacent carriage entrance room, she saw an old black man, clad in eighteenth-century clothing, kneeling on the floor and adjusting the bricks that are laid into it in a herring-bone pattern. As someone who had evidently seen ghosts before, she reportedly knew just what she was looking at and did not pay it any further heed.

Today, the bricks flooring that room are fixed in concrete, but Joanna explained to me that they were originally set in sand and periodically needed to be adjusted—a task that would likely have fallen to an older slave who might not have been capable of more rigorous duties. Joanna also vouched for Rae's sincerity, and said at the very least that she believes the woman sincerely thinks she saw a ghost in the house. Specifically who he might have been, however, is unknown and will probably never be discovered through ordinary means.

Another series of ghostly incidents associated with the Beall-Dawson House involve a dollhouse that was given on her second birthday to one of the girls who lived there but who, sadly, died just a few years later. Volunteer staff members at the house were periodically disquieted to discover the tiny pieces of toy furniture moved around within the dollhouse even when no one living had access to it, as if little spectral hands had been moving them around. And after the miniature furnishings were removed from the dollhouse, people reported hearing wailing sounds around the little structure.

Other areas of the house are also somewhat strange—especially those in which the floor plan has evidently been changed over the years, leaving it unclear exactly how certain parts of

Today, the Beall-Dawson House serves as the headquarters of the Montgomery County Historical Society, which maintains a library and exhibit in it.

the house were originally laid out—and, while overt paranormal activity may not have been reported in them, I suspect a full investigation would likely reveal something in some of them. For example, what is now the middle section of the house was originally a kitchen wing, the second floor of which served as quarters for six to eight household slaves. This room had no doors leading into it from the floor on which it was located and could only be accessed via a trapdoor in its floor, reached by a ladder from the kitchen, making it an isolated and almost secret chamber within the house.

My hopes that a hereditary connection to the original owners of the Beall-Dawson house would give me some sensitivity to whatever spirits yet haunt it were, alas, not realized by me in any palpable way—either while I was there or during a later examination of my photographs and audio tape. Throughout the house, however, there did seem to be something lurking just out of sight, and I could easily sense why Joanna was nervous when she was in it by herself. And so perhaps a future visit to the house, and more time spent within its walls, will be the key to unlocking some of its otherworldly mysteries.

CHAPTER 9

Bladensburg Dueling Grounds
Colmar Manor

A historical marker describing the significance of the Bladensburg Dueling Grounds is located in front of them on Route 450/Bladensburg Road.

Police are investigating a shooting in front of a Bladensburg nightclub that injured three people early this morning . . . when multiple shots were fired by an unidentified person . . . Police believe an altercation that took place at the club about 11 P.M. may be linked to the shooting.

—The *Washington Post*, March 26, 2007

ALTHOUGH DUELING WAS MADE ILLEGAL within the limits of the District of Columbia early on in the history of the American republic, there was nonetheless a violent streak in the souls of many contemporary gentlemen that compelled them to settle their differences through single combat. The place where they would go to exchange gunfire at close quarters was a narrow strip of ground along the banks of the Eastern Branch—also known as Dueling Creek and Blood Run—a tributary of the Anacostia River, just across the district line in Maryland. This infamous site became known as the Bladensburg Dueling Grounds.

More than fifty duels are known to have been fought at the site—although there were certainly many more—most of them over questions of honor and settled at sunrise with pistols discharged at a range of just twelve paces. Many men died here as a result, and their deaths and the powerful emotions they felt in their last moments—fear, anger, despair—have contributed to its reputation as a very haunted place. It is also compelling to consider whether or not the powerful violence and negative emotions of the spot might have persisted into our own age and influenced the actions of some residents of the surrounding communities.

The most famous person to have been mortally wounded in a duel at the site was Commodore Stephen Decatur, one of the greatest American heroes in the first decades of the nineteenth century, who lost a fight with rival Commodore James Barron in 1820. (Decatur did not actually die at the Bladensburg Dueling Grounds and was taken to his home in the heart of Washington, D.C., where he succumbed to his wounds. Some people believe his ghost is among those that haunt the dueling area but it is actually much more likely that it instead inhabits his house, the subject of one of the chapters in *Ghosthunting Virginia*, which also includes Washington, D.C.).

Many other prominent citizens also fought at the site, many of them either killing or wounding their opponents, suffering the same fates themselves, or both. From the perspective of ghosthunters, knowing who these people are can actually be quite helpful in that it establishes a possible pool from which any encountered specters might be identified. Indeed, many of the revenants seen at the sight have been described as dark, corpselike, and opaque, perhaps allowing for key details to be spotted as they replay the events of their deaths into eternity.

Another famous incident occurred in February 1819, when General Armistead T. Mason, a former Virginia senator, dueled his cousin, Colonel John M. McCarty, over the honor of a woman. Mason was killed, and McCarty, struck in the hand, was maimed and lost the use of his right arm. But it was his mind that was most profoundly wounded, and the episode so upset McCarty that he became somewhat unhinged and was haunted by it—and possibly the spirit of his cousin—thereafter. Some even believe that upon his own death, the spirit of McCarty returned to the Dueling Grounds to join that of his slain cousin.

As more and more people were killed at the site, reports of apparitions spotted on the dueling grounds began to appear, and ghost stories started to be told about the place perhaps as much as two centuries ago. Some people were unhappy that lethal gun battles, sometimes amounting to cold-blooded murder when inexperienced duelists were the victims, were taking place just outside the capital city. Maryland laws did not apply to citizens of Washington, D.C., however, so even if the state legislature passed a law banning duels in the state, it would not be binding upon the people most likely to use the Bladensburg grounds.

One incident at the dueling grounds, however, caused such public outrage that even Congress was finally forced to act.

In February 1838, Representative William Graves of Kentucky challenged Representative John Cilley of Maine to a duel after taking offense at comments the latter had made about a newspaper article that smeared a third party. Cilley apparently never really expected the duel to take place but, nonetheless, eventually ended up at Bladensburg across from Graves, each armed with a rifle and eighty yards apart from each other. Cilley had little experience with weapons, while Graves had a lot and is furthermore reported to have been armed with a much more powerful firearm than his overwhelmed opponent. Twice the two men fired at each other and missed. The third time, however, Cilley was struck in the leg, one of his arteries was severed, and he bled to death in less than two minutes. He left behind a wife, three small children, and an enraged constituency.

Congress responded during its next session and made both dueling and making or accepting a challenge a criminal offense. But while this legislation appeased the public, it actually did very little to curtail dueling, and the practice continued for more than two more decades, until the more industrialized carnage of the Civil War reduced its allure to the point where it ceased altogether.

Violence throughout the surrounding area has continued up into the current era, of course, and in recent years the District of Columbia and adjacent areas like Bladensburg have been consumed by it. People should therefore be open to the idea that any ghosts they do spot may be the spirits of those killed under different conditions or in some other age than that traditionally associated with the dueling grounds.

And the gentlemen of yore, however courageous, were generally willing to face each other only with single-shot, muzzle-loading pistols, while the urban gentry of our own age regularly face each other with powerful automatic pistols that frequently have magazine capacities of fifteen rounds or more.

Questions of honor are probably no less meaningful today than they ever were. In June 1836, for example, twenty-two-year-old Daniel Key, the son of "Star-Spangled Banner" author Francis Scott Key, was gunned down in a duel with fellow U.S. Naval Academy student John Sherbourne over an argument about the speed of two steamboats. His death would certainly have not been more or less significant if it had been caused by a disagreement over the relative merits of Olde English 800 versus King Cobra forty-ounce malt liquors.

Today, the dueling grounds are located not in Bladensburg itself, but in the little adjacent township of Colmar Manor that was incorporated in the area in 1927—displaying a pair of dueling pistols, a pair of swords, and "Blood Run" on its municipal coat of arms—and next to the sprawling Fort Lincoln Cemetery. A historical marker describing the significance of the site is located in front of the grounds on Route 450/Bladensburg Road.

Author Michael H. Varhola paces off the Bladensburg Dueling Grounds, site of countless duels of honor and now believed to be haunted by the shades of men slain there.

My father and co-author accompanied me to the Bladensburg Dueling Grounds on a pleasant, slightly overcast day in
May 2009. Passing by the gray historical sign that marked the
entrance to the dueling ground—on the corner of Bladensburg
Road and 38th Avenue, and right across the latter road from an
IHOP—we turned around and parked in front of a large parking center and then walked over to the site, crossing a small
pedestrian bridge parallel with the highway and then clamber-
ing down a path to the tree-lined lawn below.

The dueling ground itself is a few hundred yards long and
surrounded by vegetation that includes massive trees. A chain-
link fence blocked access to the concrete viaduct that now marks
the course of Dueling Creek. At the far end, we discovered a
gazebo and commemorative plaque placed there by the town of
Colmar Manor and a very quiet, pleasant, surrounding neighborhood that was in sharp contrast to the dingy edifices along
the nearby highway.

Some writers have suggested that the dueling grounds used to
be larger, but they hardly would have needed to be, and I suspect
that what we were seeing would not have been much extended in
the past. While we were surveying and chatting about all of this,
a Colmar Manor police cruiser drove by, as if to remind us that it
is no longer legal for anyone to duel at the site.

We did not see any ghosts while we were at the Bladensburg
Dueling Grounds, although we did stay vigilant, and I kept my
eyes on the dark spaces between the surrounding trees, half
expecting to see something moving there. If you go there, however, especially at night, and see something spectral moving about
at the edges of the old killing field, pray that it is indeed a ghost,
and not a young man of a more corporeal nature eager to defend
their own fragile honor against offenses real or imagined.

Spotlight on Ghosts:
The Battle of Bladensburg

It bears mentioning that the Bladensburg Dueling Grounds are set within a larger area that was once also the scene of wartime violence.

On August 24, 1814, during the War of 1812, U.S. military forces massed in Bladensburg to block the advance of the invading British troops toward Washington. A force of British regulars and troops of the Corps of Colonial Marines, a unit of newly freed slaves organized for service in the Americas, joined combat with an American force of militia, sailors, and Marines.

Most of the U.S. troops were driven from the field, the exception being the sailors and Marines, who battled the redcoats hand to hand with cutlasses and pikes until withdrawing to avoid being cut off.

The victorious British marched on and burned the U.S. capital city, and it is possible that the spirits of men slain that day, perhaps even those still suffering shame from a defeat that had such serious consequences, continue to haunt the area.

CHAPTER 10

Exorcist House
MOUNT RAINIER

Children's handprints mark a path running alongside the little park that fills the lot where the "Exorcist house" once sat, a creepy addition to an already creepy site.

. . . *she had noticed a sudden and dramatic change in her daughter's behavior and disposition. Insomnia. Quarrelsome. Fits of temper. Kicked things. Threw things. Screamed. Wouldn't eat. In addition, her energy seemed abnormal. She was constantly touching, turning; tapping; running and jumping about. Doing poorly with schoolwork. Fantasy playmate . . .*

—William Peter Blatty, *The Exorcist*

EVER SINCE IT WAS RELEASED IN 1973, *The Exorcist* has widely been considered to be among the most frightening and disturbing horror films ever made; the book on which it's based holds a similar position in modern horror fiction. It is thus all the more unsettling to learn that the story is not merely the product of a fevered imagination but is instead based on an actual series of events that occurred six decades ago.

I had long had a vague awareness that *The Exorcist* was supposed to be based on a real incident but had never really known the particulars. As a resident of the Washington, D.C., area, however, I periodically heard references to the locations where the real events behind the story were believed to have taken place.

Author William Peter Blatty's story of *The Exorcist* unfolds largely in a house on M Street in the Georgetown neighborhood of Washington, D.C., and involves the eleven-year-old daughter of a famous actress, their household servants, and Jesuit priests from nearby Georgetown University, along with various other residents of the local area. The actual incident took place about seven miles to the northeast, just across the D.C. line in Mount Rainier, Maryland, and involved the thirteen-year-old son of a blue-collar family and a priest from the local Catholic parish. Blatty's story ends a few months after it begins. The real story that inspired it, however, continues to this day.

Indeed, to say that the site where the house once sat is haunted—the residence itself having been deliberately burned down in 1962 in what has, strangely, been officially characterized as a firefighter training exercise—is probably to oversimplify and even trivialize the case. To say that it remains occupied by a malignant entity that has provoked murder, poltergeist activity, demonic possession, and innumerable other episodes of human grief probably comes much closer to the truth.

A CASE OF POSSESSION

In 1949, a teen-aged resident of Mount Rainier who has been pseudonymously identified in various written sources as "Robbie Mannheim" began to suffer severe emotional problems and manifest paranormal phenomena similar to those associated with poltergeist activity, such as objects flying through the air of their own volition (*The Possessed*, a book by Thomas B. Allen that covers this incident—and is based in part on the diary of one of the priests involved in it—was released in 1993 and turned into a film of the same name in 2000.).

Conventional means of dealing with Robbie's problems—including claims of possession, cackling, writhing, spitting, and urinating—proved ineffective as they escalated and spun out of control. The family, who were Lutherans, successively consulted a physician, a psychologist, and then a Protestant minister, who examined the boy and at one point believed him to be the victim of poltergeist activity. When he witnessed phenomena that included the appearance of bloody words raised on the boy's body—including "Christ" and "Hell"—he became concerned that he was witnessing something more serious.

"You have to see a Catholic priest," he told the family, realizing that he was confronted with something paranormal in nature that went beyond his abilities to address. "The Catholics know about things like this."

And so the family turned to Father Edward Albert Hughes, a priest in his early thirties who had been the assistant pastor of nearby St. James Roman Catholic Church since the previous year. He examined Robbie, learned that the boy's problems had originated at about the same time that he had begun playing with a Ouija board, and ultimately came to the conclusion that he was suffering from demonic possession. This determination prompted him to seek permission from his superiors to perform an exorcism, which was eventually granted.

Robbie was moved to Georgetown University Medical Center, and it was there that Hughes attempted an exorcism. During the ritual, Robbie broke free of his restraints, tore a spring from his bed, and attacked the priest, slashing him severely from shoulder to wrist. Injured, Hughes withdrew, and the exorcism ended in failure.

Soon thereafter, Robbie's family moved him to the home of relatives in Bel-Nor, Missouri, where their ordeal continued and was eventually concluded two days after Easter in a successful, six-week-long exorcism by a team of local priests. Hughes continued to serve as the assistant pastor at St. James until 1960, when he departed the parish, returning in 1973 to serve as its pastor until his death in 1980.

Publisher Dominick Salemi at the small park that now sits on the site of the "Exorcist house."

Blatty, a student at Georgetown University at the time the incident took place, learned about it and, with some prompting from a priest he knew, eventually adapted it into *The Exorcist*.

A Persistent Evil

In February 2009, I met Dominick Salemi, a lawyer and the publisher of the pop culture magazine *Brutarian*, at a convention in Roanoke, Virginia, where we were both speaking on a number of panels. Over a couple of drinks one evening, I mentioned that I was working on this book.

He in turn told me about a strange and disturbing series of events he had experienced at the site of the house where the incidents on which *The Exorcist* was based had taken place. I was surprised to learn that it was located in Mount Rainier, just four miles down Route 1 from the University of Maryland College Park, where I had lived for one semester and gone to school for three years—graduating in 1993, the year that Dom's experiences had taken place. We agreed to visit the site together and, four weeks later, in late March, we hit the Capital Beltway and headed up across the Potomac River, en route for Mount Rainier.

Our first stop was in Cottage City, a little quarter-square-mile town of about 1,100 people tucked in next to Mount Rainier. Dom had done some research into the subject of the "Exorcist house" and found a detailed article whose author claimed that the site most people associated with it was incorrect and that he had found the right one. We figured it would not hurt to check it out.

We found the house easily enough—near the modest town hall and police station, where we parked—on the two-block stretch of 40th Avenue that runs through Cottage City, between Cottage Terrace and Bladensburg Road (Alternate Route 1). It was clearly occupied, well-maintained, and a private residence, nothing about it seemed in any way exceptional or ominous, and, after taking a few pictures, we walked back to the town hall. There, we chatted for a little while with police Chief Stephen Watkins, and asked him whether he had ever noticed any sort of strange activity, mundane or occult, in the vicinity of the house. He did not have anything of that sort to report, but gave us directions to the other stops on our tour.

The next one was the St. James Roman Catholic Church complex, home of exorcist Father Hughes, an easy six-block walk on nearby Rhode Island Avenue (Route 1) in Mount Rainier. It looked the part of a spiritual fortress to be sure, and it was easy to see, from the perspectives of both proximity and appearance, why the Mannheim family would have turned to it for succor. We walked around a little bit, took some pictures, and tried to enter the church itself—an effort that proved unsuccessful, all of its entrances being locked.

Returning to our car, we moved on to the object of our visit to the area. It was located on the other side of Bladensburg Road, about exactly the same distance from the church as the "alternate" house we had visited but in the opposite direction from it.

This location was the northwest corner of Bunker Hill Road and 33rd Street in Mount Rainier, where today there is a tiny, nameless, municipal park—about the size of the neighboring residential lots—fenced off from the adjacent thoroughfares and crowned by a tall wooden gazebo. A concrete path along one side of it was emblazoned with the prints of many small, outstretched hands, evocative of the operations of a planchette on a Ouija board. To the south and the west, heading up Bunker Hill Road, were houses dating to the era of the 1940s. To the north was a playground and the back of Mount Rainier Elementary School. To the east a church. To the southeast a community arts center.

This was the site that Dom had visited sixteen years earlier, but no park had been there then. Instead, there had been nothing but a vacant lot and the foundation of the ruined house, its outline marked off with posts and cord. Nothing else remained then but the gate that once led into the front yard, and as we approached the lot and began to move into it, Dom explained to me what it had looked like then. The gazebo, he said, was located on the site of the old house, and probably set right on its original foundations.

We walked around a little bit and then entered the gazebo and picked a spot that we thought probably corresponded to the front parlor of the home, where Robbie Mannheim had played with his Ouija board, triggering the events that would affect his life so profoundly. We both felt a little uneasy in this spot, and I reflected aloud that this was probably just a psychosomatic effect.

"You didn't feel that way in front of the other house, though, did you?" Dom asked me pointedly. It struck me that he was right, and that we had not felt anything particular at all in front of the other house, much less a sense of disquiet. "No," I said. "I didn't."

Dom then proceeded to tell me the story of what had happened to him sixteen years earlier.

A PLACE CURSED

"I had known that the area, the town, in which the possession had taken place in 1949, was Mount Rainier, but didn't know the address," Dom said. One day in early 1993, however, a banner headline on the front page of the *Washington Post* declared something to the effect of "Horrific Incidents on Bunker Hill Road Raise Specter of *Exorcist*."

The article associated with this headline, Dom said, described "an unrelated series of horrific incidents occurred on this street, one of which involved the discovery of a mummified body that turned out to be the mother of a man who lived on this street, Bunker Hill Road. She died, he mummified her, and he kept her in the attic for some twenty years."

A few days after this gruesome revelation, Dom said,

"another man who lived on the street and owned some properties in Washington, D.C., went downtown and, in an obvious fit of rage, dragged out one or two of the residents who were delinquent in their rent and set them on fire."

That article, he said, gave the address of the original "Exorcist house," 3210 Bunker Hill Road.

"And it revisited the story of *The Exorcist* and the possession of the young man," Dom explained. "So now my interest was really peaked because I knew where the house was and, of course, wanted to visit it."

He mentioned this to a close friend of his from Columbus, Ohio, Jim S., who asked Dom to wait a few weeks before visiting it so that he could accompany him. Dom agreed, his friend came to town, and they took a day trip out to the site—much like our own trip, I observed somewhat shakily.

"Here is what was different about it," he said. "When we pulled up on a bright sunny day like this—it was in July, I believe—it was a typical, lazy summer afternoon in the suburbs. You heard lawnmowers running, people talking, the clink of ice in glasses." Dom somewhat sheepishly admitted how kitsch all that sounds, but insists his description is accurate.

"We pulled up in front of what used to be the house, and as soon as we got out of the car," Dom said, "the seven or eight workers sitting outside the mail order warehouse, who had been laughing, and playing cards, and talking, *stopped*. They just looked at us, didn't say a word. A window was open on the side of the church and we could hear an organist practicing, and the organ playing stopped at the same time. The lawnmowers, there were a couple—it sounds incredible, but this is what happened—switched off. And really, suddenly, there was an eerie silence, up and down the length of the street."

"'Okay, we've seen the site, let's get the hell out of here; this is very weird,' I said to my friend.

"'I don't believe in this crap,' he said to me," however, and insisted they stay, so they stepped up onto the sidewalk and started to walk toward the house.

"There was a lady pushing a baby carriage right in front of us," Dom continued. "She took one look at us, crossed herself, and quickly pushed the cart up the street. At the same time, a very grotesque, severely retarded man began to lurch down the street toward us. This was the final touch; it's a long street, nothing's obscured on it, he seemed to come out of nowhere. And I turned to my friend again and said, 'This is too much like a Lovecraft story, we need to go.'" Jim was having too much fun, however, and didn't want to leave and, because he had driven, Dom could not just get back in the car and insist they depart.

"This is all true," Dom emphasized to me, adding ominously, "It's too bad I can't get Jim to corroborate it . . . "

Our conversation was interrupted at this point by an episode that almost seemed to emphasize the persistence of some psychically disturbing force over the local area.

"Excuse me! Hello! Hey! I don't *want* no more of that stuff put on my porch, Okay? I'm talking to *you*!" we heard a woman's angry voice calling from the direction of the street. Our view was blocked by some trees and, while it sounded like the words were being directed at us, we could not at first see who was speaking.

The action then moved into our field of vision, and we could see a black woman in a black SUV following an Asian man on foot, screaming threats at him. He seemed baffled or scared, and kept walking away even as she stalked him from her vehicle and spewed venom for a minute or two before finally turning and driving off. Dom and I were afraid she was going to attack or kill him and had been getting ready to render assistance and dial 911 on our cell phones.

The crisis averted, Dom returned to his story.

He and Jim approached the remains of the house, Dom said,

which consisted of little more than the foundation and, in front of it, a gate that would have once allowed access through a now-nonexistent fence into the front yard.

"In fact, there was a latch still on it," Dom said of the gate, and Jim "went up to it and he pried off the latch, which was very rusty and hanging from one rusty bolt."

"'What are you doing?' I asked him."

"'Oh, I'm just taking a souvenir,' he said." He also collected another small piece of debris before leaving the site.

"'Are you crazy?' I asked him. 'This place is probably haunted!'" Jim, however, continued to dismiss Dom's concerns.

"I started to get back in the car, but he said, 'No, no, no, we've got to walk all around it. Look how they've cordoned off the property.' And what they had done is put wooden stakes at all four corners of the house," and connected them with heavy-duty rope a couple of feet off the ground.

"There was all sorts of detritus, empty beer bottles, condoms, cigarette butts, trash all around it. But there was nothing inside the square, just grass and weeds," Dom said. This disquieted even Jim enough that he would not step across the rope into the space where the house had once sat. "And it was obvious that kids, drunks, came out at night to ponder the mysteries of the place—and I say 'ponder the mysteries of the place,' because there was nothing inside the roped-off area. And why wouldn't a drunk just throw his bottle in the middle when he was finished? Why didn't you see that?"

Unfortunately, Dom and Jim were going to learn one possible answer to this question.

"At that point, my friend said, 'This is pretty eerie.' And for some reason, I don't know what possessed me, I said, 'Oh, it's not that big a deal,' and I did something I'll always regret: I unzipped my pants and I urinated in the roped-off area." That apparently prompted the workers down by the mail-order center to start yelling at them, "so we beat a hasty retreat," Dom told me.

"After that, all manner of setbacks occurred in my life," Dom said. "At that point, my wife and I had a pretty good relationship and had been together about nine years. It really went south from there, and my wife ended up leaving me."

Within a few weeks, Dom also came down with a painful and debilitating medical condition.

"I got very, very sick, I didn't know what the problem was, and . . . for the next six months I suffered extraordinary back pains and had severe headaches. I had CAT scans, I went to the best specialists." He also experienced a series of financial difficulties and problems with his magazine. Things went badly for Jim, too.

"He had been a very wealthy man," Dom said. "Within six months, he was totally broke, had the IRS chasing him, actually had to go into hiding to keep them from throwing him in jail. Two of his dogs died mysteriously. His girlfriend, claiming he'd changed for reasons she really couldn't understand, left him."

"After about six months of this—and we talked every week or two, commiserating about who had it worse—I told him that I thought that we made a mistake in doing what we did here and that we had a curse or hex on us."

Jim concurred with this and asked what they should do. Dom told him he needed to fly back to Maryland immediately with the items he had taken from the site of the house. Destitute, Jim said he could not, but agreed to mail the items to Dom.

"'I know what you're going to do,' he told me. 'Please say that I'm sorry, too,'" Dom said.

"And so I came back up here," on a winter day in early 1994, Dom said, "and I went to the top of the hill, outside the roped-off square, threw the latch back in, and said, 'I'm sorry. I'm so sorry. And my friend Jim S. is sorry, too.'"

By all accounts, it worked for him.

"Things immediately got better for me after that," Dom said. "I felt a tremendous weight lifted from me; I just felt lighter." He felt, he said, as if he had succeeded in placating some entity that he had offended during his first visit several months before. "My financial situation stabilized. I found a doctor who could treat me, and the headaches and the back pain went away and they've never come back. I started feeling better about myself and life in general. This dark cloud was gone. Things started getting better."

But not for Jim.

"Things continued to get worse for him," Dom said. "I really felt that he needed to make the apology in person. He didn't do

St. James Roman Catholic Church, former parish of exorcist Father Edward Albert Hughes, is located a short distance away from the home occupied by possessed child Robbie Mannheim.

that, and things have never really been the same for him. Curiously, he lives in Maryland now, probably about half an hour from here, and several years after settling here had a horrible stroke. He was in perfect health, but now he's a cripple. He walks occasionally, and when he does, it is very much like the person we saw walking down the street toward us. He's never been able to hold a job, he's had drinking problems . . . things never really got better for him, and he's never been the same."

A LEGACY OF FEAR

"I still feel like there's something here," Dom said. "I recognize that there is something evil here. I've always felt that it's a conscious entity, an evil spirit, and it's never really left the place. I've made my peace with this place, but I still feel a little uneasy here."

Dom is clearly not the only one who has felt that way at the site, which, in the thirteen years following the incident with Robbie Mannheim, was occupied only sporadically and for short periods of time.

"Several people rented it after that and left almost immediately," Dom said. "No one stayed in the house for an appreciable amount of time. And then it remained empty for years. Why would this house sit abandoned when all the other houses here were occupied?" And it certainly had a premium location, sitting on an enviable little corner hillock.

Eventually, "no one would rent it. And I remember in the *Washington Post* article, they talked to realtors, who said it was haunted, nobody wanted to live there, they couldn't sell it. The few people they rented it to in the early years after the exorcism were furious when they found out why so many strange things were happening there and wanted to know 'Why did you rent it to us?'" Being deliberately burned to the ground in a fire training exercise seems to be all that was left for it.

Before leaving the site of the house altogether, we went to

visit the church across the street from it but found it locked and, as far as we could tell, unoccupied. A man pulled up and parked a car emblazoned with Christian stickers in the church lot, regarded us briefly, and then walked up the street toward one of the houses.

We then walked over to the community arts center, Joe's Movement Emporium, which had been a mail-order warehouse when Dom and Jim had visited the area. We spoke with Development Director David Robinson Slemp, who explained that there were not many people still in the area who remembered the events that transpired on the site since the release of the book and movie *The Exorcist* in the early 1970s. It is not a subject approached lightly, however, or one that evokes pleasant memories.

"They don't like to talk about it," he said. He did mention a show produced at the center last Halloween by a local troupe called "Haunted" that was inspired by the events that began just a block away.

There is little doubt in either my mind—and certainly not Dom's—that the site of the former "Exorcist house" in Mount Rainier is, indeed, haunted, that it is in many ways ideal for paranormal investigation. I also have little doubt that such an investigation might produce some striking results, as my own experience revealed: When I listened to the tape of my interview with Dom at the site, at the point where he begins to tell me about the troubles he suffered after visiting the site, I could make out a low, groaning voice separate from Dom's. It uttered two or three phrases, some of which contained words I thought I could make out, some of which were less clear. But they were there, and their effect on my psyche was unsettling.

Needing a level of technical expertise beyond my own, I turned the tape over to the Maryland-based Gabriel's Paranormal Society for analysis. They were, indeed, able to isolate the sounds I identified on the tape, and their results were striking and somewhat ominous.

One was some sort of chanting.

The other was a deep voice, which clearly asks, "Who are you?"

"It is possible that the two phenomena are unrelated," said Carol LaRiviere, Director of the Gabriel's Paranormal Society. "One might be residual and one might be 'intelligent.'"

So there is pretty likely an other-wordly presence of some sort at the site and, quite possibly, enough associated hazards that I would personally be hesitant to try to learn too much more about it, or about what haunts it. Dom has certainly had more than enough experience with it for one lifetime. And, suffice it to say, we were careful not to take any souvenirs with us when we left.

CHAPTER 11

Surratt House Museum
CLINTON

"If any place should be haunted, it is the Surratt House," says Laurie Verge, director of the restored nineteenth-century home and tavern, who believes it is occupied by the spirit of Lincoln assassination conspirator John M. Lloyd.

. . . it was a place where people could go to converse with friends and strangers alike about the problems that were dividing the country in the crucial decade before the dawn of the Civil War. The Surratts' sympathies lay with the Southern cause during that great war, and there is ample evidence that the tavern was a safe house in the Confederate underground network which flourished in southern Maryland.

—"Surratt House and Tavern . . . A Page in American History"

"IF ANY PLACE SHOULD BE HAUNTED, it is the Surratt House," said Laurie Verge, director of the restored nineteenth century home and tavern. Verge has worked at the house in some capacity for more than three decades, so if there is anyone who would know it is certainly her.

Mary Surratt, the namesake of the house and its former owner, was convicted of treason and the first woman executed by the U.S. government for whatever role she might have played in the conspiracy to assassinate President Abraham Lincoln. Many believe her to have been falsely convicted in the witch hunt that followed the murder of the wartime president; others believe her to have been a martyr to the Southern cause; and the controversy surrounding the issue is enough to keep the spirits of the dead from resting peacefully.

Many visitors to the house are apparently able to sense this on some level.

"That's the number-one question we get from visitors, even those who aren't ghosthunters," Verge said. "'Is the old place haunted?'" Whatever the case, the Surratt House has certainly gained a reputation over the years for being haunted and, being a fairly high-profile site readily accessible to visitors from Washington, D.C., it has been featured in this context in numerous book, articles, and even television shows.

While Verge is by all accounts a believer in the paranormal, she is concerned about this aspect of the Surratt House getting too much attention and overshadowing the vital and fascinating history of the place, and the role it played in one of the most tragic episodes in American history.

In the decade leading up to the Civil War and the events that would forever ensure its notoriety, the house was a hub of local activity and the property of Mary Surratt, who also owned a townhouse in nearby Washington, D.C. At the time of the assassination, she was living there, rather than in Maryland.

"Built in 1852 as a middle-class plantation home, historic Surratt House also served as a tavern and hostelry, a post office, and polling place during the crucial decade before the Civil War. During the war, it was a safe house for the Confederate underground which flourished in Southern Maryland," say museum materials describing the house. Today, the site is "dedicated to fostering an appreciation for the history and culture of nineteenth-century Maryland and Prince George's County with special emphasis on the crucial years from 1840 to 1865" and seeks "to interpret the impact of this period on our national history as well as on the family of John and Mary Surratt, who became entangled in the web of conspiracy surrounding the assassination of President Abraham Lincoln." Costumed docents—members of the Surratt Society—guide visitors through the house and describe everyday life in the nineteenth century.

Physically, the Surratt House is a two-story, Federalist style, clapboarded wood-frame structure with a rectangular plan, a gabled roof, interior chimneys, wrap-around hip-roofed porch

Some people have claimed to see the ghost of Mary Surratt standing on the stairway leading up to the second floor of her former home.

with decorative brackets, and a centered main door that includes sidelights and a transom. It includes a one-and-a-half story wing on its southeast end that was constructed in the 1980s as a replacement for the original ground-floor areas include a small, one-room tavern that also served as a post office and tobacconist's, a guest dining room, a family dining room, a parlor, and a large, beautifully restored kitchen. Areas on the upper level include a guest bedroom, family bedrooms, and a somewhat strange, unfinished room above the kitchen that may have been used as slave quarters. It was here that the Lincoln assassination conspirators hid a Spencer carbine, lowering it down into the space between the walls in an unsuccessful attempt to keep it from being discovered by U.S. authorities.

Hard financial times plagued the Surratt family in the years leading up to the Civil War, in part because of the dissolute lifestyle of Mary's hard-drinking husband, John Harrison Surratt, and were exacerbated when he died suddenly in 1862 (likely of a heart attack). Proceeds from the sale of tobacco grown on the 287 acres surrounding the house were not enough to meet the family's needs and Mary was forced to run it as an inn and tavern and to turn her home in Washington into a boarding house (now the Wok and Roll Restaurant in the city's Chinatown).

Mary Surratt's Washington boarders included a number of the people convicted as members of the conspiracy to kill Lincoln, and her house in Clinton was used to store arms, ammunition, and other supplies by the conspirators. It was to obtain some of these items that an injured John Wilkes Booth stopped at the house in the middle of the night after shooting Lincoln at Ford's Theater and fleeing the city by way of Maryland, along with his co-conspirator David Herold. (Ford's Theater, by the way, is one of the haunted sites I cover in *Ghosthunting Virginia*, which also includes the District of Columbia.)

This strange, unfinished room above the kitchen may have been used as slave quarters and it was here that the Lincoln assassination conspirators hid a Spencer carbine, lowering it down into the space between the walls.

The extent to which Mary Surratt was actually involved in the conspiracy and whether she deserved to be executed and have her reputation forever tarnished has long been debated by historians. Verge has little doubt on this score, however, and says that the unfortunate woman was almost definitely involved, along with her son, John. Verge also has little doubt that the house is, indeed, haunted—but probably not by the ghost of Mary Surratt.

"We think we have a male ghost," Verge said. She went on to admit that when she started working at the house as a volunteer in 1975—she became manager of the site eight years later—she was skeptical about ghosts on the property. "But I'm not a disbeliever anymore."

In 1983, Verge's office was not in the museum annex where it is currently located but upstairs in the Surratt House itself, and it was there that she began to experience things she could not readily explain.

"I started hearing footsteps," Verge said, during times when no one but she was in the house. "And if it was Mary Surratt, then she was wearing army boots!" The sound was more suggestive of a man's heavy tread. "If I was upstairs, I heard it downstairs, and if I was downstairs, I heard it upstairs."

And sometimes when Verge was sitting at her desk, with her back to the entrance to her office, she "would have the sensation of someone walking out of what was then the master bedroom, standing in my office doorway looking at me, and then walking into an adjacent bedroom."

Verge was unsettled by these experiences but figured there was a chance that they might just be her imagination, until one morning in the 1980s when she and her secretary arrived at the house together and, entering it, turned off the alarm system, and started getting the place ready for visitors.

"We stopped at the foot of the stairs and were just talking," Verge said, when all of a sudden both of them gasped simultaneously. "Because at the same time, *both* of us had heard footsteps above our heads."

Verge and her secretary are by no means the only people who have reported odd occurrences at the Surratt House. One of the volunteers at the site many years ago, for example, saw a tall man in black period clothing at the door to the house as he was approaching it. He lost sight of the man when he was parking, and when asked other people already at the house who the costumed visitor was, they said that nobody else had been there.

"And, of course, through the years—the house was lived in continuously until 1965 by a variety of families—there have always been ghost stories," Verge said. A family that lived here in the 1950s reported to the famous ghost chaser Hans Holzer that they heard men talking at the back of the house. (Holzer made this information the basis of Chapter Three in his *Window to the Past: Exploring History Through ESP.*)

"But everything has been sort of male-oriented," Verge said. And, she noted, the appearance of the man people described seeing was consistent with that of a man who did have a connection with the house during the period of its brush with great events: John M. Lloyd, a former policeman who was renting the property from Mary Surratt and serving as its innkeeper.

"If there is a ghost here, I believe that it is John Lloyd," Verge said. Lloyd would certainly appear to have been a member of the assassination conspiracy and, when Booth and Herold arrived at the Surratt tavern the night of Lincoln's murder, he gave the fugitives food, whiskey, field glasses, pistols, and one of the two carbines stored at the house (proceeding thereafter to hide the other one in the walls, where it was subsequently discovered by Federal troops who raided the place). But Lloyd did not share the fates of the other people convicted in the conspiracy. Instead, he became a state's witness and testified against them, saving his own life but helping to send four of them to the gallows and a number of others to prison. It is certainly easy to see how the emotions associated with such a betrayal could contribute to a place being haunted and how the guilt of such an act might hang over someone and torment them even beyond their death.

Over the years, many other people have had experiences at the house similar to those of Verge and her coworkers, and published accounts of paranormal phenomena also describe disembodied voices of men talking together and the apparition of a man. Other people have also claimed to see the shade of Mary Surratt standing on the porch of the house and on the stairway leading up to the second floor. In the absence of any particularly strong evidence for this, however, I am inclined to defer to Verge's well-considered position that, if the place really is haunted, it is by the ghost of Lloyd and not that of Surratt. In any event, Surratt's ghost has been much more strongly and credibly associated with the site of her death, Fort Lesley J. McNair.

My wife, Diane, and I visited the Surratt House and met with Verge in mid-February 2009, on the typically bright and sunny—albeit cold—sort of day that makes travel easy but does not seem to be very auspicious for ghosthunting, and none of our photos or audio recordings revealed any anomalies. But there was, nonetheless, an ironic twist: the date of our visit to Surratt House was February 12, 2009—Abraham Lincoln's two-hundredth birthday.

Mary Surratt was imprisoned and executed at what is now U.S. Army Fort Lesley J. McNair in Washington, D.C., and her ghost is believed to haunt one of the buildings there.

Spotlight on Ghosts: Fort Lesley J. McNair

While Mary Surratt's ghost is not among those generally believed to haunt her house in Clinton, Maryland, a shade believed to be hers has been reported many times over the years at the military facility where she spent her last days and was ultimately executed on July 7, 1865, at the age of forty-two.

Surratt was imprisoned at the federal penitentiary adjacent to the Washington Arsenal, on the site of what is today the U.S. Army's Fort Lesley J. McNair, located in Washington, D.C., about fifteen miles from the Surratt House Museum on a point of land where the Anacostia and Potomac Rivers meet. This location has housed a military facility of some sort since 1791, so it is a reasonable bet that Surratt's ghost is not the only one that haunts its grounds.

When the British sacked Washington in 1814, for example, a group of about four dozen redcoats was detailed to locate and destroy a Federal powder magazine at the arsenal. Finding the magazine empty, the troops began to search the surrounding area, and one threw a match into the well where the U.S. troops had hidden the powder.

"A tremendous explosion ensued," a witness to the scene reported, "whereby the officers and about thirty of the men were killed and the rest most shockingly mangled."

U.S. Army Major Walter Reed, a physician famous for his research into treatments for malaria and yellow fever, also died at the facility in 1902, and the building where he succumbed to a failed appendectomy at the age of fifty-one is still in use today.

The building where Surratt was incarcerated has since been put to other uses, including housing for military personnel. In fact, my wife, Diane, had a friend who lived in them around 1980, when they were bachelor officer quarters. An Army captain at the time, he

Spotlight on Ghosts:
Fort Lesley J. McNair
(continued)

heard accounts of weird phenomena from other people who lived in the building but only experienced one thing firsthand which, if not irrefutable evidence of the paranormal, was certainly unnerving: His dog would sit and stare for long periods of time (at nothing its owner could see) into one particular corner of the house.

Laurie Verge, director of the Surratt House Museum, has heard similar stories over the years.

"I had one guy call up and identify himself as an officer moving into 'Quarters 20,'" Verge said of someone who had contacted her in the 1990s. "'I understand that I'm going to be living with the ghost of Mary Surratt, so please fill me in on the history of the place,' he said."

"We used to laugh, because most of the sightings there had her floating down the hall from the bathroom," Verge said. But, she said, historian Michael Kaufman, an authority on the history of the place, studied the floor plans of the building from 1865—and determined that the prisoner's box where Surratt was held was located where the bathroom is now.

Nonmilitary visitors cannot gain unrestricted access to Fort McNair, but tours of it are sometimes available for those who are interested.

CHAPTER 12

Mount Airy Mansion
UPPER MARLBORO

So much paranormal phenomena has occurred at Mount Airy Mansion that it prompted the London-based Society for Psychical Research to conduct an investigation of the site in 1931.

Something is rotten in the state of Denmark.

—William Shakespeare, *Hamlet*

IN HIS BLOOD-DRENCHED TRAGEDY *HAMLET,* William Shakespeare postulates that political malfeasance can prevent the dead from resting soundly and prompt them to haunt the earth as ghosts. If that is indeed the case, it might go a long way toward explaining the high incidence of ghosts in the state of Maryland, where a great many things in officialdom are, most assuredly, rotten. Maryland has traditionally been a den of political corruption, its most famous blackguard being perhaps Spiro Agnew, forced to resign as vice president of the United States after it was discovered that he had solicited and received bribes while serving as governor of the state. My initial personal exposure to inappropriate behavior by public servants in the state came during my first week as a student at the University of Maryland in 1989, when I witnessed Prince George's County policemen putting tape over their nametags so that they could beat with impunity people standing in a public area. And it would certainly be fair to say that during the time of my association with various Maryland state institutions that I routinely witnessed activity ranging from questionable to almost openly illegal.

So I should not necessarily have been surprised to have encountered behavior at Mount Airy Mansion of a sort that my kids and their friends would call "sheisty": perhaps not strictly in violation of the law but certainly somewhat shady and on the ethically questionable side. And, if Shakespeare is right, then the shenanigans at Mount Airy Mansion might suggest that the place is as haunted now as it has been reputed to be in the past.

Mount Airy Mansion is one of the places I was most excited about including in this book, and for good reason. Not only has the historic mansion long had a reputation for being haunted, it also has a distinguished history as a venue of paranormal investigation.

Located in southern Prince George's County, the property, along with the surrounding ninety-two hundred acres, was owned by the Calvert family, the Lords Baltimore, who ruled Maryland as a hereditary barony. There is some dispute as to when the various portions of the house were built, but some historians claim that its oldest section—a single, fifty-foot-long hall with fireplaces at each end—dates to as early as the 1660s and that it was used as a hunting lodge. There is also some disagreement as to whether some or all of this original part was destroyed in a fire that ravaged the building in 1752.

Frederick Calvert, the sixth and final Baron Baltimore, never set foot in Maryland, regarded it only as a source of income, and led a short but dissolute life that included a period in Constantinople, where he created a scandal by keeping a private harem. (Alas, it would seem that Maryland has suffered from bad government since its earliest days.) Lord Frederick bequeathed the colony to one of his illegitimate sons, but the American Revolution was in full swing by the time he tried to claim his properties there, and he was thereby despoiled of them.

Other Calverts, however, supported the American bid for independence—aristocrats are nothing if not pragmatic—and so the estate remained under their control. George Washington himself was their close friend, and visited the house many times, including the wedding of his stepson, John Parke Custis, to the beautiful Eleanor "Nellie" Calvert. Their son, George Washington Parke Custis, was born at the plantation, and went

One of the ghosts believed to haunt Mount Airy Mansion is that of Eleanor Bresco Calvert, an obsessive woman who disliked using the front parlor of the house in life and searches for some of her missing jewelry in death.

on to marry Mary Lee Fitzhugh Custis, become father-in-law to Confederate General Robert E. Lee, and build the Arlington mansion on the banks of the Potomac River (to which a chapter is devoted in my *Ghosthunting Virginia*).

Mount Airy Mansion remained in the Calvert family until 1902, when its last occupant, eccentric Eleanor Bresco Calvert, died there at the age of eighty-one as the result of a tumble down the stairs. After her death, it was converted to a restaurant. In 1931, when it was a fashionable restaurant named Dower House, there was a fire. According to the Rosaryville Conservancy: "It was after this fire that Cissy Patterson, the illustrious owner of the [Washington] *Times-Herald*, bought and restored the mansion. She also added the swimming pool, tennis court, guest cottages, and a large green house [for] her fabulous collection of orchids. She entertained lavishly, and her guests included Mr. and Mrs. Franklin Delano Roosevelt, Alice Roosevelt Longworth, Robert Considine, author Adela St. John, and other well-known people of the time."

"In spite of the fact that she had several other homes, one as close as Dupont Circle, she spent summers as well as frequent weekends at Mount Airy from 1931 until her death in the house in 1948," the Rosaryville Conservancy account continues. "She died in what was then her bedroom, now the offices for Pineapple Alley Catering. That ended a very public and glamorous era for Mount Airy, but it's far from the whole story of the house."

No indeed. But that "whole story," unfortunately, cannot be found on any of the sites run by the Maryland Department of Natural Resources, the Rosaryville Conservancy, or the afore-mentioned catering company, which we will discuss more presently.

In fact, during the twenty-eight-year period that the house was operated as a restaurant, its residents began to suffer increasingly from all manner of ghostly phenomena. Most significant of these was the haunting by a spirit identified as Elea-

nor Bresco Calvert, the last member family member to occupy
the house, who wandered its halls by night and was believed to
be searching for some of the family's missing jewels. She is,
indeed, believed to have begun haunting the place even before
she was buried.

According to the story, Eleanor disliked using the front parlor
of the house and kept the door to it locked. When she died, she
was laid out in this very room the evening before her funeral,
and it was left unlocked, the preferences of the fussy old woman
no longer being important to anyone. The next day, however, the
door was found to be locked, and after an exhaustive search for
the key, the door had to be broken in. It was then that the key
was discovered—sitting on a table next to Eleanor's coffin.

A whole repertoire of gothic legends has been associated

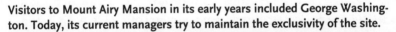

Visitors to Mount Airy Mansion in its early years included George Washington. Today, its current managers try to maintain the exclusivity of the site.

with the house, including stories of a spectral woman in white looking out from one of the windows in the house; a ghostly horseman in archaic attire (who, in some stories, is the man the woman is watching for); an old woman who wanders from room to room, waking sleeping people; and a haunted room where candles will not remain lit.

Paranormal phenomena at the place became, in fact, so much of a problem that the owners had the London-based Society for Psychical Research do an investigation of the site. This investigation, which apparently took place in 1931, just before the fire that ended the place's days as a restaurant, did in fact confirm the claims of the beleaguered owners.

Clearly, this was a place that warranted visitation and inclusion in this book, and it was near the top of my list from the start. In my naive but fevered mind, I could imagine being in the parlor, wearing my finest Edwardian-era suit (which I don't actually own), and sitting around a levitating table with a group of similarly clad people (none of whom I bothered to clearly identify). Sadly, the reality of these things are almost always much less glamorous.

In February 2009, I started to make the necessary preparations to visit Mount Airy Mansion. Some online research indicated that it belongs to the Maryland Department of Natural Resources, which acquired it with state and federal funds in 1973 from the family to whom Cissy Patterson had bequeathed it, and that it is on the grounds of the Rosaryville State Park. This clearly meant, I assumed, that the site was publicly accessible and administered by dispassionate state employees who would not have any reasons to prevent me from visiting it and perhaps even conducting some measure of an investigation at it.

When I called the number provided for the mansion, however, I was rudely disabused of this notion. As usual, when the woman at the other end of the line answered the phone, I identified myself and started to explain that I was working on a book called *Ghosthunting Maryland.*

"We're not interested in ghosthunters," she said, cutting me off before I could get any further into my explanation—and then abruptly hung up the phone! I immediately called back and, when the same person answered, introduced myself and, before trying to explain myself again, asked for the name of the person with whom I was speaking. Anonymity tends to breed rudeness, it seems, and from that point forward the person who identified herself as Marsha Schlossberg—an employee of a private company and not the state of Maryland at all—was markedly more cooperative with me.

Schlossberg told me that the company she worked for, Pineapple Alley Catering Company, had been approached many times by ghosthunters wanting to conduct investigations. My impression from our conversation was that none of them had been accommodated but she stopped short of clearly confirming that for me.

When I expressed my understanding that Mount Airy Mansion was a public site administered by the state of Maryland (the implication being that I could visit and write about it whether or not she or her company liked it), she said that was not exactly true, and that Pineapple Alley Catering Company had an exclusive twenty-year-year lease to manage the mansion and park (the implication being that they could decide who got to visit the house and what they were allowed to do there).

She was also adamant not just that the house *was not* haunted but, indeed, that it *could not* be haunted.

"I've worked ten years at the house and spent hundreds of hours in it, and I've never seen evidence of a ghost," Schlossberg said. "The house is not haunted, and I can tell you why I believe that." She then went on to give me her brief take on the haunted history of the place (which, while full of perfectly valid opinions, did not actually include any reasons for why the place might not actually be haunted).

According to Schlossberg, rumors of Mount Airy being haunted originated with a couple who many years ago operated the mansion as a bed-and-breakfast (presumably her description of the Dower House restaurant). She said that they manufactured the stories of haunting merely as a publicity stunt and that they brought the English psychic research group to the house at their own expense in order to bolster their fraudulent claims (although one might certainly have thought such a move would have increased the chances that their duplicity would be revealed).

Finally, according to Schlossberg, both Rosaryville State Park and Mount Airy Mansion are limited-access facilities open to the

While Mount Airy Mansion is ostensibly open to the public, locked gates require visitors to park elsewhere and make their way to it on foot.

public only certain days and times. Well, a perusal of the state of Maryland Web site devoted to the site revealed that to be true in the sense that it is true for all state-run parks—but Rosaryville is apparently no more restrictive than any other parks in the Maryland DNR system, and there is nothing online to indicate that the house cannot simply be visited like any other historic site. There is also nothing to indicate that Pineapple Alley is also the manager of the park itself (but who the hell knows just how much the DNR has washed its hands of its citizenry's assets).

And so my wife and I decided to take a day trip out to it one bright, sunny day in mid-February 2009. Everything started off pretty well as we followed the directions from our GPS system, corroborating them with the regular state-funded brown attraction signs for Mount Airy Mansion that we started to see soon after getting off the appropriate exit from the Capitol Beltway. We made good time and before long we reached the address for the place on Rosaryville Road and saw . . . a locked iron gate blocking a road that led away northward into the woods. Huh? Well, this was the address that had been provided for the house itself, not Rosaryville State Park, and so we figured we just needed to go to it.

The entrance to the park was just a few miles away, off connecting MD 301, and we made it there in a few minutes, paid the fee to enter via an automated kiosk, and drove to the parking area. There, we found some display cases with information about Rosaryville State Park and Mount Airy Mansion but . . . no house. No signs indicating which trails might lead to the house. No maps showing the relative location of the house. No state personnel to approach with questions about the house.

There was, however, a phone number for the ranger station at another Maryland DNS park nearby that people could call for more information. I did, and the woman at the other end of the line was very pleasant but completely uninformed about the site she was supposed to be able to provide information about, directing us back to the place where our progress had been blocked by a gate and surprised to hear that one was there. It was her impression that we should have been able to simply drive up to the house and visit it.

And so we drove back, parked on the street in a residential neighborhood across the highway from the gate, and walked over to it. Examination revealed a sign claiming the area was under video surveillance—although, like much else we had been told, this did not appear to be true—but no prohibitions against entering the area. Accordingly, we walked around the gate and started up the road.

After about three-quarters of a mile, we reached the house, a beautiful mansion surrounded by gardens and several outbuildings, including an old gatehouse. We only passed one person on the way, an old man who appeared to be coming and going from a small, relatively modern house that we took to be a caretaker's residence.

Approaching the right side of house, we began to walk around it, looking through the windows and trying the front door, which was locked. We continued clockwise around it, and on the left side of the State-of-Maryland-owned building, we discovered a person . . . washing a privately owned vehicle with State-of-Maryland-owned water. Ah.

We engaged her as much as we could in conversation, but she was somewhat evasive and sullen, clearly didn't want us there, but clearly was not empowered to just make us leave; she sounded like Schlossberg, gave us the same sort of spiel, but I don't know for sure if it was Schlossberg. In short, she told us not just that we could not visit the house that day, but that it was *never* open to the public. The old man we had seen earlier showed up during this fruitless interchange, provided similar discouragement, and, like her, avoided making eye contact with us. We thanked them for their "help," looked around a bit more, and then hiked out. We never mentioned ghosthunting or anything of a similar nature, so it seems even normal people are treated badly at the site.

Later, some additional research revealed a few more things. One is that the distance from the Rosaryville State Park parking area to the house was less than what we had walked, probably under half a mile, making it the preferred way to approach the house for those with the time and inclination to do some exploring. Another is that the house is actually open to the public a couple of times a year for various special events, but perhaps that is just a pro forma thing required by the state, and is certainly nothing the people we spoke with bothered to mention. The rest of the time, anyone who wants to visit the house needs to rent it, with rates that vary by day and duration. This, in fact, may be the easiest way for a paranormal group with some resources to get into the place and conduct an investigation, but it was beyond what we were able to do as individuals.

And so, just as Maryland itself was once a hereditary barony, it would seem that Mount Airy Mansion is today operated as a private fief to the greatest extent its caretakers can manage—and apparently with the blessings of the Maryland state authorities charged with oversight of such properties. Mount Airy Mansion is, nonetheless, a place warranting paranormal investigation and where such investigation is indeed possible. It just takes a bit more diligence than most publicly accessible sites—and the knowledge that it is, indeed, open to the public, despite the attitudes and efforts of its custodians.

CHAPTER 13

St. Mary's Cemetery
ROCKVILLE

F. Scott Fitzgerald is buried next to his wife, Zelda Sayre, and near several members of his family, including his parents and daughter.

I wouldn't mind a bit if in a few years Zelda and I could snuggle up together under a stone in some graveyard. That is really a happy thought, and not melancholy at all.

—F. Scott Fitzgerald

SET NEXT TO ONE OF Maryland's oldest churches and just a few blocks from one of the state's busiest roads, St. Mary's Cemetery is an ancient little wedge of crumbling gravestones and overhanging trees not much more than a few acres in size. It is a little oasis of solitude, its wrought iron fence forming a barrier that makes the nearby heavy press of traffic moving toward the Rockville Pike seem far away and somewhat unreal, like images viewed through a spyglass.

Many of the people buried in the cemetery established next to old St. Mary's Church—a house of worship dating to 1817 and still used along with a new structure next door to it—lived during the Revolutionary War, and the burial ground was closed to new internments many years ago. One of the last people to be buried there, however, is associated with a much more recent era and remembered as one of the greatest of American authors.

That F. Scott Fitzgerald had any connection in life with Rockville, the town where he now rests in death, comes as a surprise to many people. He was, after all, born in St. Paul, Minnesota, and spent the last years of his life in faraway Hollywood, California, where he died from a heart attack, caused at least in part by his heavy drinking.

As a boy, however, Fitzgerald had often visited his father's relatives in Montgomery County, and is believed to have returned to the area many times over the years even as an adult (although the historic record is a bit sparse in this regard). We know for certain that he visited St. Mary's Cemetery itself in 1931, traveling there from Paris, when his father died and was buried there.

"It was very friendly leaving him there with all his relations around him," Fitzgerald wrote at least semi-autobiographically in *Tender is the Night* a few years later. "Good-by, my father."

And it was beside his father that Fitzgerald himself wished to be laid upon his own death just nine years later. Unfortunately, due to circumstances that are now somewhat unclear and in dispute, Fitzgerald was buried initially not at St. Mary's Cemetery but at nearby Rockville Union Cemetery, a mile and a half to the east. Eight years later, his wife Zelda Sayre was laid to rest beside him, after she herself was killed in a tragic fire that swept through the North Carolina sanatorium in which she had been committed off and on since 1936 because of her mental illness.

The couple lay together at that cemetery for more than three decades, until they were relocated to St. Mary's Cemetery through the combined efforts of their only child, Frances "Scottie" Fitzgerald Lanahan Smith, and the Women's Club of Rockville. (Despite the fact that the cemetery was subsequently closed to new interments, Scottie herself received permission in 1985 to be buried there, and the following year was laid to rest beside her parents.)

Although I have long been a big fan of Fitzgerald, have for many years loved his greatest work, *The Great Gatsby*, and have driven through Rockville countless times, I had never actually visited the author's grave. But in the years since Fitzgerald was finally laid to rest in St. Mary's Cemetery, people have claimed to sense the presence of his spirit there, and it was those stories that prompted me to finally venture there on a gloomy day in mid-March, 2009.

It was early afternoon when I pulled into the church parking lot and, figuring that a visit to the cemetery constituted legitimate business, decided to brave the prominent "violators will be towed" signs. Wending my way between the rectory and the new church building and up to the front of the old church building, I came to the entrance of the cemetery.

Any concerns I had that I would have trouble finding Fitzgerald's grave were alleviated when I saw how small the cemetery was and realized that, if necessary, I could just go through it marker by marker until I found it. It didn't take long, and as I walked up the single path that leads through the grounds, my eyes were drawn to a large, relatively new marker off to my right that I was sure was the object of my visit. I walked over toward it, careful not to step on any of the small, low markers that dotted the intervening ground, and confirmed that my intuition was correct.

The first thing that struck me when I stepped around to the front of the author's grave was that he and I share the same birthday—September 24—and that he was born exactly seventy years before me, something I had not recalled noting previously. Sadly, however, he did not survive the span of years separating us, and died at the age of just forty-four, on December 21, 1940.

As I photographed the area around the gravesite, I took note of other details. An epitaph was carved into the slab laying over the plot, and bore the closing words to *The Great Gatsby*: "So we beat on, boats against the current, borne back ceaselessly into the past." Votive offerings of various sorts lay on and around the marker and slab, including a number of small jars containing pennies and a few quarters, a rock, and a variety of pens. A half dozen other Fitzgerald family tombstones were clustered around that of the author, and nine other relatives—members of the Scott, Delihant, and Robertson families—were buried nearby.

I also noted a faint shimmering over the author's white rock tombstone, but figured it must have just been a trick of the light which, combined with my aging eyes, prevented me from focusing clearly on its surface. Stepping up to the stone, I placed my hand upon it, and was astounded to feel it—albeit almost imperceptibly—quivering! A few hundred feet away I could see heavy traffic moving along Veirs Mill Road and wondered if it, or the subterranean Metro line that ran somewhere nearby, might not be causing this strange effect. I nonetheless closed my eyes and tried to commune with whatever part of the author might still be there and, as I did, began to sense a low, audible humming that seemed to surround me. I then felt a thumping, like a heartbeat, that seemed to emanate from the cold, hard, but almost shimmering tombstone which, through a seemingly mystical combination of traffic vibration, my own pulse, and the power of suggestion made the rock feel as it were alive.

Starting to feel overcome by this effect, I opened my eyes and lifted my hand from Fitzgerald's tombstone and, in so doing, was startled by my abrupt return to the sights and sounds of the mundane world. Wanting to explain away if possible any of the sensations I had felt, I placed my hand in the same way upon the tombstone right beside the one I had just been touching. I was surprised to note how relatively cold and dead this stone was and that the quivering I had taken to be traffic vibration was not present in it. I quickly returned my hand to the author's marker, and was stunned to once again feel the quivering and pulsation, along with a nonphysical sense of warmth.

Sensing that I had achieved more than I could have reasonably expected and that any further experimentation would be somewhat vulgar and disrespectful, I removed my hand, took a few more pictures, and then walked away from the gravesite and exited the cemetery in a state of euphoria. Stepping through

Located near one of the busiest roads in the state, St. Mary's Cemetery is an oasis of solitude in a bustling metropolitan area.

the gate, I walked up to the adjacent entrance to the old church building, which I had seen a few people passing through, and entered it.

The small, consecrated area within felt like a microcosm, silent and peaceful as a sepulcher. A scattered dozen or so faithful knelt at the pews within. I made my own oblations and then, almost reluctantly, stepped back out into the gloomy and noisy outside world.

Someone else was entering the cemetery as I left the church and, deciding to chat him up a bit and introduce myself, was pleased to make the acquaintance of Kevin D., property manager of the church for the past three years. He confirmed that at least one person had reported experiencing something of a supernatural sort in the cemetery, but he did not believe it had been associated with the Fitzgerald gravesite. He said the main sorts of weirdness he has encountered in the cemetery are the vestiges of voodoo-like rituals conducted during hours of darkness, to include chickens—both dead and alive—and invocations stuffed into buried bottles.

Kevin did note that the Fitzgerald grave does get an inordinate amount of attention, most of it positive in nature, such as offerings like those I had seen, flowers, and even bottles of wine (which does seem a bit cavalier to be leaving for someone whose health was shattered by alcoholism). At least once a year, he said, a large group of people holds some sort of memorial at the graveside.

"I'm not sure what the pens are all about," Kevin said. Having just left my own pen at Fitzgerald's grave, following a tradition that I first observed at Marcel Proust's gravesite at Pere Lachaise Cemetery in Paris, I explained that it is something done by writers hoping to obtain some of the blessings of those most revered members of their vocation.

I accompanied Kevin to the rectory, where he introduced me

to Monsignor John Myslinski, pastor of St. Mary's Church, who graciously took the time to chat with me not just about the history of his church, but also about such topics as lingering spirits in particular and religion in general. A native of Salem, Massachusetts, as well as a priest, he was open to the idea of earth-bound spirits, and when I asked him directly if he thought Fitzgerald's ghost lingered in the cemetery of his church, he shrugged and said, "Sure, it might."

An easygoing acceptance of the unseen world that is at the same time devoid of any apparent gullibility is a rare thing indeed, and I found myself not just liking smart and loquacious Monsignor Myslinski but also being impressed with his good sense and sincerity. (He made an interesting distinction in our conversation, by the way, between the terms "supernatural" and

Author F. Scott Fitzgerald, a descendant of Francis Scott Key who loved visiting relatives in Maryland as a boy, is buried at St. Mary's Cemetery in Rockville.

"preternatural," associating the former with the positive domain of angels and good spirits and the latter with the dangerous realms of demons, devils, and evil spirits.)

When my interview with the monsignor ended and I returned to my car and drove away from the church, it was with an effervescent positive feeling, almost giddiness but not quite approaching euphoria. It was, in short, the reverse of feelings I have had at negatively haunted sites (e.g., disquiet that did not quite rise to the level of actual fear), and was reminiscent of positive supernatural experiences I had read about in association with other sites, especially burial grounds, such as Arlington National Cemetery.

So does the spirit of F. Scott Fitzgerald linger on in St. Mary's Cemetery in Rockville? Well, as the current pastor of the adjacent church observed, it very well might, and I would be inclined to say that it does. And, if it does, it seems to me that it is a very benign haunting, and that part of what made the author great in life is what has remained behind to commune with those who would still seek to receive inspiration from his words.

CHAPTER 14

University of Maryland
COLLEGE PARK

Strange phenomena have been reported at Cole Field House since it was opened in 1955. Current legends involve Maryland basketball player Len Bias, who died nearby in 1986, and a spectral runner.

Night watchmen and building inhabitants ... reported sensing other-worldly presences, doors opening and shutting on their own, toilets flushing when no one was there, and matches blowing out when all the doors and windows were closed. Perhaps these occurrences can be tied to Dean Marie Mount's ghost, who, on dark and stormy nights, as the wind blows through the building, and the rain pounds on the window panes, allegedly can be heard vigorously playing a piano.

—Anne Turkos and Liz McAllister, University of Maryland Ghost Tour

AS HOME TO MORE THAN thirty thousand people, the University of Maryland's flagship campus in College Park is virtually a small city. Like any other community of similar size, chances are it is going to have some ghost stories associated with it. University of Maryland College Park, it turns out, has a lot.

During the years I was a student at the UM campus, from 1990–1993, and then as an editor for University of Maryland University College, the institution's affiliated night school, I heard many rumors about paranormal activities at several sites in and around the campus. Some of them were connected to an unfortunate spate of suicides that occurred in a block of high-rise undergraduate dormitories along the north edge of the university's grounds, and raised the question of whether they were haunted as a result—or, already being haunted, whether they had somehow played a role in the deaths. A number of these North Campus Dorms have been considered by many to be venues for paranormal activity, particularly Easton Hall, constructed in 1965.

Such rumors are certainly nothing new and go back many decades. My friend Bob Waters, for example, who graduated from the University of Maryland in the 1970s, told me that he heard rumors about strange occurrences at several of its locations during his time there. He also served as a member of the campus police force in those days and recalls getting calls about odd things at various sites, especially Cole Field House.

I decided to learn a bit more about what haunts the buildings, and my inquiries ultimately led me to Anne Turkos, the university archivist. When queries about ghosts on campus come in to various departments, many ultimately work their way through the system until they reach Anne and two of her colleagues, Liz McAllister and Jennie Levine. The three of them have collected the various stories associated with the university and the surrounding area and are, as a result, collectively considered to be the resident experts on them. Over the years, they have also organized a number of activities tying in with the subject, including an exhibit at the Hornbake Library and a ghost tour that they organized as part of a family weekend event in October 2006.

I met with Anne, Liz, and Jennie in May 2009, and spent a couple of hours chatting with them and visiting reputedly haunted sites around the sprawling campus. They acknowledged that many people believe that certain locations on the campus are haunted, and Anne said she has talked to people she considers credible who have reported paranormal experiences at the school. Anne admitted that she herself has had at least one experience on campus that she believes to be supernatural in character (although it was of a personal nature and not associated with one of the sites we subsequently discussed or visited).

After chatting for awhile in her office, Anne and I set out to visit some of the most reputedly haunted sites on the University of Maryland College Park campus, starting with one of its original buildings. For convenience, those that follow are in the order presented in her tour.

ROSSBOROUGH INN

Built between 1804 and 1812 and named for tavern keeper John Ross, the Rossborough Inn is the oldest building on campus and was one of the original buildings included in what started off in 1856 as the Maryland Agricultural College. It is located on a e 428-acre tract of land that was owned by Charles Benedict Calvert and his brother George, who pushed for establishment of the college and helped it raise the funds needed to buy their land. Over the years, the building has been used as headquarters for various departments, housing for faculty and students, a faculty-staff club, and office space.

Located along the main route between Baltimore and Washington, D.C., the inn served as a way station for people traveling between the two cities. Some of them were on their way to the Bladensburg Dueling Grounds, a site four miles to the south used by statesmen and military officers to settle their differences. (See the separate chapter in this book on the Bladensburg Dueling Grounds.) Two of these men could apparently not

Built in the early nineteenth century, the Rossborough Inn is the oldest building on campus and is believed to be haunted by a man killed in a duel on its grounds and the woman who ran it during the Civil War.

wait to resolve their dispute and, accordingly, paced off and then discharged their pistols at each other beside the Rossborough Inn. One of them was mortally wounded, and he was taken into one of the inn's third-floor rooms to die. His blood reportedly still stains the floor of that room, and his spirit is one of those believed to haunt the building.

During the Civil War, the inn served briefly as the headquarters of Confederate General Bradley T. Johnson in April 1864, during a rebel incursion into the Old Line State, and between April and June of that year, the area around the campus was occupied by both blue and gray troops. The inn was managed at that time by a woman known as Miss Bettie, and her ghost, clad in a long yellow gown, is one of those that has been seen walking the halls of the building. She is also held accountable for various other phenomena at the inn: vases of flowers appearing out of nowhere, lights inexplicably turning off, doors opening of their own accord, footsteps in empty upstairs area, and a face that has been spotted in windows and mirrors.

Marie Mount Hall

Constructed in 1940 and known since 1967 for Marie Mount—who came to the university in 1919 and served as dean of the College of Home Economics from 1927 until her death in 1957—this building is reputed to be one of the most haunted on campus. Its namesake actually dwelled within the building in a special dean's apartment. She was a beloved figure on campus, and the president of the university eulogized her during her memorial service: "The character of Marie Mount will live forever."

And perhaps her spirit does, indeed, dwell within the building to this day. Since the late 1970s, people in Marie Mount Hall at odd times of the day have reported all sorts of weird phenomena. These include the awareness of an invisible entity, toilets flushing of their own volition, doors opening and closing on their own, and open flames blowing out in closed areas in which there is no breeze. Strangest of all, perhaps, is the loud piano music that people have heard within the hall on dark and stormy nights, pounded out, some believe, by the spectral fingers of Marie Mount herself.

Marie Mount Hall is one of the areas that has been investigated in the past by the Maryland Ghosts and Spirits Association, which claims to have also detected the presence of several other ghosts in the building.

Morrill Hall

Another place on campus investigated by the Maryland Ghosts and Spirits Association is Morrill Hall—named for Vermont Congressman Justin Smith Morrill, who introduced the Land-Grant Colleges Act that allowed formation of the school—which is also believed to be haunted. It is the oldest academic building on campus that has been in continuous use.

Some of the most prolific phenomena reported in and around this building include the smell of smoke and other, stranger odors, especially in the basement, when no fire or other apparent source is present. Some people believe that these events are the spiritual residuum of the "Great Fire of 1912," a powerful Thanksgiving conflagration that completely destroyed two nearby buildings, the largest ones on campus at that time (located on the spots where the South Campus Dining Hall and LeFrak Hall are now).

People have also reported hearing the sound of marching feet from an area outside the building. That location was, in fact, used as a drill ground in the days of the Maryland Agricultural College, when, starting in the early 1860s, students were organized as cadets and required by the state legislature to undergo military training under the provisions of the land-grant act. Many of those cadets went on to fight for one side or the other during the Civil War and were killed in the bloody conflict, and it seems that some part of their spirits may yet reside on the campus.

TAWES FINE ARTS BUILDING

Prior to the opening of the Clarice Smith Performing Arts Center in 2001, the Tawes Fine Arts Building served as the home for performing arts on the UM campus, and today it houses a theater and a number of specialized facilities.

People have been reporting strange phenomena in the building since soon after it was completed in 1965, including inhuman, disembodied footsteps that echo throughout the theater. Many of the events that have happened in the building, however, are much more inexplicable, and have sometimes been characterized, for want of a better term, as "practical jokes." The mischievous ghost responsible for these activities has, for whatever reasons, been dubbed Mortimer.

The sorts of things people have experienced make somewhat more sense, however, when one considers evidence that the playful Mortimer is the spirit not of a person but, rather, a dog once owned by someone who worked at the theater. The fun-loving animal, sadly, apparently suffered an awful demise at the site.

"When they were building the theater, the seats were put in but they weren't completed yet," Jennie told me. "Mortimer used to frolic on the stage and he jumped off and actually impaled himself on the frame of one of the uncompleted seats. It's a horrible story. The rumor is that they buried Mortimer in the basement and then put all the sound equipment on top of the spot."

COLE FIELD HOUSE

Ever since it was built in 1955, strange phenomena have been reported at this cavernous building, which until 2002 was home to the University of Maryland's basketball program.

One of the most famous episodes involves Maryland basketball player Len Bias, a Boston Celtics draft pick in June 1986 who tragically died just two days later of a cocaine overdose while celebrating his professional success. Some people believe his spirit never left the campus where so many people once cheered him on, and people have heard the disembodied sounds of a bouncing basketball in both Cole Field House and the Washington Hall dorm room where the athlete died.

Other incidents associated with the field house have involved a nearby track, where people have reported seeing dust kicked up from the footsteps of an invisible runner.

STAMP STUDENT UNION

Originally opened in 1955 and named for Adele Hagner Stamp, the university's first dean of women students, Stamp Student Union has undergone numerous expansions and renovations over the past sixty years, particularly during the last decade.

"Because of these renovations, the building has turned into a vast maze of various floors, oddly connected hallways, strange stairways, and confusing floor plans, leading visitors to unexpected destinations," Anne and Liz's ghost tour states (and to which I can personally attest). Strange phenomena people have encountered during these perambulations and attributed to spirits that they believe haunt the building include elevators that move suddenly on their own and abrupt, unexplained spots of intense cold.

H.J. Patterson Hall

Built in 1931 and named for Harry Jacob Patterson, president of the university from 1913 to 1917 and director of its Maryland Agricultural Experiment Station from 1898 to 1937, H.J. Patterson Hall has been used over the years for various engineering science and science classes.

Paranormal phenomena have been reported at the building since a university maintenance employee working in the attic felt an eerie presence come into the room with him and then spotted what has been described as "a strange, misshapen shadow" moving across the wall. Who or what it may have been remains unknown.

Francis Scott Key Hall

"I've heard from numerous people that Francis Scott Key Hall is haunted, up on the fourth floor," Jennie said of the building that houses the campus's Department of History. Built in the 1930s, it is now one of the older buildings on campus, and it thus makes sense that it would have some ghostly lore associated with it, including reports of strange noises when no one is in the area in question. Anne and Liz did not actually include it on their ghost tour, and it is noted here as an example of one of the many other sites on the university grounds that has over the years acquired a reputation for being haunted.

McNamee Family Cemetery

One of the most fascinating things I learned during my visit with Anne was that there is a small family graveyard on the campus. Established on land the school bought in 1938, it is today bricked over and without any individual markers, surrounded by a wrought-iron fence, and graced by a single magnolia. An iron shield on the padlocked gate identifies it as the burying ground of the McNamee family, but no signs of recent mourning or devotion were present at the site.

This little site is tucked away largely out of view, and, speaking from personal experience, it is possible for a student to spend years on campus without ever knowing about it.

"The university had the cemetery bricked over, supposedly to prevent anyone from disturbing the graves," Anne and Liz's ghost tour says. "Although some speculate that it may have been to keep whoever is buried in the graves from disturbing the campus."

Its location struck me as very interesting: It is located between Byrd Stadium and the row of high-rise dorms that includes haunted Easton Hall. And so, perhaps, merely bricking over the cemetery is not enough to keep spirits associated with it from making their presence felt to people in the nearby buildings.

Tucked largely out of sight at the north end of campus is the tiny McNamee family graveyard, which is today bricked over and contains no individual markers.

CHAPTER 15

Waters House
GERMANTOWN

During the latter half of the twentieth century, the Waters House fell into disrepair and acquired a reputation for being haunted. Today, it is beautifully restored and managed by the Montgomery County Historical Society.

Pleasant Fields was a beautiful farm of good tillable soil and splendid woodland. And how my Grandfather loved it and never wanted to leave it. He requested that he be buried in the family graveyard there where the Basil Waterses had been placed. He also requested that he be carried to his last resting place by the men who worked on the farm. His wishes were respected and he was laid to rest there on December 24, 1907, with the farm hands as pall bearers.

—Maria E. L. Waters, on her grandfather
Dr. William A. Waters

SET IN AN AREA ONCE KNOWN as Pleasant Fields, the Waters House is still very pleasant but no longer surrounded by many fields, and the previously scenic, open approaches to it are now clogged by the suburban sprawl emanating from Washington, D.C. At one time easily visible from nearby Father Hurley Boulevard and Interstate 270, the house no longer beckons to travelers unaware of its existence, and is now likely to be found only by those deliberately seeking it out.

Today, the Waters House is the oldest house in Germantown, a community with roots in the eighteenth century that gained its name from the German-speaking merchants who once plied their trade at its main crossroads. The earliest and smallest of its three sections was built in the 1790s by Basil Waters, one of three brothers who inherited land in the area from his father, William Waters, of Brookeville, Maryland, a village about a dozen miles to the east (a fourth brother inherited the family home there).

Basil made good use of his inheritance, constructing a compact, two-story brick house for his family and, ultimately, more than tripling the two hundred acres bequeathed to him. He married Anne Pottinger Magruder, the daughter of a Revolutionary War hero, and with her had six children. Their youngest son, Zachariah, inherited the estate upon his father's death.

Sometime in the 1850s, Zachariah built the two-story brick-and-frame addition that is now the center and second-largest portion of the house, which his wife Eliza inherited when first their son and then her husband predeceased her.

In 1882, the widow Waters sold the house to her brother, Dr. William Alexander Waters, who built the third, final, and largest section of the house the following decade to make room for his growing family.

"This large, three-story frame addition includes a magnificent spiral staircase in the center hallway that extends to the roof," the Montgomery County Historical Society's description of the newest portion of the structure says. "Porches and ornamental details in the Victorian Italianate style, such as carved brackets and scrolls, were added to unify the exterior."

After Dr. Water's death, Pleasant Fields passed to his son, Charles Clark Waters. Hard times fell on the family in the 1920s with the onset of the Great Depression and, in 1932, the house and the 988-acre estate surrounding it were sold to pay off the family's debts.

During the last half of the twentieth century, the former Waters house fell into disrepair and was occupied sporadically and then abandoned. It was during this period that it began to acquire a widespread reputation for being haunted. People began to report the usual sorts of paranormal phenomena—inexplicable lights and sounds, problems with the electrical system, some incidents of moving objects, an apparition or two—and stories about it began to spring up, including some lurid explanations for what has caused the place to become haunted.

Paranormal phenomena reported at the Waters House include inexplicable lights and sounds, problems with the electrical system, incidents of moving objects, and a number of apparitions.

Undaunted by any ghosts the place might harbor, the Mary-
land-National Capital Park and Planning Commission acquired
the house in the late 1990s, beautifully restored it, and in 2002
turned it over to the Montgomery County Historical Society to
manage. It has since been used for exhibits, storage, and office
space. (The Waters House can also be rented for special events
for rates that vary by time and day but which seem very reasonable and which might provide paranormal groups with their best
opportunities for the time and elbow room they need to conduct
investigations. It is not, however, available for overnight rentals.)

Most of the ground floor is open to visitors a couple days a
week and by appointment. In the foyer there is a display about
the house itself, which includes a number of historic photos
and information about its history and restoration; the newest
wing of the house is an open area setup to accommodate exhibits of various sorts (e.g., a historic exhibit on local department
stores during our visit, and one on wedding dresses at the time
of this writing); and, in the original brick structure, there is a
gift shop. Most of the upper floors are not generally open to the
public, and are variously used for storage, leased to three different nonprofit organizations for use as office space, and used for
archiving county records and special collections.

In the first few years that it was open to the public, a local paranormal group conducted ghost tours of the house, but then stopped,
suggesting to some that the place just might not be haunted.

That is certainly the opinion of Alison Dineen, site adminis-
trator of the Waters House since 2005, who said she was certain
the place is not home to any ghosts. My wife, Diane, and I met
with her on a bright, sunny, but very cold and windy day in February 2009, so that she could show us around the house and tell
us about its history.

Despite her assertions that the Waters House could not be
haunted, many of the details Alison told us about it are the sorts

of the things that are at the very least suggestive of ghost stories and likely to pique the interest of paranormal investigators, their actual validity notwithstanding.

"There were some sad circumstances about how the Waters left this house," Alison pointed out, and went on to explain how the family had come to lose the property it had held for the better part of two centuries. It is a story of failure and heartbreak, almost gothic in its overtones, and the ghosts of the dispossessed dead can almost be sensed in its details, even if they are never mentioned.

When I asked Alison about the accounts I had read of a double murder at some indeterminate point in the history of the house, she said that she had never heard any such story and knew of no records that supported it. It probably bears mentioning here that during the course of our visit with Alison, she

Reputed to be haunted, the little Waters burial plot is located about three blocks from the Waters House in a residential neighborhood, and it is the final resting place for several family members.

alluded several times to her ongoing efforts to fill in the blanks in the history of the house, so if there is anyone who would be familiar with such an episode, were it documented it would likely be her. It should also be noted that at one time there were several other historic Waters houses in the local area, none of which remain, and it is certainly possible that a particular bit of lore might instead be associated with one of them.

If there is one thing I have learned, however, it is that whether or not the stories people tell about a particular place can be refuted has little to do with whether it is actually haunted. It would seem, rather, that if a place exhibits paranormal phenomena but does not have an appropriate story, people will make up one that seems to fit (one of the best examples of this is the case of Bunny Man Bridge, which I investigated in my *Ghosthunting Virginia*). And the one consistent criterion I have seen with regard to haunted places is their age: in short, a sufficiently old site is almost guaranteed to have some haunted lore associated with it, regardless of its actual history.

And opinions as to whether the place is haunted do vary considerably. Two members of the investigative group Maryland TriState Paranormal Members, Executive Director Ana Bruder and her husband, Technical Director Chris Wojtaszek, have conducted two cursory investigations at the site. Both were unofficial and they thus did not attempt to capture EVPs or use EMF meters.

"The back of the house outside was active and our camera equipment kept going off by itself. While in the backyard, we felt we were being watched," Ana said of their visit to the site in 2008. "The barn was very creepy and the energy of the horses was still there—we could also smell them, even though no horses have been stabled there for many, many years."

Ana and Chris made their second visit the Waters House again in March 2009. At that time they also asked about the urban legends of the murders that were supposed to have occurred at the house, and the two docents working at the site said they had not heard anything about them (but did acknowledge that the house had been around so long that plenty of people had likely died in it from a variety of other causes). The two MTSP investigators then proceeded to walk around the grounds and take some pictures.

"While we were walking around we smelled the horses again, like we did the first time there," Ana told me. As someone with psychic sensitivity to paranormal phenomena, she also said that she sensed the spirit of a slave behind some of the outbuildings behind the house.

"He was an older, large black man with white hair and overalls, beige shirt with rolled-up sleeves, and a handkerchief in his back pocket," she said. "He was pulling an old, wood land tiller, and he followed Chris and me all the way back to the edge of the house."

Wondering about the presence of this spirit in the location where she had sensed it, Ana returned to the Waters House and asked the docents about where the family's slaves had been quartered. She was pleasantly surprised to learn that slave quarters had been located behind the old horse paddocks—right where she had sensed the spirit of the old man.

So perhaps sensitivity to the unseen world and a desire to peer into it is what is needed to detect the shades of Pleasant Fields' former residents, who may simply be carrying on in death with the activities that occupied them in life. Colorful legends like unverifiable double murders aside, the Waters House certainly does have a history that could support a haunting, and profound melancholy is just about as likely to be associated with such phenomena as violence. And so the place remains unquiet—but whether that is from ghosts that haunt its aged rooms and grounds or just the wind rattling its old bones remains a matter of perspective.

SPOTLIGHT ON GHOSTS:
Waters Burial Plot

Many descendants of the Waters family live in both the vicinity of Pleasant Fields and throughout the state of Maryland today. (My wife's ex-husband is, in fact, a Waters whose family hails from Maryland, and during our visit we speculated as to the probabilities that he and his relatives might have some historical connection to the Waters of Germantown and Brookeville.) Beyond them, of course, are members of the family who died at Pleasant Fields and are buried there.

A small family burial plot is located about three blocks from the Waters House in what is now Hawk's Nest Lane, and it is the final resting place of Basil and Anne Waters; their children, Susannah, Robert, Zachariah, and Mary; Zachariah's wife, Eliza, and son, Bazil; and Dr. William Waters.

Presumably, the little burial ground was once located within a copse of trees or in conjunction with some other geographical feature, but it is very hard to visualize any of that today. It is a somewhat strange site in that it is situated in the middle of a residential development and surrounded by hundreds of relatively new family homes. Just seven upright grave markers are currently visible, three of them stunted and low to the ground, all set within a small, locked, fenced area.

The Waters burial plot is reputed to be haunted but we visited it during the day and did not pick up any anomalies, either personally or via digital photography. The site is located along a public street, however, so further investigation could certainly be conducted at just about any time of day or night if discrete enough. (Although it's possible someone in one of the nearby homes would respond to a prolonged presence by calling the authorities, who might then require "permission" for the activities to continue). And, while obtaining consent for access to the plot from the managers of the Waters House to conduct an investigation might be more trouble than it is worth and would not likely be forthcoming anyway, anything that could be done without actually touching the markers could readily be accomplished without entering the enclosure.

Eastern Shore

Eastern Shore
  Ghost of the Shore

Finchville/Reliance
  Patty Cannon's House

Snow Hill
  Furnace Town

Talbot County
  White Marsh Church

CHAPTER 16

Ghosts of the Shore
EASTERN SHORE

Numerous people have killed themselves at Suicide Bridge and the site is, not surprisingly, widely believed to be haunted by the spirits of people whose lives ended there.

Ghosts . . . have been around here as long as there have been people to talk about them. Spirit tales of the Indians have given way to supernatural traditions that have lingered around the towns here on the Eastern Shore, and the stately halls that dot the countryside have their own secrets to keep.

—Andy Nunez, *Ghosts of the Eastern Shore*

MARYLAND'S EASTERN SHORE shares the DelMarVa Peninsula with Delaware and Virginia and comprises nine counties, Caroline, Cecil, Dorchester, Kent, Queen Anne's, Somerset, Talbot, Wicomico, and Worcester. It is predominantly an agricultural region, but also includes large areas of marsh, river, and shoreline—as well as numerous islands—used for commercial fishing and is a popular vacation destination for people interested in the attractions of the Chesapeake Bay and

Atlantic Coast. It is significant in many ways, as the largest of the state's six regions, with about a third of its land area; the most sparsely populated, being home to a mere 8 percent of the population; and one of the most haunted, with some sort of ghost story, macabre legend, or other weird tale being associated with just about every crossroads, bridge, or town.

"With hundreds of waterways, streams, and hidden coves, the names of pirates, watermen, sea monsters, and swamp ghosts are an accepted and natural part of Eastern Shore residents' vocabulary," author Ed Okonowicz says in his *Haunted Maryland*. A number of notable haunted sites in the region are covered in their own chapters in this book, and some of the other most famous ghost legends associated with it follow.

BLACKWATER NATIONAL WILDLIFE REFUGE
Dorchester County

The Blackwater National Wildlife Refuge is a sprawling, twenty-seven hundred acre tract of tidal marshlands, freshwater ponds, and mixed evergreen and deciduous forests located south of Cambridge. It feels wild today, and the area it occupies would have seemed even more so in decades past, so it is easy to understand why a number of ghostly tales have been associated with it.

One of the most famous weird stories associated specifically with the refuge involves a malignant mule that is said to have preyed upon loggers and fisherman working in the area in the early 1800s. It was horrible and persistent enough, in fact, that people believed it to actually be demonically possessed and not just especially irascible or rabid. A group of teamsters eventually hunted down the troublesome beast, luring it into a pool of quicksand and drowning it. That, however, was apparently not enough to be rid of the creature, and since that time people have reported encountering its spirit deep in the marshland, where they have seen its red, glowing eyes peering angrily at them from the underbrush; heard its hot, snorting breath; or experienced it trying to drive or lure them to their own dooms in the marshy ground.

Big Liz
Dorchester County

Another legend sometimes associated with the Blackwater National Wildlife Refuge in particular but also with surrounding Dorchester County in general is that of Big Liz, whose story is almost universally known throughout the region and has been covered in innumerable articles, books, and other media.

Big Liz was a hulking slave woman who was owned by a Dorchester County plantation holder during the era of the Civil War. Like many people throughout the Eastern and Western Shore regions of Maryland, this planter was pro-Confederate enough in his sympathies that he was actively providing support for the Southern war effort. Expecting Big Liz would be grateful for what he believed to be good treatment, the owner apparently trusted the dependable and hardworking Big Liz and made her party to his various secessionist activities, which included raising money for the Confederate cause. Big Liz, however, was also a Union spy, and reported her master's activities to the Federal intelligence services for which she worked. He was, suffice it to say, not pleased to discover this about his servant.

One night, the master ordered Big Liz to load a chest of coins gathered for the Confederacy into the back of a wagon, and the two of them then headed off into gloomy Greenbriar Swamp (which is now part of the Blackwater National Wildlife Refuge). After reaching a spot he had selected, the owner directed Big Liz to dig a deep hole in which to secrete the treasure, which she proceeded to do. Then, after she had placed the chest into the pit and begun to fill it in, her master stole up behind her, stabbed her in the neck with a tobacco knife, and decapitated her with it. He shoved her mutilated body into the pit and filled it in, leaving her head to lay where it was, and then returned home and retired for the night.

According to legend, the headless body of Big Liz visited him in his bedroom that very night, clutching her head in one hand and the knife used to execute her in the other. Differing versions of the tale describe various ends for him, such as dying of fright, or perhaps even suicide to avoid having his own head cut off. All agree that he did not survive the encounter with the vengeful remains of his murdered slave.

The legends also agree that the buried treasure was never recovered and that the headless corpse of Big Liz continues to stalk the swamps and forests of Dorchester County—especially in the swamps about ten miles south of Cambridge around Bucktown and Decoursey Bridge Road—both guarding the hidden wealth and bringing harm to anyone who gets too close to finding it. Many people over the years have, in fact, claimed to have had terrifying encounters with Big Liz during the excursions into the swamps. And, as far as anyone knows, the treasure she is said to guard has still never been found.

GYPSY LOVERS
Henry's Crossroads

One of the most persistent legends associated with Dorchester County involves what are generally referred to as a pair of "Gypsy lovers," whose shades are reputed to haunt the roads southwest of Cambridge and to the west of the Blackwater National Wildlife Refuge.

According to the legend, which reads like a version of *Romeo and Juliet*, a young man and woman fell in love some time during the early twentieth century and were kept apart by their families (e.g., because they were members of opposing Gypsy clans or because he was a Gypsy and she was not). Defying their stuffy relatives, the two star-crossed lovers endeavored to be together anyway, ultimately leading to their deaths by misfortune. In a common version of the tale, her family murders the young man and she then drowns herself in grief in one of the nearby waterways.

Since those tragic events about one hundred years ago, people have reported seeing the ghosts of the young couple riding a white horse along the roads running through the swamps around the area known as Henry's Crossroads (sometimes also called Drawbridge, and right around the three-way intersection of Drawbridge Road, Steele Neck Road, and Griffith Neck Road). In some versions of the tale, the pair died in August, and it is during that month that they are said to be most likely seen.

My friend Chip Cassano and I visited the vicinity of this legend in June 2009 and—perhaps because the ghosts associated with it are sometimes supposed to manifest themselves two months later—we could not find any direct evidence for its truth. (We also did not see very many people of any description in the area, much less "Gypsies," but who knows what that term might be a euphemism for.) We did discover it to be a very creepy area, however, rife with crumbling, abandoned farmsteads, ruins just inside of the woods running alongside the roads, and dilapidated above-ground cemeteries that in some cases included breached vaults. Gypsy lovers or not, there is plenty to investigate here, and the atmospherics at least will not likely disappoint.

CRY BABY BRIDGE
Greensboro

One of the most archetypal sites I encountered while exploring the various regions of Maryland was that of the "Cry Baby Bridge." My mother and I identified what we were pretty sure was the "true" site of this legend in southern Maryland, but we heard about several other locations in the same region identified with the same or similar stories. Likewise, when my friend Chip Cassano and I were exploring the Eastern Shore in June 2009, we heard the story repeated there.

"Basically, it was a young girl from back in like the early 1800s," Ashley, a young woman we spoke with, told us in a story that expressed universal and timeless concerns. "She got pregnant with an illegitimate child by a father who was married to some other woman." Renounced by her parents, the young mother carried her child to term, gave birth to it beneath a nearby bridge along the banks of the stream it crossed, and then drowned both the infant and herself in the waters.

The bridge in this particular version of the story is supposed to be located on Still Road, just outside of Greensboro, in Caroline County.

"If you go to the bridge and sit there at midnight and flash your lights, you can hear a baby crying," Ashley told us. "I personally haven't, but my mom says she has, and so have other people I know."

GHOST LIGHT ROAD
Hebron

For as long as anyone can remember, people have witnessed strange phenomena along this lonely stretch of road. These have included yellow balls of light that have been known to chase people and cars alike, poltergeist activity in nearby homes, and at least one abandoned house that is widely believed to be haunted.

These phenomena reached their peak during a period of several weeks in 1952, when dozens of people reported them and hundreds came from all over in hopes of seeing them. Explanations for the weird lights have included the spirits of ghosts, especially a slave who was lynched during the era of the Civil

Some sort of ghost story, macabre legend, or other weird tale is associated with just about every town, bridge, or lonely stretch of road on the Eastern Shore.

War; UFOs, which were just coming into vogue during the peak of the sightings some six decades past; and the overly dismissive claim by dull-witted skeptics that the erratically moving balls of light were merely swamp gas.

My friend Chip Cassano and I located "Ghost Light Road" during a trip through Hebron in June 2009. A few queries around town quickly produced good-natured laughter from the people we approached and directions to what is actually known as Old Railroad Road (there being no Ghost Light Roads indicated on any maps we could find). This road runs for about three miles, from where it ends with Delmar Road at its north end to where is meets South Main Street in Hebron at its south end, and intersects with Route 50/Ocean Gateway a few miles north of town, making it very easy to access. It was too much to hope that we would encounter anything during our brief exploration of the road, but it is off a major thoroughfare through the Eastern Shore and thus easily investigated as part of a larger expedition to the region.

SAINT MICHAELS
Talbot County

Founded in the seventeenth century, Saint Michaels derived its name from the Church of England parish established there in 1677. According to local legend, the town played a critical role during the War of 1812, when a British fleet was moving up the Chesapeake Bay with the intent of attacking St. Michaels and destroying its shipyards. As the stories go, the British gun ships unleashed a withering nighttime bombardment on the town but, much to their disappointment, inflicted very little damage. This was supposedly thanks to a ruse by the townsmen, who put out all the lights in town and hung lanterns in the surrounding woods, causing the British to fire on the wrong locations. Because of this stratagem, Saint Michaels has dubbed itself "the town that fooled the British" (it may actually be "the town that fooled the tourists," however, as many curmudgeonly historians claim the incident never really happened).

Whether the many ghost stories associated with the town are true or not is presumably a question that needs to be answered by paranormal investigators, and there are numerous historic sites throughout the town and its environs reputed to be haunted. These include the Cannonball House, the only building believed to have been struck during the British bombardment of 1813, and where people have reported hearing disembodied footsteps; the John Thompson House, an eighteenth-century structure where people have reported seeing everything from spectral hands coming through the walls to full apparitions, and feeling invisible presences do things like poke them in the ribs or sit down next to them; and at least three of the local inns. On a more modern note, outside of town on Saint Michaels Road there is a spot beneath a tree where a motorcyclist is said to have been decapitated in an accident around which people have claimed to see a light believed by some to be his ghost.

When my friend Chip Cassano and I visited the picturesque little Eastern Shore community in June 2009, one of the places we visited was the Chesapeake Bay Maritime Museum, which is located on part of the area occupied by the historic shipyards. It is home to a number of unique exhibits, including a complete, relocated lighthouse; the bugeye *Edna E. Lockwood* and several skipjacks, all vessels characteristic of the Chesapeake Bay area; and the bell tower from Point Lookout on the adjacent Western

One of the reputedly haunted sites in historic Saint Michaels is the current Chesapeake Bay Maritime Museum giftshop, which was apparently once used as a brothel and may now be occupied by the ghost of a former lady-of-the-evening.

Shore of the state. (See the chapter on Point Lookout State Park in the section of this book on Southern Maryland.)

The historic building that houses the museum store is also reputed to be haunted, as we learned when we spoke to its manager, Mitch Anderson. Clearly a refined soul, Mitch tried to be very delicate in explaining to us the sorts of disembodied sounds people have reported coming from the upper floors of this building. Between mercilessly pressing him for more information and reading between the lines, however, we were able to determine that the building had served as a brothel as recently as the mid-twentieth century and that people had likely died there—presumably under sordid circumstances—during that time. It is now believed to be haunted by the vocal shade of at least one of its former ladies of the evening.

Suicide Bridge
Dorchester County

How could something called Suicide Bridge not be haunted? That is its real name, too, not just a local nickname, as indicated by official state of Maryland road signs and nearby establishments, such as the Suicide Bridge Restaurant.

People have been ending it all at the span over Cabin Creek, a few miles northwest of Cambridge, since a bridge was first built there in 1888 and the postmaster from Hurlock shot himself and then pitched into the waters below. Since then, numerous other people have either successfully killed themselves at the site or attempted to do so, some by shooting themselves before going over the side, others by driving cars off the bridge into the creek, and others simply by jumping into the water. Many of these latter victims slammed their heads into pilings in the water and, stunned or knocked unconscious, drowned in the muddy creek.

The current, twenty-one-foot-high bridge is the third one

over Cabin Creek at this particular point and does not at first glance look like a very auspicious place to attempt doing oneself in. This begs the question, of course, of whether or not the bridge itself might be cursed or on the site of some significant supernatural activity, like an Indian burial ground (a distinct possibility almost anywhere on the Eastern Shore). It does, not surprisingly, have a reputation for being haunted, and for more than 120 years, people have reported seeing spectral forms drifting across the bridge and along the nearby shore—although whether they are ghosts or merely people who have come to cross prematurely to the other side may not always be clear.

There are numerous other haunted sites and ghostly legends associated with the Eastern Shore as well, many of them as rich and colorful as the coastal area that is their home, and ghost-hunters will certainly have no trouble finding plenty of locations to investigate during a visit to the region. Read on for the individual chapters devoted to the Eastern Shore sites of Furnace Town, Patty Cannon's House, and White Marsh Church.

CHAPTER 17

Furnace Town
SNOW HILL

Old Nazareth Church, relocated to the grounds of Furnace Town several years ago, is the subject of some weird local legends in its own right.

"The earliest fools who turned up the bog ores for wealth,"
he said, "released the miasmas which slew all the people
roundabout. They killed all my family, but set me free."

—George Alfred Townsend, *The Entailed Hat*

OF ALL THE HAUNTED PLACES on the Eastern Shore, the area around Furnace Town is perhaps the one reputed to have claimed the most lives during the era of its early settlement. It should thus not be too surprising that it said to be haunted by the spirits of colonists who died from what at the time was believed to be poisonous emanations from the surrounding swamps.

Those were the stories people had told about Furnace Town for many years when, in 1884, author George Alfred Townsend wrote his eerie novel *The Entailed Hat*. Interestingly, the ghost stories people have told over the last century involve a character from that book, who spent most of his long life in the area of the ironworks—and died only years after publication of the story.

Widely known as "Sampson Hat," Sampson Harmon was a burly former slave who even into his sixties would challenge much younger men to hand-to-hand fights, only rarely losing such contests. He was a colorful character, noted in his later years for always being barefoot, always having a cat with him, and always wearing a hat—this former characteristic leading to his nickname.

Sampson Hat had been the manservant of the owner of the Nassawango Ironworks in the community known as Furnace Town. When the site was abandoned, he stayed on as its guard and caretaker. For whatever reasons, the abandoned village was apparently more than just a home to Sampson Hat, and he was compelled to spend his life there and also desired to have his remains buried there as well.

The Nassawango Ironworks were constructed in 1829 by the Maryland Iron Company to produce pig iron using ore deposits gathered from the surrounding wetlands. It was a cutting-edge operation in its day and, about eight years after it opened, upgraded its facilities to utilize an innovative "hot blast" iron refining technique that had been developed in England less than a decade earlier. A small, bustling community grew up around the furnace and supported its activities.

"From 1830 to 1850, this was a booming little iron-making village," said Elvira, our guide when my friend Chip Cassano and I visited the site in June 2009. For those two decades, the village was a flourishing and self-supporting regional center of commerce that was home to about three hundred men, women, and children, including many artisans employed by either the furnace or the community. It included a company store, boarding house, post office, a printer, a blacksmith shop, a woodworking shop, and broom-maker's shop. It also had a little church known simply as the "Shingled Meetinghouse," which was part of the Snow Hill Circuit of the Methodist Episcopal Church and was used by an itinerant preacher to hold a service once or twice a month. (See the Spotlight on Ghosts in this chapter for the story of the Old Nazareth Church, which sits on the grounds of Furnace Town today).

"The company went bankrupt in 1850 and, of course, everybody started leaving for other employment," Elvira told us. One of the reasons the ironworks went out of business, apparently, was the impure nature of the "bog ore" upon which it depended, an impure ferrous aggregation from which it was ultimately too costly to remove contaminants.

The Nassawango Ironworks were constructed in 1829 by the Maryland Iron Company to produce pig iron using ore deposits gathered from the surrounding wetlands, emanations from which claimed many lives in Colonial times.

"The furnace stack deteriorated and fell to ruin; the canal, which once turned the waterwheel and pumped the huge bellows, filled with silt and debris; the few remaining villagers left their homes, which soon burned or collapsed under the weight of neglect; trees and brush grew up around the abandoned foundations, and the great Pocomoke Forest reclaimed its depleted beds of ore," writes Alice Paterra of the community in *A Brief History of Nassawango Iron.*

Even after everyone else left and the place had deteriorated into a ghost town, one person remained: the aging Sampson Hat. He stayed there alone, year after year, guarding the deteriorating remains of the village and foundry and supporting himself in part by tilling corn.

"He was an old man when the company went bankrupt and had lived here all his life," Elvira told us. "He didn't know anything else and wanted to stay here. So his owner gave him his free papers and let him."

More than a decade after release of *The Entailed Hat*, and perhaps inspired by its story, at least one group of people ventured out to the site and there encountered the legendary Sampson Hat.

"We found him sitting on a handcart that was filled with firewood he had just cut," a visitor to the ghost town wrote in 1895, when Sampson Hat was more than one hundred years old. "He lives there destitute of every comfort that makes life desirable— entirely forsaken and alone, except that he has the company of a cat; yet he seems to be in perfect harmony with his surroundings."

When he became too old to care for himself any longer— around age 106—the local authorities moved Sampson Hat into the Worcester County Poor House in nearby Snow Hill. Maybe it was the desolate old village in the swamp that had sustained him so long, for he died a year later, and on his deathbed begged to be buried in the ground of the place that had been so dear to him. Sadly, the people charged with disposing of his remains ignored his wishes, and interred him instead at the County Almshouse Farm, a paupers' field.

And this is likely where the ghost story associated with the man began. Because of his profound desire to remain at the site, even after death, many people believe that Sampson Hat's spirit made its way back to Furnace Town and that it haunts the site to this day. Since then, people have reported the sensation of being watched while at the site, and some have even claimed they saw shabbily dressed old black man lurking in the shadows of the woods surrounding the abandoned village

"They say that his spirit roams around and guards Furnace Town," said Elvira, who has worked at the site for three years. Like many people I have talked to at haunted sites, she said that she does not believe in ghosts—but, nonetheless, speaks to Sampson Hat when no one else is around. "I usually say 'good morning' and 'good evening' to him."

Today, the site is once again used by people and is operated as the Furnace Town Living Heritage Museum. Many of the original buildings have been reconstructed or restored, including the thirty-five-foot-tall red brick furnace that is the namesake of the place and a number of the craftsmen's shops.

"This is the museum," Elvira said when we reached a restored wood frame structure. "Sampson resides here." She was referring, of course, to a statue of the former caretaker that had been sculpted by one of the volunteers at the site, but this was the second time she had referred to the long-dead man as if he still lived there. The life-sized statue of Sampson Hat, displaying his characteristic headgear and bare feet, and holding a cat with one hand and a broom in the other, did almost make it feel like the longtime caretaker of Furnace Town might still be there.

It would not be fair to say, however, that we actually felt any sign of his presence at the site during our brief, daytime visit to Furnace Town, and we certainly did not detect any overt para-

normal phenomena. And, although I could almost sense a presence in the shadowy woods surrounding the place, I was certainly
unable to spot a spectral old man watching us from the tree line.

But as we were getting ready to leave the place, we caught
some movement out of the corners of our eyes and were surprised
to see that we were being watched by a large cat, not unlike the
one we had seen in the sculpture of Sampson Hat. No one had
said anything to us about cats living on the site, and our guide
had already left us, so there was no one we could ask. We tried to
pet it, but it stayed just out of reach, and then was gone.

And so the spirit of Sampson Hat may very well yet reside
in the remains of Furnace Town. For my part, I am open to the
idea that the ghost of his cat might as well.

Sampson Harmon,
model for a character
in author George Alfred
Townsend's *The Entailed
Hat*, lived at Furnace
Town until the age of 106,
and some people believe
his spirit dwells at the site
to this day.

Ghosts:
Old Nazareth Church

Furnace Town has become the focus of a weird legend that originally had its roots elsewhere. Set on the grounds of the historical site is an old church that had previously been located about five miles to the west, down Old Furnace Road, at the entrance to what is now the Pusey Branch Nature Trail. The owner of the land on which the church rested, however, did not want it and planned to tear it down. He agreed instead to allow the historic site to have it, and it was relocated there in 1980. The cemetery associated with it, of course, had to remain in its original location.

Known as the Old Nazareth Church, the building currently on display at Furnace Town was a country Methodist church from 1874 through the middle of the twentieth century, after which it was abandoned. According to local legend, the large bible displayed on the lectern at the front of the church could not easily be moved, and would grow incredibly and unnaturally heavy when anyone would try to remove it from the small building—as if a pair of spectral hands were pressing down upon it.

In one episode associated with this story, two boys broke into the church and tried to lift the bible from its resting place. Try as they might, however, they couldn't move it, and the more they struggled with it, the heavier it became.

In another incident, two men attempted to remove the bible from the church, coming equipped with a wheelbarrow to help accomplish this task. (Could they have been the boys of the previous story, returned years later in hopes of succeeding where they had failed before?) After struggling to get the book into the wheelbarrow, it became increasingly heavy and difficult to move the further they got from the church, and eventually the conveyance collapsed. Fearing the consequences of their actions, the men then struggled to take the bible back to the church, during which it grew lighter and easier to handle the closer they got it to its rightful place.

CHAPTER 18

Patty Cannon's House
CAROLINE AND DORCHESTER COUNTIES

A historic marker implies that the historic home behind it was used as the headquarters for Patty Cannon's gang of murderers and kidnappers, but it was likely located a few hundred yards away in what is now a field.

> *A most villainous system of kidnapping has been extensively carried on in the state of Delaware by a gang of scoundrels residing there, aided and abetted by a number of confederates living on the Eastern Shore of this state.*

—*The Baltimore Sun*, 1840

ONE OF THE MOST WELL-KNOWN GHOSTS believed to haunt the lonely roads of the Eastern Shore is that of the loathsome Patty Cannon. She is just one of a number of female specters, including bogeywomen like Big Lizz and Screaming Polly, that has haunted the region about as long as anyone can remember. What makes Patty Cannon more tangible and horrible than most of the others, of course, is that she is more than just a legendary figure, she is a historical person, and an especially awful one at that.

"That gang of Patty Cannon's is the curse of the Eastern Shore," wrote author George Alfred Townsend in his macabre novel *The Entailed Hat*, in which he describes the activities of the murderess and her accomplices. The full extent of her criminal activities will probably never be known, but the ones she is known to have committed are bad enough.

Cannon was the boss of a ruthless gang that in the early nineteenth century kidnapped both free blacks and slaves from the area of the DelMarVa Peninsula and sold them to slavers, who then transported them to plantations in the Deep South. She was also an innkeeper who ran an establishment that was right on both the Caroline County-Dorchester County line and the Maryland-Delaware state line, and the jurisdictional gray area she operated in enabled her to evade arrest and prosecution for many years. Her accomplices included her husband until his death in 1826; her daughter and two of her own husbands, including one, Robert Brereton, who was convicted of murder and hanged, and another, Joe Johnson, who became Cannon's closest cohort; and numerous other white criminals and black slaves.

Cannon kept her victims in the attic and basement of her establishment and in a warren of secret chambers and tunnels beneath it. She is known to have tortured and beaten many of her victims and to have killed several people in support of her activities, including a number of children, some slaves who died in her custody, and possibly even some white slavers who fell afoul of her. She is also reputed to have killed and robbed a number of travelers who stayed at her inn, although she was never actually charged with these or her other probable crimes.

Delaware authorities eventually managed to capture Cannon and charge her with four murders, and she died in custody on May 11, 1829, while awaiting trial, somewhere between the age of sixty and seventy. The circumstances of her death remain a mystery to this day, and it is disputed whether she was murdered to keep her from revealing secrets she shared with others, died of natural causes, or killed herself with a dose of poison kept hidden on her person. Townsend, for his part, favors the latter possibility.

This aura of mystery has doubtless contributed to stories that her malignant spirit haunts any number of sites that have been associated with her: the site of her inn and tavern, a nearby house that is sometimes mistaken for her establishment, the jail where she died, the pauper's field where her remains are buried, and, perhaps strangest of all, the Public Library of Dover, Delaware, which is believed to be the current custodian of her skull.

There does indeed seem to be a substantial amount of confusion in the local area over the Patty Cannon legend, as my friend Chip Cassano and I discovered when we investigated it in June 2009. We decided to visit the location where the horrible woman lived and conducted her operations, which is indicated with a historical marker located at the juncture of Maryland Route 392/Finchville Reliance Road and Maryland Route 577/ Reliance Road. This marker, suffice it to say, does not do Cannon justice, and says simply:

"Patty Cannon's House. At Johnson's Crossroads where the noted kidnapping group had headquarters as described in George Alfred Townsend's novel 'The Entailed Hat.' The house borders on Caroline and Dorchester Counties and the State of Delaware."

Behind the marker is a large, well-maintained, nineteenth-century historic structure that is now a private home. Astute visitors will notice, however, that it is not actually on the state line at all, and could thus not be the house where Cannon purportedly walked to the Maryland side of her parlor when Delaware authorities arrived with a warrant for her arrest and vice versa when dealing with their Free State counterparts.

A number of investigators have, in fact, debunked the notion that this is actually Cannon's house and have determined that it was instead located a few hundred yards away in what is now a farmer's field right on the Delaware state line.

In his book *Roadside Markers in Maryland*, for example, author Charles Adams explains that the actual house was still standing when the marker was erected by State Roads Commission in 1939 (although it still would have implied the wrong house was Cannon's, as the apparent real site is some distance away and in the direction opposite indicated by the sign).

Likewise, an episode of the PBS television series *History Detectives* claims to have learned that the extant house was constructed sometime after Patty Cannon's death in 1829 and that the remains of her actual residence in the nearby field were torn down in 1948.

It would seem, however, that the land where the ersatz slaver house sits is, indeed, on land that belonged to Cannon.

In any event, it being a private residence, Chip and I decided not to bother the people who currently live in the house and, instead, speak to the proprietors of the surrounding businesses, which consist primarily of a florist and a convenience store.

I chatted briefly with the florist, whose establishment at the crossroads is adjacent to the field where Patty Cannon's actual house is believed to have once stood, which he confirmed. I then walked through his parking lot over to the edge of the field and examined it for signs of a former structure or anything else. Over the years, visitors to the site have reported both seeing the apparition of a hideous old woman and hearing the despairing, spectral cries of the people she imprisoned, killed, and abused. During my brief daytime sojourn there, however, I did not see, hear, or otherwise sense anything out of the ordinary.

After a bit I crossed to the south side of the highway to a sign indicating the boundary between Maryland and Delaware. Looking along the line of the sign to a point in the middle of the field, it was easy to envision Cannon's actual headquarters, and the jurisdictional shenanigans that allowed her to pursue her evil trade for so long. That field, I reflected, would be the perfect area to conduct any sort of paranormal investigation related to Cannon and her uncounted victims, and I wondered whether any traces of the hidden chambers and tunnels that had once lain below the house still remained beneath the tilled earth.

I then went over to the convenience store, where Chip and I spoke with some of the people working and shopping there. Our conversations added to our impressions that there is some uncertainty where the legend of Patty Cannon is concerned.

Located on both the Maryland and Delaware state line and the Caroline and Dorchester County lines, the site of Patty Cannon's former house made it possible for her to pursue a hideous criminal career for many years.

Some of it is pretty straightforward, such as the misimpression given by the historical marker as to the actual location of Patty's house. Some of the misunderstandings associated with her, however, completely bypass the ironic and move straight into the grotesque.

One woman we spoke with, for example, seemed a little indignant at the version of the Patty Cannon story we recited and expressed to us her impression that Cannon had actually helped slaves! When we pressed her for details about what she thought Cannon had really done, she essentially told us the story of another native of Dorchester County and the Eastern Shore—Harriet Tubman, herself a former slave and the most famous conductor on the Underground Railroad. We had not encountered any Harriet Tubman ghost stories, but this kind of misimpression would presumably be just the sort of thing that might keep her spirit from resting soundly and elicit a chuckle from the evil shade of Patty Cannon.

We also spoke with a man who said he had been a long-time friend of the residents of the house by the marker and had in fact visited the house many years before. He said that the existing house does, in fact, have several hidden rooms and tunnels beneath it, begging all sorts of questions in light of the fact that it is not supposed to have actually been Cannon's house. It occurred to us that perhaps it had actually been a stop on the Underground Railroad, the system of moving escaped slaves north, even as people like Patty Cannon moved free and enslaved blacks alike south. This could certainly account for some of the existing confusion over the opposing activities of these two networks. And, while we could not find any record of the existing house having been a stop on the Underground Railroad, this is not unusual and the secrecy associated with many such locations is known to have extended into our own era.

Some research after my return from the Eastern Shore also

revealed the existence of a housing development in nearby Sea-
ford, Delaware, called the Patty Cannon estates! That is pretty
much like naming a subdivision after John Wayne Gacy or Ted
Bundy, and one has to wonder whether the people who did so
have a perverse or seditious sense of humor or are just plain
dumb. Various roads through the development are named for
Cannon and her accomplices.

And so, the legend of Patty Cannon persists into our own
time, distorted, in many cases, like the soul of the horrible
woman herself. Since the time of her death, parents on the Eastern Shore have scared their children with cautionary tales of her
crimes. And innumerable people have claimed to see a strange
and misshapen old woman that they have identified as the terrifying specter of Patty Cannon, shambling along the bleak
and darkened roads that form the border with Maryland and
Delaware—forever searching for people to kidnap, torture, and
murder.

CHAPTER 19

White Marsh Church
TALBOT COUNTY

For many years, people have reported seeing spectral forms around the historic graveyard at old White Marsh Church, which has been in continuous use for more than three centuries.

Two strangers . . . had attended the funeral and observed this valuable ring and determined to secure it that night, so they went to the old church yard, for it was over half a century old, and digging into the grave, removed the coffin, broke it open and attempted to take the ring off the woman's finger. It would not come off, and so a knife was used to sever the joint, and this revived the woman, who, not being dead, suddenly uttered a cry and sat up in her coffin. Tradition does not say

what became of the two grave ghouls, but it is to be hoped that
the fright they received turned them from their evil ways.

—Prentiss Ingraham, *Land of Legendary Lore*

FOR MANY YEARS, passersby and nighttime visitors have reported seeing spectral forms walking amidst the ancient ruins of White Marsh Church and the weathered stones of its surrounding graveyard. So macabre and even bizarre are the actual events associated with the place, however—which includes desecration by what the locals have described as "ghouls"—that it is little wonder that it should be haunted.

My friend Chip Cassano and I visited the remains of White Marsh Church and the few hundred scattered stones clustered around it in June 2009, spotting it as we headed south along Route 50 toward Cambridge. The single remaining red brick wall of the church is pierced by a doorway leading into an open area in which only an altar still stands. Surrounded by gravestones spanning some three hundred years in age, the ruins struck us as portentous and worthy of investigation.

The faithful of Talbot County established a wood-frame church at White Marsh in the 1670s, expanding it with a brick addition some seven decades later, in 1745. It became the seat of St. Peter's Parish, a sprawling spiritual community that covered a large portion of the county, including the towns of Trappe, Easton, and Oxford. A number of prominent local people were buried in the yard surrounding the church during its early years, including tobacco farmer Robert Morris Sr., father of Robert Morris Jr., one of the signers of the Declaration of Independence.

Although the church is now ruined and long abandoned as a site of worship, the cemetery is still in use. Numerous stones are so old and weathered that the words on them have been worn away, and a number of large slabs set into the ground have become cracked or partially covered with turf. Even more markers have crumbled away entirely or been completely obscured by vegetation.

Establishment of Christ Church in Easton and Holy Trinity Church in Oxford drew much of the congregation away from centrally located but increasingly isolated White Marsh. By 1856, the parish was divided, and the older church became the seat of what was initially referred to as South St. Peter's Parish and, eventually, White Marsh Parish. The number of parishioners attending services at the church continued to diminish, especially after the construction of St. Paul's Chapel in nearby Trappe. The church remained the official but largely forsaken seat of the parish until the 1890s, when a brush fire destroyed it and the site was finally abandoned.

While White Marsh Church had become associated with the Church of England by 1692, when the Maryland General Assembly declared it the colony's official religion, some of its early members were Huguenots, or French Calvinists, many of whom

At least two incidents of grave robbery, one of which involved the theft of interred human remains, have taken place in the burying ground of the old White Marsh Church.

emigrated to North America in the seventeenth century. One of these was Daniel Maynadier, the rector of St. Peter's Parish from 1711 to 1745, whose family is the subject of a strange local legend.

Sometime during Maynadier's tenure as rector of St. Peter's Parish, his wife, Hannah, died and was buried in the cemetery adjacent to the church. Present at Hannah's funeral were two unidentified guests, who very likely attended the ceremony with bad intentions in mind. Noticing while the deceased woman lay in state that she had a valuable gold ring on her hand, the custom at that time being to bury people with jewelry they had regularly worn, they determined to steal it.

That night, while the ground over her grave was still relatively soft, the two vagabonds returned and dug it up. Opening her exposed coffin, the ghouls crouched over the woman and attempted to remove the coveted ring from her finger. Having trouble pulling it off, however, one of them drew a knife and endeavored to cut off the stiffened digit.

When Hannah Maynadier bolted upright, screaming and thrashing, the grave robbers were duly horrified, scrambled out of the hole in a panic, disappearing with due haste into the night, never to be heard from again.

Mrs. Maynadier had, apparently, not really died, but instead been in some sort of cataleptic state; accidental burials were not completely uncommon in that era, and were the subject of weird tales by a number of authors, most notably Edgar Allan Poe. Crawling up out of her own open grave, the stunned, disheveled, and now-injured woman stumbled back to her home, where she collapsed against the door and was discovered by her grieving husband.

Numerous variations on this story exist and any of them might be true. In some versions, for example, Hannah Maynadier was interred in an above-ground sepulcher, and this detail does jibe well with events and certainly could be correct. In one account, Reverend Maynadier is literally scared to death when his wife, risen from the grave, arrives back at their home, fresh earth from her grave still clinging to her funerary clothes. The chair he supposedly died in was itself the object of local legends for many years.

Some spin-off legends evolved and persisted for many years about the "death" chair, the idea being that the piece of historic furniture had acquired the ability to claim lives in its own right and not just in conjunction with other horrifying events (e.g., having someone's dead spouse turn up at the door). Its ownership was a matter of public record through at least 1962 but has since fallen into obscurity. It is very likely still owned by the same family that had it then, but anyone antiquing in the area should nonetheless probably exercise caution.

Just when Hannah Maynadier actually died is unknown, as no record still exists in the county of her dying and being buried even once, much less twice. A bronze marker set into a slab in the floor of the ruined church—which, by implication, marks the spot where the couple was finally interred—is of no help in this regard, even for purposes of knowing just how old the rector was, and simply says:

Daniel Maynadier

Huguenot

16__–1745

Rector of St. Peter's Parish

1711–1745

And His Wife

Hannah Martin

Even death, however, could not protect the Maynadiers from further travails and indignities. In the winter of 1915, robbers who very likely were motivated by legends of wealth buried in the Maynadier vaults violated not just Hannah's grave but Daniel's as well—and went so far as to steal everything that had been interred there, including the bodily remains of the couple!

"For at least the second time in the history of the ancient burial ground in which sleep some of the noblest of Maryland's early settlers, ghouls within the past two weeks desecrated a grave at White Marsh Church by exhuming the remains of one who is believed . . . to have been the Rev. Daniel Maynadier," the *Easton Star Democrat* reported in December 1915. "The sole motive for this act of vandalism seems to have been the procuring of any valuables buried with the deceased . . . the earth had been removed to a depth of five or six feet, laying bare the brick vault in which the coffin had rested. The remains had been removed . . ."

The lonely spot would seem to have been even more isolated a hundred years ago, and it is believed that the graves had been despoiled at least two weeks before this act had been discovered. For some years, the pillaged vault lay empty and open to the sky. It was during the period of this unfortunate state of affairs that

Many of the markers in the graveyard of old White Marsh Church are so ancient that their words have been obscured and some have crumbled and become nearly completely buried.

people reported witnessing an increasing number of phantasmal phenomena at the site and that ghost stories about it and the associated incidents proliferated throughout the surrounding area.

Ghostly tales associated with the Maynadiers and White Marsh Church persisted even after someone filled in the empty tomb, bricked it over, and added the bronze plaque that now marks the defiled graves. Even the best of intentions, it would seem, are sometimes not enough to mollify restless spirits.

So, the spirit of Hannah Maynadier—and some believe that of her husband Daniel as well—is still said to haunt the graveyard of Old White Marsh Church and to walk the lonely roads surrounding it, forever trying to find her way home and retrieve the ring that was so special to her in life and denied to her in death. And there is little doubt in many people's minds that it is, in fact, the spirit of the grave-robbed woman who wanders the area by night. For in addition to the apparition of an unhappy woman swathed in burial dress, elements associated with stories about the place have also included a voice, calling plaintively from the darkness, "Who's got my golden ring?"

Southern

CHAPTER 20

Ghosts of the South
SOUTHERN MARYLAND

Over the years, people have reported various sorts of paranormal phenomena at Piney Point Lighthouse, including being spoken to when no one else was present.

[The British] conduct would have disgraced cannibals; the houses were torn to pieces, the well which afforded water for the inhabitants was filled up . . . What was still worse, the church and the ashes of the dead shared an equally bad or worse fate. Will you believe me when I tell you the sunken graves were converted in barbecue holes, the remaining glass in the church windows broken, the communion table used as a dinner table, and then broken to pieces . . . and a vault was entered and the remains of the dead disturbed. Yes, my friend, the winding sheet was torn from the body of a lady of the first respectability and the whole contents of the vault entirely deranged!

—Maryland Governor Robert Wright

SOUTHERN MARYLAND is the oldest inhabited area of a very old state and has a rich, varied, and sometimes dark and violent, history with which many strong passions have been associated. A coastal region, it has also witnessed many shipwrecks over the past four hundred years. It should thus not be surprising that the area is home to many ghosts and may, in fact, be the most haunted of the Old Line State's regions.

Today, Southern Maryland comprises three counties, Calvert, Charles, and St. Mary's. It is a beautiful area, more lush and less windswept than the nearby Eastern Shore. Numerous historic placards are reminders of the region's heritage and point to many formerly flourishing towns, ports, and estates that no longer exist, marked today only by copses of trees, open meadows, or handfuls of restored structures.

The region's first inhabitants were drawn to this western shore of the Chesapeake Bay by the abundance of seafood and the fruits of its fertile forests and fields, which they eventually tilled as farmers. In the early seventeenth century, when the first Europeans explored the area, several tribes of Indians lived there, the most powerful being the Piscataway. Most of the Indians are long gone, but their memories live on in place names like Chaptico, Mattawoman, Patuxent, Piscataway, and Wicomico.

In 1634, St. Mary's City became the first Roman Catholic English settlement in North America, and the area quickly became a bastion of Catholicism in the New World, with vast tracts of land being acquired by the Society of Jesus. A strong Catholic presence is obvious in Southern Maryland even today, and the names of the many places founded by the Jesuits can be found on churches, historical markers, and place names throughout the region.

Culturally, the area developed as part of the American South. Visitors or even residents who have not traveled out from the National Capital region of Maryland might consider it to be a Northern state in its traditions, history, and attitudes, but those who venture into its hinterlands will discover that it is far more Southern in many respects. A slave state located below the famous Mason-Dixon line, traditional line of demarcation between the North and the South, Maryland would likely, in fact, have seceded from the Union prior to the Civil War had not fears of having Washington, D.C., surrounded by hostile states prompted the Federal government to militarily occupy it. A characteristic line from the state song, "Maryland, My Maryland," composed during the Civil War but still official to this day, underlines these senti-ments: "Huzza! she spurns the Northern scum!"

Nowhere are these attitudes more obvious than in South-ern Maryland, the inhabitants of which are often noted as hav-ing had Confederate "sympathies" during the Civil War. This somewhat understates the case; the local people gathered intel-ligence for the Confederate military, provided aid to escaped Southern prisoners of war, smuggled supplies into blockaded Virginia, and formed up into Maryland regiments that fought for the rebel cause. It is no coincidence that, after John Wilkes Booth assassinated President Abraham Lincoln in April 1865, he made his escape through Southern Maryland, a region where he rightly expected he might receive assistance.

The history of Southern Maryland being what it is, many well-known ghost stories have become associated with the area over the years. During the visit my mother and I made to the region in June 2009, in fact, almost every single person we spoke with was able to recite the basics of at least one or two of them. Separate chapters in this book are dedicated to two of them, Point Lookout and the Mudd House, and following are some of the other ones we heard about.

CHARLOTTE HALL HISTORIC DISTRICT

This historic district in the hamlet of Charlotte Hall includes thirteen buildings of historic or architectural interest and two natural springs, the "Coole Springs of St. Marie's" [sic], which were once believed to have healing properties. It also includes the former Charlotte Hall Military Academy, a military boarding school until the 1970s—attended by, among other people, actor Sylvester Stallone—which is now used as a Maryland state home for historic veterans.

Various ghost stories are associated with the district and its buildings. One that the helpful ladies at the St. Mary's County visitor's center at the site told us about involved a French cadet at the school named Pierre, who is believed to have drowned in the healing springs and to haunt the little park surrounding them.

Ghost stories aside, the springs are surprisingly picturesque and worth a look, and the visitor's center has all sorts of information useful to anyone continuing into St. Mary's County.

MOLL DYER

Just about everyone in the area seems to have heard the legend of Moll Dyer, a woman who in the late seventeenth century was suspected of being a witch, had her home burned down by the locals, and subsequently froze to death. As with many such tales, there are variations of the story often of a contradictory nature, and there is reason to think Dyer may not have actually been a witch at all, but was merely an unsightly old woman who kept to herself and became a scapegoat for local ills. She was also said to have been an herbalist, been Irish, been an impoverished noblewoman, and traded with Indians—none of which was likely to have been in her favor.

In all versions of the story as we heard it, the old woman had long been regarded as a witch and lived a few miles outside of town, according to some along a short country lane now known as Moll Dyer Road. (Some people we spoke with say the remains of her house can still be found, but there are a number of private residences along this road and we decided to forego wander-

ing around in search of them on property that was likely private.)
Dyer's story, incidentally, might be the origin of the story presented
in *The Blair Witch Project*, which appears to encompass elements
of legends from around Maryland, rather than just the mountain
town 125 miles to the northwest, where the film is set.

One winter around 1697, a number of hardships afflicted
the people of Leonardtown, including hunger brought on by
a meager harvest and many children fallen sick. Eager to find
a scapegoat for their problems, and maybe even a solution to
them, the populace turned their attentions to the local witch. In
some variations of the story, the colonial governor of Maryland
himself plays a role, his own children having been made ill by
the malign sorceries of Moll Dyer, prompting him to provide
troops for an attack on the suspected sorceress.

On a freezing winter night, the people of Leonardtown ventured to Moll Dyer's house and burned it down. The old woman
escaped the conflagration—according, to some sources, with the
direct assistance of Satan. The powers of the devil would seem,
however, to be very limited—or were being used on behalf of
someone else just then—because the homeless old woman froze
to death that very night.

Moll Dyer was found the next day, dead from exposure and
clutching a boulder. To their horror, when the townspeople
pulled her corpse from the rock, they discovered her handprint
permanently imprinted on it! As the story goes, the folk of Leonardtown then buried her nearby, upright according to some
sources and not far from what is now the Willows Restaurant
and Tavern on MD 5.

In 1972, an 875-pound boulder was found in a wooded ravine
near the town, and, marks upon it being reminiscent of a hand
print, it was identified with the legend of Moll Dyer. The rock
was moved to the grounds of Tudor Hall, a historic property next
to the courthouse in Leonardtown that is now home to the St.

Mary's County Historical Society Museum.

To this day, many people in Southern Maryland hold the ghost of Moll Dyer accountable for misfortunes that occur in and around Leonardtown, believing that she continues after more than three centuries to wreak vengeance upon the community that killed her. Some also believe that the rock itself is a source of malign power and that the dead witch's soul resides within it.

CRY BABY BRIDGE

Another legend prevalent in the area of Leonardtown is that of "Cry Baby Bridge," which has at least a couple of ghost stories associated with it. It is a creepy site, especially down around the base of the bridge, and is a popular destination for ghosthunters.

In one story, a slave woman who was thought to have killed her owner was hunted down and killed in the swamps

"Cry Baby Bridge" is a very creepy site, especially down around the base of the bridge, and is a popular destination for ghosthunters.

surrounding the bridge. Her spirit haunts the swampy area around the site to this day. Whether she is believed to be the source of the crying that people have reported around the span is unclear.

In another tale associated with the site, the desolate stretch is held to be haunted by the ghosts of a woman and her baby who were run down just after the end of World War II by the woman's husband. Having been gone too long to be the father of the child, he murdered her in anger over her infidelity. In this story the infantile crying is much easier to account for.

There have actually been numerous published references to this site. The majority of them seem to have pilfered information from each other and most of them incorrectly list the location of this haunting as St. Andrew's Church Road. The bridge, however, is actually located toward the lower end of Indian Bridge Road, which originates around the middle of St. Andrew's Church Road in the north and terminates about five miles later at MD 5 in the south.

Parking for this site can be found a few hundred yards south of it at the Cecil's Mill Historic District, which consists of a few stores set up in historic buildings (markers all around the site indicate that several more structures were present at its height around one hundred years ago). The walk down the road to the bridge can be a bit hazardous, however, as there is not much shoulder to the road before it drops off into the marshy ground; ghosthunters need to be careful that they don't become one of the spirits haunting the site.

PEDDLER'S ROCK AND THE BLUE DOG

Several variations of a legend about a murdered man and his loyal dog are told in Southern Maryland and are associated with what remains of Port Tobacco, in Charles County. In some versions the victim is a traveling merchant and the bloodstained boulder where he was killed is dubbed Peddler's Rock. That was our initial introduction to the story and the one we set out to track down. In another, more specific version of the story that we discovered later, the victim is a Revolutionary War soldier named Charles Thomas Sims, returning home from the war with a pouch full of gold and the deed to an estate, who, along with his dog, was ambushed and killed by a Port Tobacco man named Henry Hanos.

The location of the murder is a bit unclear in most of the accounts, and we started our search in Port Tobacco. A thriving river port in the seventeenth century, it is today a virtual ghost town, no pun intended, with just fifteen inhabitants in five households. There is an historic courthouse, which is sometimes open to visitors. At its height, the town included port facilities,

Author Michael J. Varhola investigates the legend of Peddler's Rock, believed to be haunted by a ghostly dog whose master was murdered around the era of the Revolutionary War.

warehouses, a hotel, and many more homes. We visited the site on a Saturday and did not see a single person during the time we were there.

At one side of the courthouse there is a pile of rocks, and on one of them are reddish streaks that look like spectral blood. This did not seem like a very compelling artifact, however, and we certainly did not get any sort of a haunted vibe from it. Unless the stone had been moved to the site at some later date, the implication is that the peddler/soldier/whoever would have been murdered pretty much in what had been the town square. Not impossible, but not very likely, either.

Leaving the abandoned historic site, we made some inquiries at a gas station down the road, where someone told us that the site of the legend was not actually in Port Tobacco but just outside it, on nearby Rose Hill Road. Precisely where was unclear, but the exact site, and any rock that is associated with it, may actually be on private property and not easily accessible.

While in the area we also spoke with a number of people who told us only about a ghostly blue hound that is sometimes seen running across the roads around Port Tobacco, they were not familiar with the legend of the rock. It is certainly possible that these are two different legends that have been combined into one, or a single root legend that has diverged into separate tales.

In any event, this is another legend that has appeared in confusing or incorrect forms in various published sources and then picked up by Web sites and other venues, all by people who have never bothered to actually walk the ground themselves. My suspicion is that the rock might not have appeared in the original version of the story and was added in more recent decades by people who wanted to associate the pile of masonry sitting next to the courthouse in Port Tobacco with the legend of the murdered man.

PINEY POINT LIGHTHOUSE

Located along the banks of the lower Potomac River near its approach to the Chesapeake Bay in St. Mary's County, Piney Point Lighthouse is a conical stone tower with a detached keeper's house that became operational in 1836. It has sometimes been called the "Lighthouse of Presidents" because of the several U.S. presidents—including James Monroe, Franklin Pierce, Theodore Roosevelt—who fished and relaxed on or near its grounds during vacations from the White House. The lighthouse was decommissioned in 1964 and it and the keeper's house were subsequently incorporated into a little historic complex that includes an adjacent building containing the Potomac River Maritime Exhibit.

Over the years, people have reported various sorts of paranormal phenomena at the place, and, while somewhat off the beaten track, it has received some attention from ghosthunters (e.g., the D.C. Hauntings paranormal group recently conducted an investigation at the site, but declined to share their results). Workers at the site have reported numerous strange phenomena, including hearing people speak to them when no one else was present.

When we visited the site, I took numerous pictures both inside and outside the lighthouse and walked around the exterior of the tower with my microcassette recorder to see whether I could capture any EVPs. While a subsequent review of my tape did not reveal anything definite, something strange happened while I was recording it: As I walked around the tower, it suddenly struck me that something I couldn't see was touching and raising up the hair on the back of my hand!

SOTTERLEY PLANTATION

Sotterley Plantation is an eighteenth-century plantation home which, along with several outbuildings, is set on a ninety-five-acre estate overlooking the Patuxent River in Hollywood,

Maryland, in St. Mary's County. A possible model for George Washington's Mount Vernon estate, it was once home to George Plater III, the sixth governor of Maryland, and powerful financier Herbert L. Satterlee. It has been a museum since 1961.

Considering its age and the varied and colorful people who have dwelled within and visited the home, it is not surprising that Sotterley Plantation has a reputation for being haunted. Several people mentioned the historic home to us during our visit to Southern Maryland; specific stories we heard involved incidents of workers hearing children laughing and crying within the house when no one else was present in it.

CHRIST EPISCOPAL CHURCH AND CEMETERY

Founded in 1683 and once a thriving port, the town of Chaptico in St. Mary's County is now little more than a crossroads, the most prominent feature of which is Christ Episcopal Church, built in 1736. The graveyard of this church is widely considered to be haunted and, when one considers its history, there is little wonder that it would be.

"The cemetery itself is filled with tales. Some people are buried upright. The Key family vault had to be welded shut because neighborhood kids kept playing in it. When digging a new plot, ancient and unknown remains are sometimes found," wrote Southern Maryland Newspapers in a 2008 article. "Hurricane Hazel blew over a red oak tree in October 1954, and up with its roots came some bones."

One of the most famous events associated with the church and its cemetery happened during the War of 1812, during which British troops frequently raided Maryland coastal communities for supplies. British Marines occupied Chaptico for one day in July 1814, as part of a raid-in-force that had included a foray into nearby Leonardtown, about ten miles to the southeast. The troops stole livestock from the local inhabitants and robbed the graves of people buried in the cemetery. A report by Maryland Governor Robert Wright, who visited the town after the British withdrew, enumerated their atrocities and was published in the *National Intelligencer* newspaper.

One of the graves we visited while at the Christ Episcopal Church cemetery was that of Catherine Hayden, the "Angel of Chaptico," a pro-Southern woman who during the Civil War provided food and other assistance to Confederate soldiers. On Christmas Day in 1872, seven years after the end of the war, she suffered an epileptic seizure and fell into a blazing fireplace, succumbing to her injuries the following day. Her grave, which is still honored with a small Confederate battle flag, is the only one on the grounds at which we found any sort of anomalies.

The graveyard at the eighteenth-century Christ Episcopal Church is widely considered to be haunted and, when one considers its macabre history, there is little wonder that it would be.

These consisted of a pale colored orb that appeared in two photos near the top of her stone and a wispy flair in the air to the left of it. While these were not overly striking, and could be explained away as a trick of the light, their position and the fact that they appeared only around this particular marker nonetheless seemed somewhat compelling.

During the time we spent exploring Southern Maryland, we heard may other ghost stories as well, or fragments of them at least, to include ones about haunted inns, marinas, and boats. There are, suffice it to say, no shortages of venues for ghosthunters to investigate in this oldest and possibly most haunted region of the old and haunted state of Maryland. Read on for individual chapters on Point Lookout State Park, the Samuel Mudd House, and the Passion of John Wilkes Booth.

CHAPTER 21

Point Lookout
St. Mary's County

People have reported all sorts of strange phenomena at Point Lookout Lighthouse, a profoundly haunted site that was investigated by paranormal researcher Hans Holzer in 1980.

On several occasions, I have witnessed a man running across the road through Point Lookout. The sightings always took place during the day on the same section of road and the man always crossed the road just after my truck had passed, causing me to view him in my rearview mirror. The man was always crossing in the same direction. Other rangers have experienced the same phenomenon while passing in other vehicles at different times of the day and different times of the year.

—Don Hammett, *True Tales of the Bizarre and Unnatural*

IN AN AREA THAT IS HOME to innumerable haunted places, Point Lookout, a spit of land the end of which is the southernmost point in the state of Maryland, is almost certainly the most haunted. A relatively quiet state park today, this peninsula was a hub of activity during the Civil War, and was inhabited by hundreds of thousands of people over the course of the war. Thousands of them, along with numerous shipwrecked mariners and others before and since, died there of causes that included violence, disease, injury, and drowning, and many of their ghosts remain behind to this day.

Washed by the waters of the Potomac River on the one side and the Chesapeake Bay on the other, what is now known as Point Lookout has been continuously occupied and used for millennia. Its first inhabitants were the native Indian tribes who grew corn and tobacco in its fertile soil and harvested clams, crabs, fish, and oysters from the surrounding waters. Spanish explorers were the first Europeans to spot the peninsula, in the early 1500s, and Englishman John Smith is the first known to have landed on and explored it, in 1612. And by 1634, Leonard Calvert, who ruled Maryland on behalf of his older brother Cecil, the second Baron Baltimore, established his personal estate on the peninsula.

The first battle of the Revolutionary War was fought about 10 miles northwest of Point Lookout, at St. George Island, when Captain Rezin Beall—one of my ancestors who help give me a sense of roots in the state of Maryland—prevented a British flotilla of more than 70 vessels from sailing up the Potomac. Vigilance against British vessels remained important in this area for the duration of that conflict and the one that followed it, the War of 1812, and it was during this period that the place obtained the name Point Lookout.

In the late 1850s, a local developer recognized the recreational merits of the peninsula and bought up much of it to build a resort. His plans were interrupted by the onset of the Civil War, which prompted the Federal government to occupy the strategic peninsula and put it to many of the uses that contributed to it becoming such a site of paranormal activity.

Today, much of the peninsula falls within Point Lookout State Park, although there are a number of sites of interest on it that lay just outside the entrance to the facility. Within the park, there are numerous specific areas that are reputed to be haunted. Moving from the point northward, these include the lighthouse itself; the site of a large military hospital; the prisoner-of-war camp; an adjacent "contraband" camp occupied by refugee blacks; and an area used during the war to house a smallpox ward. The first and last of these sites are generally regarded to be the most haunted, but many people have reported phenomena at all of them over the years. Just outside the park is the Confederate Cemetery, where prisoners who perished in the nearby prison were buried in a mass grave. A monument erected by descendants of rebels who had been incarcerated in the camp now marks the spot.

Point Lookout Lighthouse

By the early 1800s, shipwrecks had become a problem at the mouth of the Potomac and along Maryland's western shore, and people increasingly claimed to see the specters of drowned sailors in the vicinity of the point. In 1825, the U.S. government allocated funds for a lighthouse on the point, and by 1830 one built by local lighthouse architect John Donahoo was operational.

Initially, the lighthouse consisted of a one-story rectangular keeper's house equipped with a light cupola, but over the years the facility was expanded and improved. The Coast Guard took over the site in 1939 and ran it for the following twenty-six years, until 1965, when it was shut down and replaced with an automated offshore beacon. That year, the Navy purchased the facility and leased it to the state of Maryland, which subsequently rented it out to various private parties. Numerous people lived in it during this period, including park manager Gerald Sword and a woman named Laura Berg, who lived in it from December 1979 to October 1981.

During the years he spent in the house in the 1970s, Sword reported numerous inexplicable phenomena, including feeling invisible beings push past him on at least a half dozen occasions; seeing a spot of light as big as a dinner plate appear on the kitchen wall, grow to four feet across, and then disappear; seeing the specter of a drowned seaman outside the house; hearing snoring in the kitchen; personally hearing voices inside and outside the lighthouse, particularly during storms; smelling strange odors in the living room; hearing footsteps in the hallway and up and down the stairs; seeing lights turn on and off; finding doors locked that he had left unlocked; and hearing doors bang open or closed.

Berg decided that she needed to call in experts and, in January 1980, renowned paranormal investigator Hans Holzer and a team of psychics conducted one of the most famous investigations of the site, which included the capture of numerous electronic voice phenomena (EVPs). They recorded the voices of both men and women, as well as sounds like steamboat whistles, none of which had been audible to their naked ears. These included the words and phrases "vaccine," "my home," "living in the lighthouse," "fire if they get too close to you," and, incredibly, "let us not take any objections to what they are doing."

A month later, in February 1980, the Maryland Committee for Psychical Research followed up with an investigation of their own, along with a séance, and the fruits of their labors included an image of a spectral Confederate soldier.

Since those investigations, numerous individuals and groups have reported various phenomena at Point Lookout Lighthouse, much of it similar in nature to that witnessed previously. EVPs have continued to rank among the most prevalent paranormal phenomena at the site, but numerous other anomalies of the sorts described above have been recounted as well. The place is so haunted, in fact, that this is acknowledged in brochures and other literature about the site published by the state of Maryland, a rarity amongst government-owned sites.

Unfortunately, the growing reputation of the place made it a target for miscreants, many of them local youth, who in the process of "looking for ghosts" invariably also found it necessary to vandalize the historic property. As with many sites, this tainted the opportunities for legitimate ghosthunters at the site.

These prospects improved considerably, however, in 2006, when the Navy relinquished control of the site to the state of Maryland, which has allowed the Point Lookout Lighthouse Preservation Society to manage it. The PLLPS has restored the site to its 1927 appearance and made it much easier to visit the site. For decades, it was open to the public only one day a year, and now people can visit it during the day on the first Saturday of each month, April through November, and pay to participate in nighttime investigations several times a year. Other than these times, however, it remains behind a locked gate and cannot be freely accessed.

When my mother and I visited the lighthouse in June 2009, we were sensitive to audible phenomena because of what we had heard about such things at the site, and we both noticed an eerie moaning noise that, initially at least, was quite unnerving. Neither of us could determine whether the sound was natural or manmade—we were pretty sure it wasn't supernatural in any way—but, if it was something that had long been present at the site, it was easy to see how it might have been quite unnerving to lone lighthouse keepers or other individuals during dark or foggy conditions.

We were not there on a day when it was open to the public

and had to suffice with exploring the surrounding area, taking pictures, and walking along the fence with a microcassette recorder in hopes of possibly obtaining some EVPs. Upon subsequent review of my tape, I heard a strange whiffling sound that, with some isolation or adjustment of speed that had not been accomplished as of this printing, might have revealed something. Nothing, however, was readily apparent.

What was strange, however, is something that happened while I was walking the fence line with my recorder and heightened my expectations of capturing a profound EVP: Despite the fact that it is voice-activated and I was not speaking, on at least three occasions while I was walking past the middle portion of the house, the recorder turned on for no apparent reason and, each time, ran for a minute or so—giving the impression that someone was trying, if unsuccessfully, to make themselves heard.

About two-thirds of the former POW camp at Point Lookout is now underwater, which can provide some interesting challenges for ghosthunters.

OTHER HAUNTS AT POINT LOOKOUT

While Point Lookout Lighthouse itself is the site within the state park that has the greatest reputation for being haunted, people have experienced paranormal phenomena at several other nearby locations.

Just north of the lighthouse, the Federal government established in 1862 Hammond General Hospital, a sprawling military medical complex that stretched from one side of the narrow neck of land to the other. Its central feature was a massive hospital building with sixteen wings radiating out from a central hub like the spokes of a wheel. Over the remaining three years of the war, thousands of sick, wounded, and injured men were brought into the hospital by steamship, and many of them subsequently died after painful or lingering maladies. It is thus not too surprising that people have reported ghostly phenomena on the site in the 150 years since the war ended. And perhaps the incidence of such things began very early on; despite the fact that a benevolent society wanted to turn the complex into a home for disabled Union veterans, the government quickly dismantled and shut down the site right after the war was over.

Further north and on the west side of the peninsula is the site of Camp Hoffmann, the military prison camp. Established in the summer of 1863, right after the Battle of Gettysburg, it was designed to accommodate ten thousand prisoners, but frequently housed more than twice this many in cramped and unhygienic conditions. Of the roughly fifty thousand men who were incarcerated in the camp during the war, about four thousand died there. Most of the prisoners were Confederate soldiers, but some were Southern sympathizers from the surrounding countryside arrested for supporting the rebel cause.

As a result of a shifting shoreline, about two-thirds of the former camp is now underwater, and it may not be immediately apparent to visitors exactly where it is: Its northern boundary is roughly marked by a large modern fishing pier, and its southern extent by a fenced radar facility owned by the Navy. Much of the remaining area is currently off limits, but there are several stretches of woods that motivated investigators can access. With much of the site currently underwater, the pier, the associated parking lot, and the surf itself might all provide interesting possibilities for ghosthunters (i.e., those with a boat).

Across the road from the former prison is a now-wooded area that was used during the war as a campsite by refugee blacks, most of them freed or escaped slaves—referred to by Union soldiers as "contrabands." Most of them lived in marginally improved holes they had dug in the ground and covered over to somewhat protect them from the elements. Some obtained jobs at the various military facilities on the peninsula, which included forts and port facilities—a few of them as guards at the prison camp, which led to incidents of both increased brutality and, periodically, of kindness when former slaves encountered former masters now in their power. I am not specifically aware of any phenomena at the site of the "contraband camp" but believe an investigation might prove fruitful.

One of the other areas in the park in which people have reported all sorts of strange phenomena is the campground around Hoffmann Loop, which is on the site of the former smallpox ward. It is near there that park ranger Don Hammett on several occasions witnessed what appeared to be a uniformed figure running across the road. Hammett's theory is that he had witnessed the spirit of a Confederate soldier who had feigned disease in order to be transferred to the lower-security smallpox camp and then escaped from it. If so, it is not known whether the man made good his getaway—but, in light of the fact that his ghost is still making the attempt, it is more than likely he did not.

Daytime visitors to the park are required to leave at sunset, and ghosthunters who prefer to conduct their investigations during hours of darkness might thus want to consider staying at one of the park's campgrounds, which will enhance their access throughout it at the most desirable times.

Outside of Point Lookout State Park and on the main road leading up to it is the fenced Confederate Cemetery, a mass burial site marked by two obelisks that rise up suddenly and strikingly before unsuspecting visitors. The larger of the two, in the center of the plot, was erected in 1930 by the Department of Veterans Affairs—then called the Veterans Administration—and includes the names of more than three thousand of the Confederate prisoners who died at the site (a book at the site includes the names of known victims of the camp who do not appear on the memorial). The smaller one was erected by

A large obelisk erected in 1930 by the Department of Veterans Affairs marks the burial place of more than 3,000 of the Confederate prisoners who died at Point Lookout. People have, understandably, reported numerous supernatural phenomena at the site.

the state of Maryland. People have, understandably, reported numerous supernatural phenomena at the site and, being outside the park, it is one at which nighttime investigations might be more feasible.

Other people besides soldiers and shipwrecked sailors have died at Point Lookout over the centuries, and their bodies were laid to rest in graves that have since, in many cases, become covered by the waters of the Chesapeake Bay. These included, for example, nurses and nuns who tended to the sick and dying at the main hospital and the smallpox ward.

"One of them died at the hospital," wrote civilian nurse Sophronia Bucklin of one of the twenty-six Sisters of Charity from Emmitsburg, Maryland, who served at the site during the war. She "was buried in the wave-washed cemetery, surrounded by the graves of the soldiers." Her spirit is, perhaps, one of those that still haunt the wooded shores of the ancient peninsula and continue to make their presence known to the living.

CHAPTER 22

Dr. Samuel A. Mudd House
WALDORF

Many people, including some of his own descendants, believe that Dr. Samuel A. Mudd's ghost continues to haunt the home where he lived and died.

She began hearing knocking at the front door, but whenever she went to open it she found no one there. The sound of footsteps going up the stairs and down the hall was likewise not uncommon. Soon, Mrs. Arehart began to catch glimpses of a man on the grounds of her house . . . Suddenly, she realized that the man was no stranger to her—he was her grandfather, Dr. Samuel Mudd.

— Trish Gallagher, *Ghosts and Haunted Houses of Maryland*

FOR MORE THAN 140 YEARS, one of the ongoing debates in American history has been over the guilt or innocence of various people convicted in the conspiracy to assassinate President Abraham Lincoln in April 1865. The pendulum swings back and forth, with "most" people believing one thing one decade and "most" of them believing something else the next.

But from the beginning and right up to the present, the family and descendants of Samuel A. Mudd have been steadfast in their assertions that their forebear is innocent. And, for almost

As with many Southern Maryland families, the Mudds were Catholic, as indicated by the crucifix hanging on the wall of their bedroom.

as long, there have been people who have claimed that the embittered ghost of Mudd—whose name apparently became a byword
for disgrace in the well-known phrase "his name is mud"—has
continued to haunt the home where he lived and died.

Like a shade caught between this life and the next, however,
the question of whether or not Mudd is guilty may not, be as
black and white as most people would like; the truth may actually lie in a gray area in between.

At about four o'clock on the morning of April 15, six hours
after he had shot Lincoln, John Wilkes Booth and his companion, David Herold, showed up at the darkened Mudd family
farm, knocked on the door, and requested aid.

Mudd admitted setting the injured man's broken leg and
allowing him and his friend to rest at the house. At his trial,
however, Mudd claimed that when Booth came to his house he
was wearing a fake beard and used an assumed name and that,
in the darkness, he thus did not recognize him. On the face of
it, this claim seems absurd, and it is no wonder that the court
rejected it out of hand—especially when one considers that he
knew Booth at least casually and had spent time with him on
two previous occasions. One point those involved in the debate
never seem to address is the unlikelihood of Booth, fleeing and
in pain, stopping on the road in the dark to affix a fake beard to
his face.

In the witch hunt following the Lincoln assassination, no
one who had come into contact with Booth was safe. As someone the assassin had known and sought out for assistance, Mudd
was one of the people who was arrested and charged with being
a member of the conspiracy to kill the president (a plan that had,
incidentally, begun as a kidnapping plot that, when it did not
come to fruition, escalated to murder).

Mudd was convicted, but not executed, for whatever role he
might have played in the plot, dodging that fate by just a single vote

of the nine-man military court convened illegally—in that military tribunals have no authority over civilians—by President Andrew Johnson to try the conspirators. His life was nonetheless ruined as a result, and in June 1865, he was sentenced to life in prison. Mudd was sent far, far away—along with three other convicted conspirators—to the Fort Jefferson military prison in the Dry Tortugas, a group of desert islands about seventy miles west of Key West, Florida (sort of the nineteenth century equivalent of Guantanamo Bay). There he was given a job in the prison hospital.

Two months after he arrived in the Dry Tortugas, Mudd learned that the unit of New York Volunteers then assigned to the fort was being replaced by the 82nd United States Colored Infantry. This reportedly caused him to fear for his safety, being a former slave owner and a convicted member of the conspiracy to kill Lincoln, and prompted him to attempt escape by stowing away on a transport ship. He was caught and, along with three others, transferred to a more secure area referred to as the "dungeon" for three months.

In the Fall of 1865, yellow fever broke out at the prison. The prison doctor was one of its victims, allowing Mudd the opportunity to once again ply his true craft. By all accounts, he worked hard and selflessly on behalf of his patients, and they acknowledged this with a petition sent to President Johnson.

"He inspired the hopeless with courage and by his constant presence in the midst of danger and infection [they] doubtless owe their lives to the care and treatment they received at his hands," the letter said. Ultimately moved by this, Johnson pardoned Mudd in February 1869, and a month and a half later he was once again home in Maryland.

While Mudd had a tough life after his release from prison, he became active in local politics, had five more children in addition to the four he and his wife already had, and, in general, appears to have had a fulfilling life. It was, however, destined to be a short one: In January 1883, at the age of just forty-nine, Mudd contracted pneumonia and died.

The controversy over his conviction continued beyond his life, however, and ghosts—both proverbial and literal—still surround it, with passions running high at both ends of the debate over Mudd's guilt or innocence.

To those without a horse in this particular race who examine the facts, however, the actual truth is somewhat more ambiguous. What is more probable than either his absolute guilt or innocence is that Mudd was not an intimate member of the conspiracy but that he was known to be a loyal proponent of the Confederate cause and, like many other such people, had a sense that something big was afoot, even if he did not know exactly what it was.

Dr. Samuel A. Mudd was convicted of being a member of the conspiracy to assassinate President Abraham Lincoln but was imprisoned rather than executed. He was eventually pardoned and allowed to return home.

Booth is thus much more likely to have visited Mudd not because he was a member of the conspiracy but rather because he was known to be staunch a Southern sympathizer who he personally knew and who he believed would help him with his injury.

Today, Mudd's home is a museum—run largely, as my mother and I discovered when we visited it in June 2009, by a number of the doctor's relatives and descendants. They are unequivocal in the contention that Mudd is innocent and this came out, both subtly and less so, in the tour we took of the house.

Figurative ghosts aside, there would also seem to be some real ones at the Mudd house. A number of the Mudd family members we talked to acknowledged their own belief that the house is, indeed, haunted.

Ed Mudd, who dresses in a manner reminiscent of a nineteenth-century doctor and who serves as one of the guides at the house, told us that unexplainable things regularly happen there. That very morning, for example, he said that he and a number of the other people working at the house had heard what sounded like gunshots just outside the door to the room they were standing in but, when they went outside to investigate, no one was there.

Henry Mudd, a descendant who does not work at the house but who lives in part of it, said he regularly experiences things of a supernatural nature in the house. The most profound, he said, was an episode in which he saw a full apparition of a woman in Civil War-era clothing.

While at the house we also met Louise Mudd Arehart, last remaining granddaughter of Dr. Mudd. She has gone on record in the past as saying that what prompted her to lead the efforts to restore her grandparents' home were increasing visits from a spectral man that she ultimately identified as her grandfather.

Ghosthunters also regularly have "hits" at the site and generally regard it as a hotspot. While we were there, our guide told us that the members of a ghosthunting television program had recently visited the house and that it would be the subject of an upcoming episode. We also learned that ghosthunting groups can make arrangements to conduct investigations at the house and that they are generally pleased with their results.

Members of one group I spoke with got more than they bargained for during a visit to the site. A few years ago, Ana Bruder and her husband Chris Wojtaszek, co-founders of the Maryland TriState Paranormal investigative group, visited the Mudd house. At one point, Chris became agitated, angry, and began to say things that seemed to make no sense and to generally not act at all like himself. Feeling overwhelmed, he went outside, and the feeling passed. To this day, they believe Chris was temporarily possessed or at least influenced by the ghost of Mudd. While at the site, they also had good results from their dowsing rods, which directed them to a bedroom where they obtained a good photograph of an orb.

So it would seem that the Mudd house is indeed haunted and worthy of investigation. But, perhaps, based on the experiences of the Mudd descendants, the conventional view that the doctor's ghost haunts the home where he lived simply because he is bitter over what befell him may be a bit off the mark. It would seem far more likely, rather, that his spirit has been infinitely more concerned with mobilizing his descendants in an ongoing effort to preserve his legacy and tell his story the way he would have wanted it told.

CHAPTER 23

The Passion of John Wilkes Booth

SOUTHERN MARYLAND

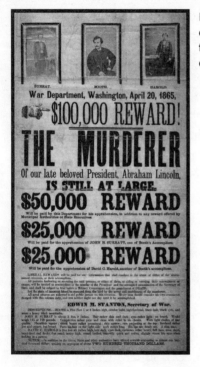

Huge rewards were offered for the capture of John Wilkes Booth and the other Lincoln assassination conspirators.

Certainly, incidents of hauntings—some involving the hated assassin—have been reported at the sites where Booth grew up, or where he killed the president and later stopped during his attempted escape.

—Ed Okonowicz,
Haunted Maryland

THE GHOST OF JOHN WILKES BOOTH has, ironically, been spotted at nearly as many places as that of President Abraham Lincoln, most of them places he visited during the last few weeks of his life or those where his body lay following his death. This is, of course, somewhat problematic for ghosthunters, and raises the sticky question of whether it is possible for the ghost of one person to haunt more than one site.

Booth's spirit is widely believed to be one of the ghosts that haunt Ford's Theatre, the place where the pro-Southern actor assassinated Lincoln in a raised theater box by shooting him in the back of the head with a .44 caliber Derringer the night of Good Friday, April 14, 1865. (I devote a chapter to Ford's Theatre and Booth's possible presence there in my Ghosthunting Virginia.) While he did not meet his own death there, the murderer did badly injure his leg, likely breaking it, when the spur on one of his boots became snagged on a flag during his leap to the stage below, causing him to land badly. He then dramatically proclaimed *"Sic semper tyrannis"*—"Thus always to tyrants"— and staggered out into the nearby alley, where a getaway horse awaited him.

Booth then set out from Washington, D.C., on a desperate, fearful, and pain-ridden twelve-day odyssey through pro-Confederate Southern Maryland, where he hoped both to receive aid and make good his escape across the Potomac River into Virginia (some say his ultimate destination was Mexico).

Booth was accompanied by co-conspirator David Herold. Their first stop, around midnight, was at the Mary Surratt house in present-day Clinton, Maryland, where they paused briefly to pick up supplies and hide a pair of rifles that they opted not to take with them. Booth's ghost, along with those of apparent accomplices John Lloyd and Mary Surratt herself, are among those people have claimed to see at this location.

The killer and his companion then continued southward, to the Mudd family farm, near the present-day community of Waldorf, Maryland, where, at 4 A.M., Dr. Mudd set Booth's leg and where he and his companion rested.

Sometime after dark, the two continued on their way, reaching their next stop, the home of rebel sympathizer Samuel Cox early on the morning of April 16, once again around 4 A.M. Cox contacted his foster brother, Thomas A. Jones—who had led

espionage efforts in Southern Maryland on behalf of the Confederacy since 1862—and hid the fugitives in a nearby thicket of
pine trees. By this time, the War Department had announced a
one-hundred-thousand-dollar reward for information leading to
the arrest of Booth and his co-conspirators, and Federal troops
were combing Southern Maryland in search of them. It was
while he waited there that, on the morning of April 20, Booth
learned from one of the newspapers brought to him by Jones
that four of his fellow conspirators had been arrested.

Booth and Herold remained within the thicket for four days
and then continued south once again, departing the night of
April 20 and thereafter reaching the banks of the Potomac,
where they once again hid in the woods.

On the night of April 21, using a boat and compass provided
by Jones, Booth and Herold attempted to cross the Potomac.
Apparently forgetting that they were characters in a tragedy and
not a comedy, the two incorrectly navigated their way upriver
and landed a few miles away—but still on the Maryland side of
the Potomac.

Discovering their error, the two went first to the nearby farm
of a Southern sympathizer known to Herold, and thenceforth to
the home of that man's son-in-law, the pro-Confederate Colonel
John J. Hughes, who hid and fed the fugitives until night fell
once again.

Booth and Herold successfully crossed to the Virginia side
of the Potomac on the night of Saturday, April 22, landing near
the mouth of Machodoc Creek before sunrise on April 23. There
they made contact with other Confederate agents, who provided
them with fresh horses and, ultimately, led them to the Garrett
family farm, which they reached around 3 P.M. on April 24. It was
here that Booth learned that the last Confederate forces of any
size had surrendered, ending the Southern war effort, and that
his attempt to save the Confederacy by killing Lincoln had failed.

Closed to the public for a couple of years, a renovated Ford's Theatre was reopened in February 2009 with the box where President Abraham Lincoln was shot restored to its 1865 appearance.

Union pursuers soon after captured the Confederate soldier who had taken Booth and Herold to the Garrett farm, to which he thereafter led the soldiers. In the predawn darkness of April 26, the Federal troops surrounded the barn in which Booth and Herold were hiding. Herold quickly surrendered himself but, when Booth refused, the soldiers set the barn on fire.

Seeing Booth silhouetted in the burning structure, one of the soldiers fired at him, striking him in the neck, shattering three vertebrae, and paralyzing him. Booth was dragged out of the blazing structure and up on to the porch of the Garrett farmhouse.

"Useless, useless," were the last despairing words he spoke as, soon after, dawn broke and he died.

Booth's journey did not end with his death, but it did reverse its direction. His corpse was transported to the Washington

Penitentiary—at what is now Fort Lesley J. McNair, in Washington, D.C.—and buried there, along with the people who had been executed following their convictions for the conspiracy to assassinate Lincoln.

Booth's body rested there for nearly three years, but his brother Edwin ultimately received permission to have it exhumed and moved to the family plot at Green Mount Cemetery in Bal-

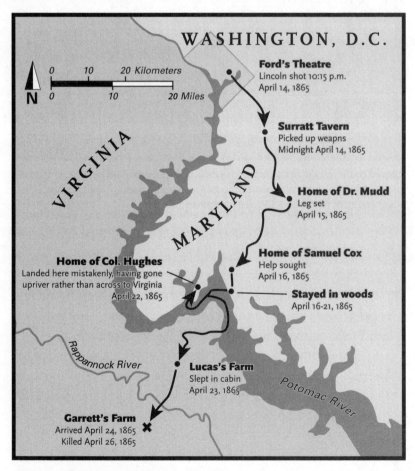

Assassin John Wilkes Booth's escape route.
(Credit: Wikimedia Commons)

timore. It arrived there in February 1869 and, the ground being too hard for burial at that point, it was stored in a holding vault until late June. It was then buried in an unmarked grave in the family plot—Edwin's desire being to keep the site from turning either into a Confederate shrine or being defiled by Union supporters—its presence acknowledged only by the addition of his name to the back of the family monument.

Over the years, people have claimed to see the apparitions of Booth at all of the sites along the route, along with orbs, mists, and the various other phenomena commonly associated with haunted sites. Most also have some other sort of haunting or ghost story associated with them, the most notable being perhaps the Dr. Samuel A. Mudd House (which has an entire chapter devoted to it in this book).

But perhaps it is not so strange after all that Booth's ghost is believed to haunt so many sites along the route of his attempted escape. He did, presumably, feel some of the strongest emotions of his life during the final two weeks of his life, during his desperate and unsuccessful attempt to reach the South and freedom. And so perhaps his earthbound ghost is not tethered to a specific location, but rather eternally fleeing through all the places he passed in his final dramatic—and tragic—role as a murder and fugitive, and itinerantly haunting all of them.

Western

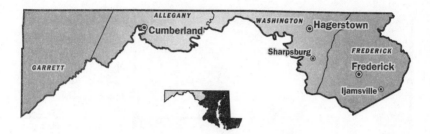

Cumberland
Church of St. Patrick

Frederick
Schifferstatd

Frederick County
Burkittsville
City of Frederick
Monocacy National Battlefield

Ijamsville
Gabriel's Inn

Sharpsburg
Antietam National Battlefield

CHAPTER 24

Antietam National Battlefield
SHARPSBURG

An estimated 22,717 were killed, wounded, captured, or missing at the Battle of Antietam, making it the bloodiest single day of combat during the Civil War, and many of their ghosts are believed to haunt the site where they died.
(Alexander Gardner)

September 17, 1862 was the bloodiest day of the American Civil War . . . With so much blood spilled in so little time, it's not surprising that the Antietam battlefield is one of America's most haunted battle sites.

—Jeff Belanger, *Ghosts of War*

IF YOU ASK MOST AMERICANS what the bloodiest day of the Civil War was, many will answer that it was the Battle of Gettysburg. This is, however, incorrect. Gettysburg was indeed the bloodiest *battle*, but it was fought over a three-day period. The war's bloodiest single day of combat took place nine-and-a-half months earlier and about fifty miles to the southwest, near the little Maryland town of Sharpsburg.

In the last days of the summer of 1862, Confederate General Robert E. Lee had led his army of forty-five thousand men in an invasion of the Northern states, hotly pursued by Union Major General George B. McClellan and his force of eighty-seven hundred troops. On September 17, the two armies fought each other to a standstill along the banks of Antietam Creek, and when the sun set, it was on combined casualties of an estimated 22,717 men (1,546 killed, 7,742 wounded, and 1,018 captured or missing Confederate; 2,108 killed, 9,540 wounded, 753 captured or missing Union).

The Battle of Antietam was characterized to a great extent by a series of ill-conceived, costly, and—for many of the men participating in them—suicidal assaults, especially by Union troops, against reinforced positions or in the face of artillery fire. On a tactical level, the battle was a stalemate with no clear victor. On a strategic level, it was a decided Confederate defeat, in that Lee and his men were forced to retreat back into the Southern states, delaying the international recognition and support a victorious Confederacy was struggling to achieve (the prospects for which were permanently laid to rest on the battlefield at Gettysburg).

In light of the above, it should not be too surprising to learn not just that the Antietam Battlefield is widely considered to be haunted, but that it is, indeed, probably one of the most haunted battlefields in the entire United States (second only, perhaps, to infinitely more famous Gettysburg, at which about twice as many casualties were suffered).

One of the things that especially struck me about Antietam when I visited the battlefield several years ago was the wide-reaching scope of the violence. In particular, I can recall being stunned to learn that nine general officers, killed on the spot or mortally wounded, were among the men consumed by that single day of apocalyptic violence. Upside-down cannon barrels set into stone cairns mark the places of the five generals who died on the field, and the four others that later succumbed to their wounds.

"Such a storm of balls I never conceived it possible for men to live through," wrote Confederate Lieutenant Colonel A.S. "Sandie" Pendleton. "Shot and shell shrieking and crashing, canister and bullets whistling and hissing most fiend-like through the air until you could almost see them. In that mile's ride I never expected to come back alive."

Tightly packed formations of troops were driven into such firestorms across open fields and along the narrow roads and bridges that crossed Antietam Creek or ran through the area and, exposed and unprotected, were cut down in droves.

"I have heard of 'the dead lying in heaps,' but never saw it till this battle," recalled Captain Emory Upton of 2nd U.S. Artillery. "Whole ranks fell together."

Over the years, innumerable witnesses have reported experiencing almost every sort of paranormal phenomena at the Antietam Battlefield, including complex manifestations like apparitions of troops marching across the fields and engaging phantasmal foes, and detailed sounds of combat, complete with barked commands, screams of anguish, musketry, and cannon fire. Lesser and more generic phenomena—such as orbs, mists, and simple EVPs—are even more commonplace at the site.

While any point on the battlefield is probably worthy of investigation and could yield some potentially interesting results, several areas of especially savage fighting have been identified as paranormal hotspots by investigators.

CORN FIELD

Located between the East Woods and the West Woods, the area remembered as the Corn Field was the scene of especially savage fighting, and costly attacks and counterattacks swept across it during the early part of the day. Blue and gray artillery alike cut through the ranks of advancing infantrymen, and casualties for both sides were heavy.

"In the time that I am writing, every stalk of corn in the northern and greater part of the field was cut as closely as could have been done with a knife, and the slain lay in rows precisely as they had stood in their ranks a few moments before," recalled U.S. Army General Joseph Hooker, one of the Union corps commanders. "It was never my fortune to witness a more bloody, dismal battlefield."

This section of the battlefield, especially around its southeastern corner, is second only to the Bloody Lane in paranormal activity and is the primary area of investigation preferred by many ghosthunters. Specific paranormal events detected here have included some of the complex apparitions and sounds of battle experienced by some visitors to the battlefield.

BLOODY LANE

Known before the Battle of Antietam merely as the Sunken Road, this country track earned the name Bloody Lane from the heavy bloodshed exacted on it in September 1862. An estimated fifty-six hundred men from both sides were killed and wounded along its length in a period of just three-and-a-half hours, during the middle segment of the battle.

Paranormal phenomena people have reported witnessing along the Bloody Lane include the sounds of gunfire and the stench of smoke and gunpowder.

"I sat down there on the ground and started taking pictures," Jim Wissert, a ghosthunter who is a member of the Maryland TriState Paranormal investigative group, told me of his visit to the Bloody Lane. "And then I just felt an overcoming sensation of grief, sadness. And that's the best way I can describe it. The atmosphere just felt really heavy and you just knew that something happened there. I just got saddened." During that visit, he also took a number of pictures in which he has identified what

Paranormal phenomena people have reported witnessing along the Bloody Lane, where an estimated 5,600 men were killed and wounded in just three-and-a-half hours, include the sounds of gunfire and the stench of smoke and gunpowder. *(Credit: Wikimedia Commons)*

he believes to be the faces of soldiers in the foliage of surrounding trees.

BURNSIDE'S BRIDGE

Constructed sixteen years before the battle that ensured its fame, this limestone and granite span was originally known as Rohrbach's Bridge for a local farmer who lived nearby, and was used for conveying livestock and produce across Antietam Creek to nearby Sharpsburg. The triple-arched bridge, 125 feet long and 12 feet wide, served as a choke point during the battle, and was assaulted multiple times over several hours by troops under the command of U.S. Major General Ambrose Burnside, commander of the Union IX Corps. A numerically inferior but dug-in Confederate force repelled three frontal assaults before finally being dislodged. Many of the IX Corps' 438 killed, 1,796 wounded, and 115 missing from the Battle of Antietam suffered their fates at the bridge, which has since borne the name of their commander.

Paranormal phenomena people have reported seeing at the bridge have included blue lights, reminiscent of the many blue-clad Federal troops who died trying to cross it.

PRY HOUSE

Built in 1844, this brick house overlooks the fields of Antietam and was commandeered by Union General McClellan for use as his headquarters during the battle. Many of the men injured in the battle—including mortally wounded Union Major General Israel Richardson and Union Major General Joseph Hooker—

Paranormal phenomena people have reported seeing at Burnside's Bridge, where the Union suffered heavy casualties, have included blue lights, reminiscent of the many blue-clad men who died trying to cross it. (Credit: Wikimedia Commons)

were brought to the Pry House barns, which were temporarily converted into a field hospital.

Today, the house contains the Pry House Field Hospital Museum, which features exhibits that focus largely on period medical care and which is sponsored by the National Museum of Civil War Medicine (the latter site is covered in the chapter in this book on the city of Frederick).

Maryland TriState Paranormal Executive Director Ana Bruder and her husband, Technical Director Chris Wojtaszek, visited the Antietam Battlefield in 2008 and detected the presence of numerous spirits in the vicinity of the Pry House, especially around the barns, the garden, and the wooded area to the left of the house. Many of the areas in and around the house

Specific sections of the Antietam Battlefield that might warrant investigation by ghosthunters include the area around the Dunker Church. *(Credit: Wikimedia Commons)*

were being renovated, and some were being used as administrative offices and were thus not open to visitors, and so Ana and Chris did not try to conduct a full, official MTSP investigation.

"I felt many a spirit ready to communicate," Ana said, but "there were a lot of people there that day, and I was unable to truly concentrate inside the house. It can be very hard when a lot of other people in my space sort of speak. I am sure if I went back, I could get some of them to appear to me."

Other specific sections of the Antietam Battlefield that might warrant investigation by ghosthunters include the area around the Dunker Church, the Mumma Cemetery, and the stands of vegetation known as the East Woods and the West Woods.

If any place could be haunted, it is certainly easy to understand why the Antietam Battlefield would be, and there is no shortage of reasons why this should be the case. An estimated 3,654 deaths alone in such a brief period of time and in such a constricted area would presumably be enough. But factor in the immense psychic trauma generated by so much collective terror, anguish, and despair—not to mention resentment of the men who may have realized, in many cases, just how carelessly their lives were thrown away by incompetent commanders—and causes for the thousands of episodes of supernatural phenomena experienced by visitors to the battlefield start to sink in.

And so Antietam Battlefield is in many ways an ideal site of investigation for ghosthunters. But there is likely much to be experienced there in the way of psychic trauma from the wholesale slaughter that occurred there, and meditation upon the sheer numbers of the dead and what they experienced could very well weigh oppressively even upon those who are non-sensitive and take a heavy toll upon those who are. It is thus not a place to be investigated lightly—or by the faint of heart.

CHAPTER 25

Burkittsville
FREDERICK COUNTY

Some scenes from *The Blair Witch Project* were filmed at the historic cemetery in Burkittsville, which has markers dating back to at least the early 1800s.

Girl: All my life I've believed in witches or ghosts and stuff.
Heather: But you believe there are some in this area?
Girl: Oh, definitely.

—The Blair Witch Project

THERE IS A COMPLICATED RELATIONSHIP at many reputedly haunted sites between the body of urban legend associated with them and the evidence that they are genuinely haunted. For some reason, many aficionados of the paranormal—veteran ghosthunters among them—assume these two conditions are mutually exclusive and that they cannot coexist in one location. Even as I write this chapter—about a place made famous because of its refutable legends rather than the ghosts that actually haunt it—I know there is a cadre of self-declared experts and critics who will attack it on that faulty basis.

That place is, of course, Burkittsville, Maryland, and the woods and hills around it, made famous by the 1999 movie *The Blair Witch Project.* Despite the acclaim it initially received, it has become fashionable in recent years among many horror and paranormal fans to pick the film apart and point out how most of it really has nothing to do with events that occurred in Burkittsville; I will have to do some "picking" as well, but only as a service to people exploring the area and without malice or a gloating attitude.

Pick as some people might, there really was a witch in Burkittsville. Her name was Elly Kedward, and she was banished in 1785 from what was then known as Blair Township for allegedly practicing her craft. Other elements from the movie, while not actually located around Burkittsville, can be found elsewhere in the state. The Black Hills, for example, can be found in adjacent Montgomery County; many of the scenes from the movie were filmed in Patapsco Valley State Park in Howard County; and the legend of Coffin Rock is reminiscent of a story from the Southern Maryland. *The Blair Witch Project* is thus, to a great extent, a tribute to creepy places and witch lore associated with the state of Maryland in general, a fact that most movie debunkers fail to discover.

Whether the shade of Elly Kedward haunts the hills, fields, and forests around Burkittsville is an open question, and the locals are disinclined to answer questions related to witches and the like one way or the other. Local ghost stories have, however, been around since long before the movie that turned Burkittsville into a mainstream attraction. Many of these stories are related to the Civil War's bloody Battle of Crampton's Gap, which was fought nearby as part of the larger Battle of South Mountain. For years, people have claimed to see the spirits of soldiers killed in the fray marching through the surrounding woods in a ghostly repetition of their last actions. And so, while it was witch lore that brought a friend of mine up to Burkittsville during the craze following the release of the movie, it may have been spectral soldiers that contributed to his strange experience in the hills above the town.

My friend—who wished to remain anonymous in this book—was working on a "Purcellville Witch Project" and dating a Wiccan from the nearby Virginia town of that name. She told him that she wanted to visit Burkittsville, and so one day they took a trip to the little town.

After exhausting the limited entertainment opportunities in Burkittsville, they continued up the road toward Gathland State Park and parked in the lot on the north side of the highway. At that point, the Purcellville Witch pulled a blanket out of the car and led my friend up into the woods, either more familiar with them than she had let on or confident that the path would lead to a spot suitable to her purposes.

They reached a moonlit clearing, where she spread out the blanket, bade my friend lie down on it, and then began dancing and performing some sort of witchy striptease. My friend was, perhaps needless to say, engaged by this, but—his senses not completely distracted—began to hear ominous noises in the surrounding woods, crunching sounds too loud to have been made by normal animals. As each piece of clothing came off the Purcellville Witch, the louder these disturbances became and the more anxious he grew (and less able to enjoy the show). By the time the arcane temptress had stripped to nothing but her witchy thong, the encroaching ghosts/ghouls/demons/hillbillies had gotten so noisy and apparently so close that his nerve broke. He jumped up and ran back to the car, the witch in tow.

My assumption would have been that this was all part of some malign spell that required a living victim—my friend—

for its completion and that the Purcellville Witch was complicit in the whole thing (absurd objections that *all* Wiccans are really good and wonderful people notwithstanding). Other explanations might include phenomena in the woods that was targeting only him or to which only he was sensitive or some sort of sensory deprivation on her part.

In any event, numerous articles and books, many published prior to the release of *The Blair Witch Project*, discuss the presence of Civil War ghosts in and around Burkittsville. Many of these are supposed to be those of Confederate soldiers, who were killed and in many cases buried improperly far from home.

One story, for example, tells the tale of a local resident, a Mr. Wise, who was paid by the retreating Confederates to bury about four dozen bodies, but who then dumped them down a well. Wise was reportedly haunted by the spirits of one of the men, a rebel sergeant named James Tabbs. Some believe that he and the other troubled spirits made their presence known so intently that the wretched Wise was eventually confronted by the local authorities and forced to bury the bodies properly.

Numerous other tales cite people hearing the whispered words of slain Civil War soldiers while walking the quiet streets of Burkittsville at night, and of a score or more haunted places in the town, especially the site of a now-razed tannery that was used as a field hospital during the fighting in the surrounding area. Other stories also indicate that the residents of Burkittsville have, in general, always tried to dismiss rumors of such things as they relate to their town.

My friend Dominick Salemi and I visited Burkittsville together in May 2009. It was my first trip up to the town but he had passed through the area numerous times and had, with the exception of Burkittsville itself, generally been quite taken with it. During our journey along the Capital Beltway and then up I-270 toward Frederick, Maryland, Dom told me about some of his experiences in the area and what we might expect while exploring it. He made it clear that we would not find many friendly faces in the place we were going.

He had visited Burkittsville shortly after *The Blair Witch Project* had been released and described some strange antics on the part of the locals. These included seeing things hung over the exit sign for Burkittsville off of US 340, the closest major highway, to obscure it from view as well as finding the main road into town blocked with traffic cones. Such ham-handed efforts were, of course, almost guaranteed to enhance people's interest in the town and make outsiders believe there was something to hide. One might even think such measures were intended to actually boost interest if the locals had then been at all accommodating toward visitors.

A decrepit little graveyard and church on the hill above Burkittsville is one of the many interesting sites in the vicinity of the little town.

"I've never seen a smiling face in Burkittsville," Dom told me during our journey, a look of distaste on his face. "The people just stand there and stare at you with their dull eyes and sweep porches that don't need sweeping as you go past. And it is obvious that they are the products of years of inbreeding." He had more to say in a similar vein and made the village sound, in short, like one of the little damned New England hamlets described in the horror novels of H.P. Lovecraft. I wasn't really buying it. His intense sincerity notwithstanding, it all sounded a little too overtly horrible, and I could think of no good reason why the locals would necessarily be inclined toward inbreeding. A patent lawyer and the publisher of the pop culture magazine *Brutarian*, Dom is smart and—often inadvertently—funny, but he is also sometimes given to hyperbole. I was, nonetheless, starting to get a little apprehensive.

Upon reaching Burkittsville we drove around a bit, eagerly seeking, at least on my part, the glowering visages of misshapen, inbred locals as they pretended to sweep their already-clean porches. Perhaps even more strangely, we simply saw . . . no one. Not a single man, woman, or child. It was a weekday, true, but you would think we would have seen *someone* moving around the town. The only exception was a police officer, who followed us in his cruiser for awhile and then pulled over and stopped. When we turned around at the edge of town and drove past him, we could see him doing what appeared to be running our plates on his onboard computer.

We stopped near the local graveyard, where some scenes from the movie had been filmed, and parked between a church and the local historical society; we heard noises of construction coming from within the latter structure but still saw no one. An exploration of the picturesque burying ground revealed it to have among its stones numerous old ones, including some from the early 1800s and others worn completely illegible by age. A later perusal of my photos revealed some odd black spots in the air over some grave markers in one of them, and I suspect a detailed investigation of the site might produce some interesting results.

Continuing westward out of town along Gapland Road, we climbed up into the hills above Burkittsville and toward Gathland State Park, which straddles Frederick and Washington Counties and through which the Appalachian Trail passes. The slope at this point is known locally as "Spook Hill" and, like "gravity hills" in other places, is known for the tendency of cars, when in neutral, to roll uphill on it. According to legend, this is caused by the spirits of Confederate soldiers who were killed while pushing heavy cannons up the hill; people who have spread flour on the back ends of their cars have reported finding handprints in it. Not wanting to accidentally get rearended by a ghosthunter-hating local, we opted to forego experimenting with this and kept our car in drive.

We had also been hoping while in the area to visit the nearby graveyard of the old Brethren church, where the body of an executed eighteenth-century German pacifist had been laid to rest. (See the chapter on the City of Frederick in this book.) So, when we saw a decrepit little graveyard and church at the right side of the road, we pulled off at an open spot a little further up the road and then walked back to it.

Exploration of the site revealed an interesting dichotomy: Many of the stones in the graveyard were falling over, or actually laying flat, but in a plot toward the rear of the site we discovered the recently turned earth of a fresh grave, along with wilting flowers and a new stone. Back along the timberline, we found a number of other recent stones, so it would seem that this aged site was still in use, perhaps by people with ancestral roots in the area who now live elsewhere and no longer use the church or maintain its graveyard.

The cornerstone of the rotting and disused little church identified it as "Geres Bethel of A.M.E. Church 1870. L. Benson Pastor." The church dated from a later time than what we were seeking and was founded by a different sort of brethren. The foundation certainly could have been older and been used for an earlier structure but we could not be sure just by looking at it. The interior of the church was in terrible shape and had apparently not been used for at least a couple of decades.

We headed on to Gathland State Park, a 140-acre site that consists of the remains of the estate of George Alfred Townsend, a war correspondent during the War Between the States who wrote under the pen name "Gath." (He is the author of an eerie story titled *The Entailed Hat*, which ties in with two of the Eastern Shore chapters in this book, the ones on Patty Cannon's House and Furnace Town.)

The most prominent feature of Gathland is the War Correspondents Memorial Arch, the first such monument in the world and still a rarity, which loomed up before us as we crested the hill. Fifty feet high and forty wide, it is a striking amalgam of arches, statues, niches, inset tablets, and inscriptions, including the names of 157 war correspondents and artists who witnessed and described in narrative and image the events of the four-year Civil War.

We parked and explored the rest of the site, which Gath had acquired in 1884 and upon which he had built numerous structures between then and 1896. These included Gapland Hall, an eleven room house; Gapland Lodge, a stone servants' quarters; a large building containing ten bedrooms, a study, and a library; a barn; a walled burial ground; and a mausoleum with a marble lintel inscribed "Good Night Gath." All of these structures are currently in various states of repair and connected with paths through the surrounding woods, creating the effect of a weird little amusement park.

The retired journalist had split his time between his estate and his home in Philadelphia and had planned to be laid to rest at Gathland. At some point, however, he decided to be buried in the former location. Gath had, perhaps, been one of the first to detect the presence of the ghostly soldiers who had fallen on the hill during the war and which are even now reputed to haunt the grounds of his estate. Having spent his professional life with them, Gath may have decided he did not want to also share eternity with their spirits and any others that might yet haunt the wooded hills above Burkittsville.

Author George Alfred Townsend had a tomb built for himself on his mountain estate outside of Burkittsville but, perhaps sensing the presence of the Civil War soldiers who haunt the area, opted to be buried in Philadelphia instead.

Spotlight on Ghosts: Brunswick

One disservice the various "Blair Witch" films did for potential ghosthunters was to portray Burkittsville as a place with a diner, convenience store, and other establishments associated with larger communities. No such amenities can actually be found in the little town, which, according to the most recent census data, is inhabited by just 171 people in seventy-two households. We thus knew we would not find a place to each lunch there and, when we reached the junction with US 340 and Route 17, decided to first go south into Brunswick, Maryland, and have lunch there before heading up to our ultimate destination.

Dom had visited the pleasant little town a number of times before and had even considered buying a home there. He had also chatted with people at a local tavern and from them heard tales of strange happenings in the area. So, while we were there we also decided to poke around for any ghost stories we could find. Suffice it to say, the residents of Brunswick, a town of about five thousand located on the upper Potomac and a bedroom community for D.C., are much more open to talking about any ghosts that haunt the local area than are those of Burkittsville. In just a few hours, we were able to uncover a number of stories without too much difficulty.

At the diner where we had lunch, the waitress told us that the municipal firehouse and adjacent ambulance company, located just a few blocks north up West Potomac Street, were believed by many in the local area to be haunted. Phenomena she described involved a pool table at the one location and some weird water effects at the other. She was, in any event, wearing a volunteer fire company T-shirt, so we had every reason to believe her information was good.

Just past the firehouse, we discovered Chesapeake & Hudson Inc., a publishers' representative located in a historic bank building, and chatted with Janine Jensen for a little bit. She and her colleague Robin Bell very generously brainstormed and made some calls on our behalf and got me on the line with a teenager of their acquaintance who was familiar with local ghostly lore.

The story he told us involved a nearby tunnel where a motorcyclist is believed to have been killed in a wreck. As with many such stories, this one involved the claim that at certain times visitors hear the sound of the dead biker's engine being gunned from the otherworld. Tunnels are, among some of the creepiest and most haunted places I have encountered in my journeys on America's Haunted Road Trip, so it would be my guess that this site would warrant investigation. (See the chapters on Bunny Man Bridge and Poor House Road Tunnel in *Ghosthunting Virginia*.)

We made a cursory attempt to find the haunted tunnel but, after several instances of failing to successfully get onto the road on which it was located and somehow accidentally getting off of it once we did find it—all in the style of the lost souls from *The Blair Witch Project*, of course—we decided to make the most of our remaining daylight and just continue onto Burkittsville.

CHAPTER 26

Church of St. Patrick
CUMBERLAND

The Church of St. Patrick is believed by some to be haunted by the ghost of a Civil War soldier executed for fratricide.

There is a tradition among Cumberland people that the night after the execution, Father Brennan heard the military tread of a soldier in the hall and opening the door, he was confronted by his dead penitent, who rebuked him for being too slow in carrying out his promise.

—"The Parish Ghost of Cumberland"

I HAVE ALWAYS LOVED DRIVING through Cumberland, a quiet little antebellum city near the western end of Maryland, and its name has always evoked a certain romance for me. Its old brick buildings spread out from the banks of the north branch of the Potomac River, like a carpet beneath the raised highway that virtually passes over the town. At one point, the fort built there in 1755—more than three decades before the town was founded and a full sixty-two years before it was incorporated—marked the furthest extent of the British Empire into North America. George Washington himself really did sleep there, and fight in the hills and forests surrounding it, before he was even an American, during the French and Indian War as an officer of colonial militia.

It was during a war a bit more than a century later, however, that Cumberland acquired one of its oldest and most persistent ghost stories.

During the Civil War, one of the Union units that passed through the area was the 15th New York Volunteer Cavalry Regiment, formed in 1863 and active as part of Brigadier General George Armstrong Custer's brigade. Discipline was often draconian during the conflict, and when twenty-four-year-old Private Francis Gillespie of the regiment's B Company violated some regulation, his commander, First Lieutenant William B. Shearer, ordered that he be hanged by his thumbs. Gillespie was reportedly left in this agonizing position almost until he was dead, at which point he was cut down, his punishment presumably complete.

Volunteers are quite often not big fans of military excess, at least as it pertains to discipline, and Gillespie is said to have sworn vengeance on Shearer. That was apparently not an idle oath and, during a march from Parkersburg, West Virginia, to Cumberland, Gillespie shot Shearer to death.

Gillespie was tried by a military tribunal that found him guilty and sentenced him to be hanged not by his thumbs until nearly dead but, rather, by his neck until completely dead.

Father Brennan of the Roman Catholic Church of St. Patrick in Cumberland, who knew Gillespie and had ministered to him, was asked to help prepare him for death, an experience that is said to have been very painful for the sensitive priest. During his final hours, Gillespie asked Brennan to ensure that various personal effects be delivered to his relatives, among them his young wife, who lived in Syracuse, New York.

Gillespie reportedly faced his death bravely, and remained steady as he ascended the scaffold erected for his execution near Rose Hill Cemetery in Cumberland.

"I forgive everybody from the bottom of my heart, and I pray God to forgive me," Gillespie is reputed to have uttered for his last words. "May the stars and stripes never be trampled on."

As previous events had shown, however, forgiveness was not exactly Gillespie's strong suit. It is not clear whether Father Brennan intended to personally deliver to the hanged man's loved ones the items entrusted to him or whether he was planning on having them delivered by someone else. Either way, he evidently did not set about accomplishing this task as quickly as Gillespie would have liked.

"There is a tradition among Cumberland people that the night after the execution, Father Brennan heard the military tread of a soldier in the hall and, opening the door, he was confronted by his dead penitent, who rebuked him for being too slow in carrying out his promise," says the local *Mountain Discoveries Magazine* in its Fall/Winter 2003 article "The Parish Ghost of Cumberland."

"This story has been part of the tradition of the history of the church of St. Patrick for over one hundred years," Monsignor Thomas R. Bevan, pastor of St. Patrick Parish, told the magazine. And some people claim that the troubled ghost of the executed Gillespie haunts the church to this day.

This story intrigued me and I resolved to visit the church the next time I passed through Cumberland. That opportunity presented itself one night in August 2008, when I was passing through Cumberland en route from Cincinnati, Ohio, to my then-home in Springfield, Virginia.

It was nearly midnight when I exited I-68 and for the first time drove down into the darkened streets of aged Cumberland. It did not take me too long to find the Church of St. Patrick, which is within several blocks of the highway, and once I figured out that the street that ran past it was one-way and maneuvered accordingly, I was able to make my way to an empty parking lot just across from the church.

Everything was quiet around the church and its various outbuildings, including the rectory, and as I approached it I could see that its looming, classical façade—an exception in church architecture in general and in this part of the country in particular—was illuminated, but everything else lay cloaked in quiet and darkness. Down the street, I could hear revelry coming from a corner bar. I set about exploring the place.

"On this site in 1791 the first mass was celebrated in Allegany County by Father Dennis Cahill," I read on a historic marker near the front of the church's grounds. This place had been, it seemed, a continuous center of worship for well over two centuries. Another, more detailed marker indicated that a log chapel had been constructed on the site the same year as that first mass and that the first parishioners were primarily English Catholics from southern Maryland. A brick church replaced the log building in 1839, and after an influx of Irish immigrants to the area—drawn by the construction of the National Road, the B&O Railroad, and the C&O Canal—the parish grew in size and wealth, allowing for the construction of the current building in 1851. It is still obviously an important religious center, another sign identifying it as the "Mother Church of Western Maryland."

I spent some time walking around the quiet churchyard, taking pictures, meditating upon a stone bench, examining a number of statues that adorned the grounds. The doors to the church itself were locked, and I could thus not extend my explorations into it at that late hour. While my sojourn on the grounds was a somewhat eerie experience during which it was easy to imagine that any number of ghosts might haunt the old place, it was by no means an unpleasant one, and I did not detect anything specific (nor did a subsequent examination of my photos reveal any anomalies indicative of paranormal activity).

After about an hour, it occurred to me that I had probably spent enough time at the site and that I needed to be on my way—motivated, perhaps, by the unquiet spirit of poor Francis Gillespie, the de facto local patron saint of promptly attending to the business at hand.

CHAPTER 27

City of Frederick
FREDERICK COUNTY

**Many of the people who have worked at Barbara Fritchie's house in Frederick believe it to be haunted by the ghost of its former owner.
(Credit: Brady and Co.)**

Up from the meadows rich with corn,
Clear in the cool September morn,
The clustered spires of Frederick stand
Green-walled by the hills of Maryland.

—John Greenleaf Whittier, "Barbara Fritchie"

FREDERICK IS CHARMING AND QUAINT, with one of the best preserved and most meticulously maintained historic districts in the state of Maryland. It has wonderful shops, a good selection of restaurants—some quite upscale—and a great museum of Civil War Medicine. It is steeped in history.

The layout of the streets and, indeed, many of the buildings themselves, have not changed much since the intrepid Barbara Fritchie faced down Stonewall Jackson's troops as they marched through Frederick on their way to Harpers Ferry. Leaning from her second-floor window and clutching the American flag in her aged hands, Fritchie uttered the words immortalized by the poet John Greenleaf Whittier and so well known to school children of earlier generations:

> *"Shoot, if you must, this old gray head,*
> *But spare your country's flag," she said.*

Or so the legend goes. Some say her house did not lie on Jackson's route through Frederick, but the Union needed heroes and—as a friend of Francis Scott Key, author of the national anthem—ninety-five-year-old Barbara Frithcie was a natural.

Her house still stands at 154 West Patrick Street and, along with a small museum, is open to visitors. Volunteers there believe she still haunts the premises. While inspecting the house during the winter months, when the museum is closed, they report having seen her chair rocking, apparently of its own volition, and then suddenly stopping as they approached it. One even thought that she could see Mrs. Fritchie's feet extending from beneath the quilt that was draped over the chair. She refused to ever again set foot alone in that house.

But it is not just Barbara Fritchie whose ghost still lingers in this charming Maryland town. Frederick, in fact, may be Maryland's most haunted city. The reason for this can surely be found in the confluence of history and geography that put Frederick into proximity with a number of the bloodiest battles of the Civil War: Gettysburg, Antietam, and Monocacy. Blood still stains the floors of Frederick's Evangelical Lutheran Church, which served as a makeshift hospital for the wounded from these gory battles. What is now the National Museum of Civil War Medicine in downtown Frederick, served then as a morgue and embalming station for dead Union officers and men.

While the Civil War did contribute its full share to the ghostly phenomena that can still be observed today, Frederick's ghostly history did not, however, begin with that conflict. The American Revolution, in particular, also left its mark. This was a time in Frederick when Tories and Patriots clashed, not in the epic blood-spilling of the Civil War, but in a colder conflict of intrigue and accusations. One casualty of that time was Peter Sueman, a German farmer from nearby Burkittsville (made famous by its association with the Blair Witch and covered in its own chapter in this book).

Sueman belonged to the Church of the Brethren—a sect often known as the German Baptist Brethren with American roots dating to 1723. Its members were pacifists and generally tried to stay

Phenomena people have reported at the Barbara Fritchie house include seeing her rocking chair moving on its own and seeing her ghostly feet sticking out from under the quilt covering the chair. (Credit: Wikipedia)

neutral during the American Revolution, refusing to swear loy-
alty to either side. In the highly charged atmosphere of the times,
such a position generated suspicions of disloyalty, leading to conspiracy theories, accusations, and sometimes retribution.

This seems to have been the fate of poor Sueman, who was
implicated with six others in a supposed plot to free prisoners of
war who were being held in Frederick. These were British troops
and Hessian mercenaries who had been captured at the battles of
Yorktown, Saratoga, and Bennington. An informer reported that
he had infiltrated a group, of which Sueman and several other
Brethren were supposedly members. According to the informer,
this group was conspiring to aid the British—supported by Indians—to come down from Canada and Detroit through Pittsburgh
to Frederick. The ostensible aim of the invasion was to free the
prisoners, then go east to help the British in Virginia.

Because of the informer's story, Sueman and six others
were tried at the courthouse house in Frederick. Sueman and
two of his co-defendants were quickly convicted. The sentence,
in keeping with the English law for treason, was draconian. It
was pronounced by Judge Alexander Contee Hanson on July 25,
1781, and read as follows:

> *You shall be carried to the gaol of Fredericktown, and be
> hanged therein; you shall be cut down to the earth alive, and
> your entrails shall be taken out and burnt while you are yet
> alive, your heads shall be cut off, your body shall be divided
> into four parts, and your heads and quarters shall be placed
> where his Excellency the Governor shall appoint. So Lord
> have mercy upon your poor souls.*

On August 17, 1781, Sueman was led to the gallows, which
had been erected in the courthouse house square, and there he
suffered the full sentence as prescribed by the judge. He was
the first of three who had been convicted. The other two—or so

the story goes—were more fortunate. The crowd was so horrified by what had been done to Sueman that it demanded that the others should be simply hanged.

It was left to Sueman's wife, Eleanor, and some friends to go around the town and pick up the pieces of the body and take them home to Burkittsville. Some accounts have Sueman buried off Broad Run Road, just below the Mount Pleasant Church in Burkittsville. In another story, he is buried at the Pleasant View Church of the Brethren in Burkittsville.

It is possible that both accounts could be true. The body could have been hastily buried in a convenient location in 1781 by an impoverished Eleanor, whose land had been confiscated by the government, and then reinterred later in the church cemetery when passions had cooled and she had won her land back in court. Possibly future investigations in the Burkittsville area, in itself a place of interest, will shed more light on this matter.

Given the gruesomeness of the punishment and the uncertainty of Peter Sueman's guilt, it would not be unexpected that a vengeful ghost might haunt the building in which the sentence was pronounced, and in front of which he suffered his agonizing death. The courthouse house itself literally rotted away after the trial and was replaced in 1787 by a second courthouse. That one was plagued by fire. The steeple and roof burned in 1842, and flames finally gutted the entire building in 1861. Not only had that fire been deliberately set, but someone had also cut off the water supply so that the firemen could do nothing but watch as the building became enveloped in flames. At the time, suspicion was cast on secessionists. Poor Peter Sueman had already faded from popular memory and has only recently been rediscovered by ghosthunters.

The current structure, which has served as the Frederick City Hall since 1983, has not suffered the fate of its predecessors. Nevertheless, some say that Peter's restless spirit is still abroad. Employees at the hall frequently report otherwise inexplicable events: lights that somehow come back on after having been turned off; water faucets that are found to be running when employees arrive to open up City Hall in the morning; and strange noises and footsteps when the occasional late worker believes he is there alone.

One must wonder, though, why these phenomena have all been attributed to Peter Sueman. Two other conspirators, after all, also died with him that day. They were Yost Flecker and Casper Fritchie, who was the father of Barbara Fritchie's husband, John Casper Fritchie. It is as logical to attribute the strange phenomena at the City Hall to Flecker and Fritchie as it is to Sueman. Or maybe they are all involved. Maybe these men, convicted of what could well have been a trumped-up charge, became the conspirators in death that they might not have been in life.

The most reputedly haunted building in Frederick, however, is not the City Hall, it is the National Museum of Civil War Medicine located at 48 East Patrick Street. Ghosts aside, this is an absolutely fascinating museum, and it alone provides ample reason for a visit to Frederick. At the time of the Civil War, this building was not a medical facility, but was instead owned by James Whitehall, furniture maker and undertaker. Today, this may seem a strange combination, but then it made perfect economic sense. The main function of an undertaker was to provide coffins. Who better than a furniture maker to provide that product?

With the onset of the Civil War, the demand for Whitehall's coffins exploded. The Army did not supply them, nor did it return the remains of deceased soldiers back to their hometowns. It was left to the families themselves to make their own arrangements— and they had need of more than just a coffin for that long trip home. The bodies needed to be embalmed. To take advantage of this need, Dr. Richard Burr, a contractor with the U.S. Army, set up an embalming station in the building in 1862, after the battles of Antietam and South Mountain. Dr. Burr's services, however, proved unsatisfactory, and the Army canceled his contract. While the details have been lost, one can only imagine the shoddy practices that would cause the Army in these desperate times to terminate a much-needed service. This may also have resulted in those desperate situations that are so often at the root of many of the supernatural phenomena that we encounter today.

While the fact that there are hauntings in the museum is well attested to, the details seem to be closely guarded. In what I have seen as a pattern since I began researching stories of ghosts, there are some institutions that shun any association with the supernatural, even when their own employees continue to report ghostly phenomena. This appears to be the case for this museum. My request to interview employees—which I provided in writing, per the request of the museum—went unanswered. I was fortunate, however, to happen upon a friendly docent, who was a bit more forthcoming. This combined with what I had learned on Frederick's late-evening ghost tour, called the Candlelight Tour, shed a bit more light on the phenomena at the museum.

There are, as to be expected, the unexplained noises. These include the sound of doors closing, footsteps on the stairs, heavy keys rattling, and the stomp of spectral boots on bare floors. These incidents, however, have not been associated with any particular person or event. What breathes life, so to speak, into these stories for me is knowing something about the spirit as a human being, as was the case with poor Peter Sueman.

There is one name that is associated with the spiritual phenomena at the museum, and that is John Failing. As the story was recounted on the Candlelight Tour, a visitor at the museum was viewing an exhibit that contained a picture of Failing. This visitor allegedly commented that Failing was an ugly brute. On saying this, the fellow felt a sharp blow to his shoulder that rocked him back. The inference was that Failing, feeling insulted, delivered the blow. Maybe it was the many years I spent with U.S. Army counterintelligence, as well as the U.S. Army Inspector General Agency, but I thought this explanation required a closer look.

Failing was an ambulance corpsman with the 9th New York Artillery Regiment. A contemporary photograph of him is part of an exhibit on the evacuation of wounded soldiers from Civil War battlefields. Other than this picture, there is nothing to associate Failing with the building. There is no reason to believe that he ever in life set foot in it. It was, after all, a mortuary, and Failing was surely fully occupied with evacuating the wounded, not transporting the dead. As far as his being ugly, that is also debatable. Yes, there is a strange cast to his eyes, but that is easily attributable to the state of the art of photography in the 1860s.

Employees at Frederick City Hall frequently report inexplicable events like lights that somehow come back on after being turned off, water faucets that start running on their own, and strange noises and footsteps.

If this visitor did receive a blow to the shoulder, it is much more likely to be from the spirit of a soldier from the regiment who had been brought to the building for embalming. The 9th New York, which had so proudly marched off on May 27, 1861, 850 strong, returned home after three years of service with a mere seventeen officers and seventy-eight enlisted men. It had participated in many brutal battles in the vicinity of Frederick, including Antietam, South Mountain, and Gettysburg.

It is easy to caricature ghosts and forget the real humans behind them. One should try to imagine the feelings of a soldier, wounded in one of these epic struggles, but evacuated, possibly under enemy fire to a field dressing station by the selfless and heroic Failing. It should not be surprising that such a soldier would take offense at hearing a visitor gratuitously insulting a valiant comrade. Good advice to any visitor to the museum is to not do that. Rather, take that opportunity to reflect on the valor and devotion of those young men, including the ambulance corpsmen, who gave their last full measure of devotion to save the Union.

There are, of course, many more ghostly phenomena associated with Frederick. The Candlelight Tour, mentioned above, provides a good introduction to many if not all of them. It does not, for example, take you to the Evangelical Lutheran Church, where Greg Glewwe reported that he had seen a full-frontal apparition. (See the separate chapter in this book on the Schifferstadt.) The tour also provides a convenient opportunity to meet other like-minded visitors who share a common interest in exploring the supernatural. And the brewery pub, where the tour begins, is a cozy place to meet afterwards and share experiences over a good beer—a pleasure reserved for the living.

CHAPTER 28

Gabriel's Inn
IJAMSVILLE

Much of the paranormal activity at Gabriel's Inn, particularly in its wine cellar, has been associated with casualties from nearby Civil War battles.

Since we formed Gabriel's Paranormal Society we have held numerous private and public investigations at the Inn. In most cases, the investigations have turned into real learning experiences for the investigators as they have been able to communicate with the Spirit World while at Gabriel's Inn and so saw their equipment and/or abilities in action.

—Carol LaRiviere, Gabriel's Paranormal Society

"I LOVE THIS HOUSE," Carol LaRiviere explained. "When I turn off the road and come up the driveway, I feel like I am going through a barrier into another world." Carol is the charming founder of Gabriel's Paranormal Society, which meets monthly at the inn. She was also our host for the evening.

I understood what she meant. I had experienced the same

feeling as we drove up the winding driveway toward the long white structure that crowned the ridge line. Gabriel's Inn seemed untouched by the twenty-first century and the urban sprawl that was transforming much of Frederick County into bedroom communities for Federal workers and contractors from the Washington, D.C., metropolitan area.

We had turned off I-270 at Urbana, where we discovered that what had been a quaint Maryland town just a decade ago was now dominated by shiny new townhouses. It was a pleasant surprise to see how quickly we left that behind as we headed a few miles further east toward Ijamsville. This was old Maryland—little changed from the nineteenth century. I suspect that General Lew Wallace's soldiers, retreating through here on July 9, 1864, after the Battle of Monocacy, would have recognized many of the wood-framed houses. The layout of the streets and roads, although now paved in asphalt, would also have been very familiar. Moreover, the tracks of the B&O railroad, one of the nation's oldest railroads, still run along the southern edge of the property on which Gabriel's Inn now sits. This line, which ran from Baltimore to the Ohio River, was undoubtedly critical to both the resupply and the evacuation of Union forces. It probably also made the buildings on the property a hub of activity during Wallace's retreat to Baltimore.

By delaying Confederate General Jubal Early by one day, Wallace's soldiers gave General Ulysses S. Grant the time he needed to reinforce Washington, D.C., thereby not only saving the nation's capital but possibly the Union itself. Because of Wallace, Early was late.

The battle still haunts the surrounding area. Visitors to Gabriel's Inn have reported hearing cannon fire in the west—in the direction of the Union line. It also haunts the inn itself. Paranormal investigators have detected significant activity in the inn's wine cellar—one, for example, reported a six-hundred milligauss hit on an EMF meter, which to paranormal investigators is phenomenal—and are gradually piecing together the human story left behind.

One source of this activity appears to be a Union soldier by the name of Patrick, who, perhaps, died in the cellar. Hopefully, future investigations will flesh out his story. Was he wounded during the battle and sought refuge here from Confederate pursuit? Did he then die of his wounds in that cold, lonely darkness? Given the number of investigators who regularly visit Gabriel's Inn, it is likely that more will be learned before too long. The fact that Maryland TriState Paranormal (MTSP) has finally confirmed that there are indeed numerous spirits residing there cannot but add to the intensity of the effort.

We had chosen the third Thursday of the month to visit the inn because this was when members of Gabriel's Paranormal Society gathered to share their experiences. Carol, a conscientious hostess, ensured that we and a few other newcomers were introduced and comfortably integrated into the group. I had never attended such a gathering before. Whatever I expected—and I am not sure what that was—this was probably not it. Over their drinks and food (crab dip seemed to be a favorite), the attendees discussed their ghostly explorations, sightings, and investigations with a calm matter-of-factness one more readily associates with birdwatchers, or maybe a book club. I, for one, am still intimidated by the thought of ghosts, but they clearly were not.

Across from me sat Jim and Chip, both relatively new but enthusiastic ghosthunters who had explored Gabriel's Inn together. Apparently, one of the female ghosts in the inn had taken a liking to Chip and was known to stroke his hair during meetings.

"Is she doing that now?" Carol asked at one point.

"Yes," Chip replied, grinning sheepishly. For once, I was glad that I am completely bald.

Jim used a K-2 meter for his investigations in the inn, while

Chip favored a trimeter. Their readings often correlated, particularly when exploring upstairs and in the wine cellar (it was Chip who had gotten the six-hundred milligauss reading in the latter location). One of the most dramatic experiences, however, was in the parlor—and there they had failed to obtain any readings. As they were leaving, Jim said, "I'm not getting anything. There must not be anything here." Chip, fortunately, had his recorder running, and when they played it back later, they heard clear as day, "I'm sitting right here."

The inn, steeped in history, filled with antiques, and projecting an aura of mystery, provides a perfect setting for the meetings, as well as the many other paranormal events that the inn hosts. What is now one long structure had originally consisted of three separate wood-framed houses that had been built in 1862 to house six Welsh mining families that had immigrated to the area to mine Ijamsville slate.

In 1896, Dr. George Henry Riggs of Ijamsville purchased the property and converted it into the Riggs Cottage Sanitarium for the "care of women with mild mental disorders." It was he who connected the buildings on the ground-floor level with windowed sunrooms. Wholesome food, light and airy surroundings, and a tranquil country environment were the key elements of Dr. Riggs' therapy. In 1938, Dr. Hosea McAdoo acquired the property, and he ran it for thirteen years before selling it to the last owner who would run it as a hospital, a Dr. Lerner, in 1952.

More than one thousand patients were treated at the facility, which was the third oldest mental hospital in the state of Maryland. Many patients died on the property, including two who stayed after Dr. Lerner sold it to restaurateur Guy Gabriel in 1968. It seems that the spirits of some of these patients still watch over the building that had been their refuge in life. According to Carol, theses spirits love the inn just as it is and will sometimes interfere with renovations and repairs. While not in any way malicious, they have been known to generally make their disapproval known in mischievous but nonthreatening ways.

Mr. Gabriel came to Ijamsville from Paris, France, where he was already an accomplished chef. His dream was to have his own farm and to raise a big family there. He converted the sanitarium into Gabriel's French Provincial Inn—but being a compassionate man by nature, he allowed the remaining two patients to live out the remainder of their lives on the property. Mr. Gabriel has since passed on, but the buildings still house an excellent restaurant specializing in French Provincial cuisine.

According to Carol, Mr. Gabriel's spirit watches over the building as well, and she said that she actually sees him there all the time, often in the bar, just standing there and looking around.

Carol's daughter can attest to this and to that the chef's pride in his culinary skills have not diminished with his passing. On one occasion, for example, she was in the kitchen assisting the current owner, Sean DeLawder, in preparing a particular salmon dish. As DeLawder worked, he commented that Mr. Gabriel used to make it one way, but he, Sean, did it this way—and he liked his way better. At that point, one of the spices on the top shelf flew across the room.

Gabriel's Inn also hosts what to me is a most remarkable and poignant event. It's called the "Mourning Tea," and it is based on nineteenth-century tradition. Participants dress in Victorian mourning clothes and recite stories, poems, and eulogies designed to remember and honor deceased family and friends. Gabriel's Inn has revived this tradition primarily because of the active spirits residing there.

"This event was one of the most interesting and emotional experiences we've ever had at MTSP," said MTSP Administrative Director Sharon Ramirez when describing the Mourning Tea.

Participating in the tea, as well as many of the other paranormal events that the inn hosts, is Terri Rodabaugh, a psychic medium. According to members of the MTSP, she is actually able to channel and convey messages of loved ones from beyond the grave, sometimes recounting the tiniest of family details with breathtaking accuracy.

Our visit to Gabriel's Inn confirmed one thing for me: it is thoroughly haunted. What perplexed me, though, was why this place in particular. There are many places that are just as old, or older, also much loved by their residents, and often the site of dramatic events. Not all such sites are haunted or have revealed any indication of paranormal activity.

My wife's theory is that it is the furniture, and, indeed, Gabriel's Inn is filled with many beautiful antiques. I believe, however, that my wife is doing some projecting here. She attaches to things, not places—like her grandmother's dining room set that we inherited. It was at that table where she had many happy Thanksgiving dinners with her family—and I suspect she can see her grandmother sitting there still. But that is not necessarily true of the spirits at Gabriel's Inn—so I posed the same question to Carol.

"It's the rocks," she answered without hesitation. She went on to say that some types of stone, like limestone, seem to attract and hold spirits—maybe because the stone is composed of material that was once alive. Here at Gabriel's Inn, she explained, it is the Ijamsville slate—and, of course, the deep affection that these souls had in life for this lovely place.

THE UPPER POND

The grounds of Gabriel's Inn once contained a working slate mine. Legend has it that a child of one of the Welsh slate-mining families drowned in the upper pond near the inn (another, lower pond can also be found by the railroad tracks at the foot of the hill on which the inn is located). It seems that the spirit of this little boy still roams the grounds, and visitors have reported such things as an unseen presence tugging on their pant legs. Also, the many glass globes that line the walkways are often found to have been moved around for no explicable reason. A number of investigators have identified the playful spirit responsible for these things variously as Josh or Jacques.

THE UPSTAIRS ROOMS

Before Gabriel's Inn was a restaurant, it was a sanitarium for the "care of women with mild mental disorders." These women had rooms on the second floor, where ghostly sightings are frequent. Recently, several members of Maryland TriState Paranormal, many of whom are sensitives and empaths, took turns individually investigating this area. Several reported seeing or feeling the presence of a well-dressed clergyman, a curly-haired woman, an older demented lady, and children playing.

CHAPTER 29

Monocacy National Battlefield
FREDERICK COUNTY

Paranormal researchers have detected significant spiritual activity around the memorial to the 14th New Jersey Infantry Regiment, which suffered heavy casualties during the Battle of Monocacy.

. . . war has its higher fields, and he who would move successfully in them must know more than to defend with shield and thrust with spear. In those fields the general finds his tasks, the greatest of which is the reduction of the many into one, and that one himself; the consummate captain is a fighting man armed with an army.

—Lew Wallace, *Ben Hur*

A RELATIVELY MINOR BATTLE when compared to bloodbaths like Antietam, the Battle of Monocacy Junction was nonetheless significant from a strategic point of view—and its site remains important today as a venue for paranormal activity. Despite this, however, the site seems to have largely been overlooked by tellers of ghost stories and paranormal investigators alike, most of whom have gravitated to the larger and better-known clashes. For those who die in them, of course, small battles are as meaningful as big ones, and the sites where they take place are just as likely to have earth-bound spirits associated with them.

In the summer of 1864, Confederate Lieutenant General Jubal Early launched a raid through the Shenandoah Valley into Maryland, in an attempt to lure Union forces away from their siege of Petersburg, Virginia.

On June 29, agents of the Baltimore & Ohio Railroad reported signs of Early's attack to their superiors. John W. Garrett, the pro-Union president of the railroad, passed this and subsequent information onto U.S. Army Major General Lew Wallace, head of the Middle Atlantic Department, which was headquartered in Baltimore. It was unclear at that point whether Early intended to advance on the national capital, and it was equally feared that he might attack Baltimore.

What information there was made its way up the chain of command, and a week later, on July 6, Lieutenant General Ulysses S. Grant, commander of the Union forces, deployed two brigades of the VI Corps—consisting of about five thousand troops—to intercept Early's advance. Pending their arrival, however, the only federal forces between Early's fourteen thousand men and the vulnerable cities were a motley crew of about twenty-three hundred soldiers, most of them inexperienced "Hundred Days Men," under the command of Wallace (who would ultimately gain his greatest fame as the author of

Ben Hur). Knowing his forces were no match for those of the advancing rebels, Wallace knew he had to delay their advance until reinforcements could arrive.

The Confederate forces advanced on Frederick—from which they could then continue south to Washington, D.C., or east to Baltimore—and their cavalry swept through the town, driving out the handful of Union troops defending it. Early then demanded and received two-hundred thousand dollars in exchange for not destroying the city.

Meanwhile, Wallace moved his troops into defensive positions centered on Monocacy Junction, just three miles southeast of Frederick and the optimal point to protect the approaches to either target city. Here, the National Road to Baltimore (now I-70), the Georgetown Pike to Washington, and the B&O railroad line all crossed the Monocacy River. Wallace hoped to screen an area six miles long along the east bank of the river, thus guarding the two turnpike bridges, the railroad bridge, and a number of fords, and thereby delay Early as much as possible and force him to disclose the objective of his attack.

Wallace did have some defensive elements at his disposal, including higher elevation along the side of the river he was holding, a pair of blockhouses, trenches some of his men had been able to dig, and the fences and fields of the surrounding farms. And his thin blue line was strengthened considerably by the arrival of the first part of the VI Corps troops, which had left the siegeworks around Petersburg, taken ship to Baltimore, and then been rushed by train to Monocacy Junction. This increased the strength of the Union forces along the river to about fifty-eight hundred men.

Wallace and his men fought fiercely and held their positions as long as they could but were soon overwhelmed by the superior Confederate force. The Union forces suffered 1,294 men killed, wounded, or captured, while the Confederate forces paid a price for their victory of 700 to 900 killed and wounded—and a day lost in increasingly hostile enemy territory. Early was, in short, running late, but the road to Washington still lay open to him.

Early rushed on, his forces strung out behind him, and by midday on July 10 he had crossed the District line. Before him lay Fort Stevens, part of the ring of steel that surrounded the capital city, and it was here that he was finally blocked. Early's units skirmished and traded artillery fire with the Union defenders for a few days while he consolidated his forces but, ultimately, he realized that he could not successfully storm the defenses of the alerted city and that its gates were now closed to him. And so on July 13, 1864, the rebel commander withdrew, leading his men back across the Potomac River and into the Old Dominion, ending the last Confederate attempt to carry the war into the North.

I ventured out to the Monocacy Battlefield for the first time in May 2009, and there rendezvoused with Ana Bruder and her husband Chris Wojtaszek, cofounders of the Maryland TriState Paranormal investigative group. Both of them had visited the site before and were familiar with it from both a physical and a spiritual point of view. It had been drizzling off and on the gray, gloomy day we met at the battlefield, and storm clouds threatened to sweep in and impede us as we decided which spots we wanted to check out.

Originally a native of Costa Rica, Ana is a natural sensitive who has been able to sense and sometimes even see ghosts for as long as she can remember; she most often seems to get impressions of individuals, often being able to pick out very precise details about them. Chris is more of a trained psychic in the process of developing his abilities and who tends to see physical objects, such as tents, weapons, and the other detritus of war, as well as large-scale things like troop movements. Together, we toured the battlefield, stopping at a number of hotspots to see what sort of spiritual activity we could pick up.

Best Farm

Combat began near the Best family farm, when Union skirmishers of the 14th New Jersey Infantry Regiment at Monocacy Junction—about a half mile away and on the same side of the river as the invading forces—began firing at Confederate troops advancing southward along the Georgetown Pike (MD 355). The rebels reacted to this by setting up artillery near the farm and shelling the Federal positions, sparking a duel with Union artillery on the far side of the river, which eventually started a fire in the Best Farm's barn.

The three of us walked around the farm house and its outbuildings, the former building shut up and obviously in precarious condition, with a skeleton-like structure of braces that supported its walls visible through the windows.

Chris said he got some impressions of Confederate snipers perched on the barn, firing at the Union artillery positions on the high ground across the river. He also said he sensed something a few hundred yards away, toward the railroad tracks, and when we investigated the spot he was drawn to, we discovered the grisly remains of a possum, apparently torn apart by what we guessed was a fox.

Ana's own primary impressions were somewhat more subdued and involved a woman in dark mourning clothes toward the rear of the farmhouse. She could not be sure that this image was actually from the period of the war, but the style of the dress seemed reminiscent of the era to her and the small, brimless hat she described seemed to me to fit with the austere styles that the economic hardships of the conflict caused many people to adopt.

Worthington and Thomas Farms

Wanting to avoid a frontal attack across the Monocacy, Early sent some of his cavalry down Buckeystown Road to find a ford and outflank the left end of the Union line. Confederate troops crossed the river at the ford near the Worthington Farm, at the western end of the battlefield, and attacked Wallace's left flank. Some of the heaviest fighting of the battle took place along the fence line separating this farm from the one directly to its east, the Thomas Farm.

The Confederates set up artillery at the Worthington Farm and began to both bombard and assault the Federal-held Thomas Farm, and fighting swept back and forth across it throughout the day.

Both of these farms still exist, although they are not in very good shape and are thus not open to the public, but it is possible to walk around them. We decided to examine the Worthington Farm and the area around it, in part because the Confederate forces had used it as a field hospital. Built in 1851, it looked like a classic haunted house, both on the outside and what we could see of its intriguingly decrepit interior through the windows.

As soon as Ana walked up onto the front porch, she said that she had the impression of numerous gray-uniformed soldiers sitting on it and resting—and that one of them even looked at her, touched the brim of his hat, and said "ma'am"! (Whether he was actually a conscious entity and, if so, whether he knew he was dead or simply thought she was a person of his own time, she could not be sure.) She was able to pick out a number of other details about their uniforms, insignia, and accoutrements as well. She also said that she experienced a strong feeling of nausea, not because of any particularly negative emotions, but simply because there was so much psychic energy present at the site.

"The ones I saw were not injured," she said in response to my observation that this house had been used as a field hospital during the battle. "They were just sitting there, exhausted, taking a break."

Chris got impressions of John Worthington, the owner of the farm, giving a slave three or four days worth of rations and directing him to flee northward with the family horses to Sugarloaf Mountain until the fighting was over.

MONOCACY JUNCTION

Wallace centered his defensive line around the convergence of roads, railway lines, and river known as Monocacy Junction, posting about 350 skirmishers on the Confederate-dominated western side of the river. Two bridges crossed the river at this point, a covered wooden bridge and an open railway trestle, and when he had to reinforce his crumbling line around the Thomas Farm, he burned the former span as an impediment to the enemy.

This wooden bridge would also have been the easiest way for the now-cut-off New Jersey soldiers to withdraw if that became

Husband and wife ghost-hunters Ana Bruder and Chris Wojtaszek, co-founders of the Maryland TriState Paranormal investigative group

necessary, which it did after a third Confederate assault on their line dislodged them. Taking heavy fire from the advancing rebels, the skirmishers broke and retreated across the exposed iron bridge, taking further casualties in the process.

In the years following the battle, a number of veterans organizations erected markers commemorating specific units on the battlefield, one of the most significant being the one to the 14th New Jersey, dedicated in 1907 at Monocacy Junction. We decided that this would be a good spot to take a reading for spiritual activity.

Ana did, indeed, say that she sensed strong impressions of agitation and commotion in the area around the memorial, as if from many people, which dovetailed well with what I knew of the retreat of the New Jersey skirmishers toward the river after they were finally dislodged by the Confederate attackers.

Here, too, Ana said she felt nauseated because of the great volume of psychic energy present, and there were patches of this that were distinctly obvious to her and which she could move in and out of. Her hands also began to twitch, something that has happened to her before in similar situations but for which she did not have an explanation.

"I'm trying to visualize why I can't stand there," she said of what was a particularly sickening spot for her. "There's actually a deceased soldier laying this way," she said, indicating, "There's another one kneeling, with his gun down there, and I think the deceased one is his son. The kneeling one is crying, and I almost started crying when I saw him. That's why I had to step back a little bit and regroup and then go back again to see it."

Interestingly, the one emotion Ana did not feel here or elsewhere on the battlefield was fear, which is one of the predominant ones that would have been experienced in a combat environment, especially in an area through which panicked troops were retreating. Her theory on this is that she probably just blocks out this emotion, and I figured it was also possible that she is simply receptive to some residual emotions and less so, or not at all, to others.

Eventually, a three-pronged Confederate attack broke the Union line and drove the surviving troops past the Gambrill Mill, near the eastern end of the battlefield, and thenceforth onto the National Road and toward Baltimore.

GAMBRILL MILL

Built in 1830, the Gambrill Mill was a stone structure that Union troops occupied during the battle and used as a field hospital.

"When I was walking down in here," Ana said, indicating an area near the pond where she said there used to be a tree that is no longer there, "there was a soldier sitting with his legs extended, he was holding a gun, and just coughing, like there was something terribly wrong with him, whether he was injured or just ill. I actually heard him coughing first, which is what caught my attention, and then saw him."

Ana also said she sensed children playing and fishing in the area but believed it was from a later period, perhaps forty years after the war, and a woman with a parasol sitting under a tree that was now just a broad stump.

For his part, Chris got an impression of troops moving across an open area beyond the mill pond. (I did not find this to be a particularly compelling reading at the time. When I got home and downloaded my pictures, however, I discovered an odd, gray mass floating right in the spot where Chris was pointing.)

While at the site of the mill, Ana also saw a spectral, gray-clad figure moving through the nearby wood line, rather than the mind's-eye impressions she received at most of the stops we made on the battlefield.

Suffice it to say, our visit to the Monocacy Battlefield revealed it to be rife with all sorts of spiritual activity. Most of what Ana and Chris sensed was along the lines of what is often referred to as a "residual haunting," a nonintelligent, noninteractive image from the past, sort of like a psychic recording. She was confident, however, that if we were to visit the battlefield after dark that we would encounter higher-order specters of a more intelligent—and more interactive—nature.

Another odd thing Chris and I both experienced were indications that the batteries in both our cameras were nearly dead, even though they were fresh. We were both, nonetheless, able to take pictures our entire time there without reloading them (about seventy in my case).

After the battle, Wallace ordered that the bodies of the Union dead be gathered into a burial ground on the battlefield and proposed a monument that would read "These men died to save the National Capital, and they did save it." And, it would seem, the spirits of some of the men who fought there still struggle to defend the capital city, standing their ground year after year against the spectral forces that continue to march against it.

CHAPTER 30

Schifferstadt

FREDERICK

The spirits of several former inhabitants are believed to haunt the Schifferstadt, a historic home built by German immigrants that is more than two-and-a-half centuries old.

Remember me in these good old days with these Yankees.

—Inscribed on a wall at Schifferstadt by Olivia Warfield, a guest in the 1860s

THE ATTIC WAS FRIGID AND BARELY ILLUMI-NATED by the glow of a single candle. We had just climbed the precarious winder staircase from the second floor—and the tension was mounting. We had explored the lower floors of the house, each room more spiritually active than its predecessor.

"The attic is a pretty active space," our guide Greg Glewwe, vice chairman, board of directors, of the Schifferstadt Architectural Museum, explained. "We have had all kinds of things up here."

I glanced at my wife. I could see that Greg's stories were getting through to her. Now he was starting another.

"A couple years ago, a little girl was taking the regular day-

279

time tour with her mother. They came up to the attic, and the mom's holding the little girl when she leans over to her mother and asks, 'Mom, who's that little boy?' 'I don't see a little boy,' her mother answers as she looks around. 'That little boy over there,' the girl replies. The mother quickly takes her back down the stairs.

"That same girl came back two years later with her mother for the spirit tour. She was six now. They were standing down there at the base of the stairs, in the hallway. The little girl looked up toward the attic, and asked her mother, 'Mom, will that little boy be here again?'"

I could see my wife and son both looking around—my son expectantly, obviously hoping to catch a glimpse of the little boy, my wife nervously and hoping not to.

"The same thing happened on a spirit tour just a little while ago. There was this big bulky black-jacketed biker fellow. You know the type—not the kind of guy to scare easily. But when we got up into the attic, he said he could have sworn that he saw a little boy in that corner there."

My son raised his camera and began walking toward the corner. My wife moved a little closer to me.

"We think his name is Isaiah," Greg said. "You see, we at Schifferstadt have a pretty good relationship with our neighbors. It's happened a couple of times now that people have stopped by and said that their son or daughter had asked to play with Isaiah. 'Is he around? They played together a couple weeks ago, and they had a really good time.'

"Well, nobody who has ever worked here has had a child by that name. But the records show that a child by the name of Isaiah once lived here."

The flash of my son's camera briefly illuminated the darkness. A few seconds later, he exclaimed, "We got an orb! Your little boy is in the corner."

My wife told me later that that was the point where she had almost decided to bolt. I, however, probably the single remaining skeptic in the group, calmly studied the orb on the viewer of my son's digital camera. It looked like a ball of fur—white, soft, a little fuzzy, and somewhat translucent. This, I guess, is what sometimes remains behind after the spirit is separated from the body.

THE HOUSE

My first view of Schifferstadt was from U.S. Route 15 as we came around the cloverleaf onto Rosemont Avenue. It was a clear, crisp February night—and the moon was full. The old stone house was bathed in the golden glow of its floodlights.

"Now, this looks like a place for ghosts," my daughter-in-law said. How right she was!

Our hosts—Greg and his wife, Diane—were expecting us. They had kindly offered to provide us a personal tour of what is now the Schifferstadt Architectural Museum and ushered us into the museum gift shop. Their son, Gareth, was engrossed with his laptop at a table in the corner and nodded politely as we entered. He was searching the files for audio-visual phenomenon (AVP) that had been recorded during previous tours. We would view them later, when, hopefully, we would also have our own recordings to add.

Schifferstadt was not always a museum, of course. Built around 1758, at the beginning of the French and Indian War as frontier settlers abandoned their western Maryland farms in fear of raids from the French and their Indian allies, this formidable stone structure could have been designed to provide a refuge for families west of Frederick who chose to stay on their land. It is now one of the oldest and most historic buildings in the City of Frederick, and among the best examples of early Colonial German architecture in the country.

The large stone house was constructed on the site of what was probably a log house, built on 303 acres of virgin timberland by Joseph Brunner, a German who emigrated with his family from their village in the Palatinate area of southwestern Germany. He named his farm Schifferstadt after his hometown.

In 1753, Joseph sold Schifferstadt to his son Elias—and it was Elias who replaced his father's original log house with the fortress-like structure we would now be touring. Although its exterior and interior have been altered over the years, it is amazing how many features of Elias's original home remain. These reflect the traditions of his homeland and include built-in cupboards around the fireplaces; a cast iron "five-plate" stove still in its original position; an ingenious "squirrel-tail" bake oven; gracefully arched windows; winder staircases; a vaulted cellar; and decorative forged hardware.

But, as we would soon learn, the Brunners and subsequent residents left behind more than just architecture and artifacts. The spirits of several of them still remain to watch over that which had been so important to them in life.

Greg and Diane led us by candlelight from the gift shop into the house proper. The house does have electricity, but we needed no explanation to understand that the bright lights were not conducive to the detection of spirits. Greg explained that we would be beginning with rooms that had shown the least paranormal activity and progressing through areas of increasing activity until we reach the most haunted room of the building. He stressed that he was a scientist by both training and profession—in other words, his first instinct was to find a natural explanation for phenomena that might initially appear to some to be supernatural. He had come to accept, however, that at Schifferstadt, that was not always possible. He had seen things that had no earthly explanation. As we moved from one dark, chilly room to the next, we gradually became acquainted with not only this remarkable old structure, but also with a few of its ghostly residents.

We were not there to for the architecture, of course, but we nevertheless could not help but be impressed by the solid German craftsmanship and with how remarkably unchanged much of the house was. Amazingly, some walls still retained their original whitewash. This was attested to by the many inscriptions on the walls that had been left by mid-nineteenth-century guests, when apparently leaving such a record of one's visit was customary. One of the most remarkable was a message left by Olivia Warfield, a North Carolina cousin of the Yonson family, who were tenant farmers at Schifferstadt in the mid-1800s. In faint but elegant script, the following was recorded, "Remember me in these good old days with these Yankees." What makes this inscription particularly noteworthy was that three Union officers had recovered from their wounds in the room directly

The attic of the Schifferstadt is one of the most paranormally active areas in the eighteenth-century house, and phenomena like orbs are frequently captured in photographs taken there.

above. One can imagine a gracious southern lady, thrown by fate into the company of the foe. Her inscription would indicate that she made the best of it.

Olivia had left her mark to be sure, but other than the inscriptions—yes, she left more than one—there was no indication that she still lingered in any form. There were many others, however, whose spiritual presence was still manifest, and Greg introduced us to several, although quite possibly not all. Much is known about some of them from the historical record. Others, Greg said, have been identified through the efforts of psychic researchers— and this record is still being added to. Two of the most active have come to be known as Wilhemina and Christian.

WILHELMINA

Death can come in many ways, and fire is certainly one of the most painful. It was also, back in the days of open hearths, one of the most common. Women, of course, were most at risk. Not only did they do the vast majority of the cooking, their layers of long skirts, often made of highly flammable cotton, put them at greater risk.

This seems to have been the fate of a young midwife by the name of Wilhelmina, who Greg said haunts the old kitchen. Psychic research conducted at the site, he said, indicates that she became a midwife at the young age of seventeen and that she met her terrible end just seven years later, when she was only twenty-four . What exactly she was doing when her clothing caught fire has not been established. The kitchen, however, is adjacent to what was once the "birthing room," a small room with good light that would have been warmed in winter by the heat emanating from the kitchen. Was she boiling water in preparation for a delivery? We do not yet know, Greg said, but research continues and further investigation of the site is certainly warranted.

One thing we do know of Wilhelmina is that she was, and still is, a compassionate person. Greg himself can attest to that. He reports that she actually hugged him. It was a cold hug, to be sure, but a sign of affection nevertheless. Women have reported that she has stroked them on the cheek. Poor Wilhelmina, her life cut short in its prime! There were many, no doubt, who grieved her passing.

It Be Christian

When Liz, the former director of the Schifferstadt Museum, first started working there, she brought some college-age girlfriends over for a wee-hours exploration of the building. The gardener and his son picked them up at nearby Hood College. The son had brought a DVD video camera with him to record the events of the evening. The girls, hyped up on caffeine and chocolate, were in high spirits. They knew, of course, that the house had a reputation of being haunted. As they explored the darkened rooms, they began to joke about it, possibly to counter some feelings of trepidation about what they were doing. The son was still recording the antics as they entered the room known as the back bedroom. Gesturing toward the bed, one of the girls observed, "It's like one of those horror films where someone is under the bed." "Yeah," one of the other girls joined in, "like there's some demonic child under the bed who reaches out and grabs your leg."

No such thing occurred, of course, at Schifferstadt. Later, however, when they were reviewing the DVD, they detected a faint whispering voice just after the comment on the demonic child. What they heard was, "It is Christian," or, possibly, "It be Christian."

The historic record confirms that three-year-old Christian Brunner died of fever in this house. The room in which the voice was recorded was his parent's bedroom. One can only imagine the unfortunate tot on a straw pallet on the floor beside his parents' bed, expiring from one of those childhood diseases that took such a terrible toll in the centuries before our time. How sad that these unsuspecting girls had referred to this innocent child as demonic. I do not doubt that even ghosts have feelings, particularly the ghost of a much-loved little boy whose short young life ended so tragically.

I also wonder if, rather than giving his name, he was assuring the girls that he was not demonic. Could he have been stating his religion, not his name? The recording is a little fuzzy. Could he have been assuring them, "I be Christian"?

THE ROOT CELLAR

We followed a passage hewn through virgin rock to a lightless room that had once been the root cellar. This was once, but is no longer, accessible via a staircase from the main kitchen. According to Greg, it is the most spiritually active room at Schifferstadt and a favorite of psychic researchers, though it's not certain why. The cellar, which maintains a constant year-round temperature of about fifty-six degrees, did serve as a temporary morgue during the winter months when the ground was too frozen to dig proper graves. Imagine the poor child, sent down into the cellar for buttermilk, navigating in the darkness around grandma's coffin.

That use undoubtedly does contribute something to the psychic activity—but, otherwise, there is little in the historical record that sheds any light on the spirits here. This is quite unlike the upper levels, where history and psychic research work together in helping us identify and understand those spirits that persist. Here, in this cold and lightless chamber, we are almost totally reliant on psychic research, on EVP and K-2 meters—but these, Greg explained, have produced some very interesting results. Just the night before he was reviewing some EVP from the cellar, when he heard a faint but distinct voice saying, "Don't leave." On other occasions he has heard voices whispering, "We are here." Once, a recording picked up, "It's me, Church."

It was therefore appropriate that Greg ended the tour in the cellar with even his small candle extinguished. You can imagine how our spines prickled in the nearly complete darkness as he sought to induce any spirits to make their presence known. My recorder was going (or so I thought), as Greg intoned, "Are there any spirits here tonight? If you are here, would you give us a sign of your presence?" But we could hear nothing with naked ears.

When I played my recording, I was edified to learn that I had a crystal-clear digital recording of the entire evening's tour. Unfortunately, the maximum length of a single recording must be two hours—because it stopped just a few minutes short of Greg's invocation. You can imagine my disappointment.

Reached by a passage hewn through virgin rock, the lightless room that had once been the root cellar is supposed to be the most spiritually active room at Schifferstadt and a favorite for paranormal investigators.

A young midwife named Wilhelmina who died in a fire is believed to haunt the kitchen of the Schifferstadt.

I don't doubt there are spirits in that root cellar who want to communicate with visitors. And so, when you visit Schifferstadt, bring a good digital recorder, and do not repeat my error. Make sure it is actually recording.

Spotlight on Ghosts:
Hide Me!

A volunteer at Schifferstadt once had a strange experience there that might be related to an event that occurred during the Civil War. The young lady was sweeping the floor in the central hallway when she heard a very clear voice saying, "Hide me!" When she turned to look in the direction of the voice, no one was there. She was alone in the hallway. An incident reported in the *Frederick Tribune* as occurring on September 12, 1862, however, may provide the basis for the volunteer's experience.

According to the historic news article, when Confederate forces under General Robert E. Lee entered Frederick as part of the invasion that would culminate in the Battle of Antietam several days later, a Mr. Gilson, the apothecary of the U.S. General Hospital, had been in the vicinity. Realizing he would have to pass through the Rebel forces to get home and being concerned for his safety, Gilson sought refuge at Schifferstadt, which at that time belonged to Dr. Lewis H. Steiner and was occupied by tenant farmers Martin Yonson and his wife. The Yonsons accommodated him and hid him with "three good Union people" in a second floor room.

When Confederate troops visited the house, Mrs. Yonson thought they were looking for Gilson, but she did not betray his presence. Instead, the Southerners commandeered a horse and other property, paying for it with $150 in Confederate currency.

Ghosthunting
Travel Guide

Additional Haunted Sites

FOLLOWING ARE MORE THAN FIFTY additional haunted sites from around the state of Maryland. Some of the sites listed here are not known to have been "active" for some time but might nonetheless warrant further investigation.

Multiple variations exist for many of the following ghost stories, and details vary from version to version. In many, the paranormal phenomena associated with the respective sites are sometimes said to manifest only on specific dates; October 30 or 31 or November 1 are typical, as is the anniversary of a specific event or during a particular month or season.

Varying versions of many stories also set them in different periods, and the events of a particular tale might be variously said to have occurred, for example, during the early Colonial Era, the War of 1812, or the Civil War. Such temporal discrepancies, presumably, have no bearing on the actual truth or lack thereof of a particular story.

Many of the ghost stories associated with a particular region refer to various social or economic factors that have traditionally existed there. Those from the Eastern Shore, for example, point to the many plantations that once dominated the countryside and to the tensions between the owners of those estates and the less affluent who dwelled on or around them.

While some effort has been made to determine the veracity of these tales, they have not been investigated to the extent to which sites covered in the various chapters have. Some may also be less accessible than those covered in the individual chapters. Ghosthunters should expect to do a little more legwork tracking them down and exercise some caution when doing so.

As it becomes available, addenda to this material will be posted on the America's Haunted Road Trip Web site. Readers should feel free to post their own additional information and experiences there as well!

BALTIMORE

Gardens of Faith (Baltimore)

People have reported seeing a number of ghosts at this cemetery at the east end of the city, including the spirit of a woman dressed in gray who floats above it by day and one of a man who leaves his grave and lurks about during the day. People have also reported hearing mumbling voices in various buildings at the site and feeling a presence by a nearby creek, where a man is said to have killed himself.

Gridiron Club (Baltimore)

The ghost of an old woman who was kidnapped and murdered by her slaves in the years prior to the Civil War is believed to haunt the house where she dwelled in life.

O'Donnell Heights (Baltimore)

For two weeks in 1951, a ghoulish figure from a nearby graveyard accosted local children and otherwise terrorized this neighborhood at the west end of the city, until an armed mob eventually drove it back into one of the tombs from where it had come.

Todds Farm (Baltimore/Dundalk)

Located in the port district of Dundalk, this home dates to before the War of 1812 and may soon be turned into an historic attraction. A family cemetery is located behind the house. This site is believed to be haunted by several ghosts. Phenomena reported at the house and its grounds include the apparition of a woman standing in the attic window holding a candle and forever waiting, as the story goes, for a slain soldier to return from the war; lynched slaves hanging from trees; and lights coming on when people enter the house—even though the house has no electricity!

Zodiac (Baltimore)

Located in downtown Baltimore, many people believe this trendy restaurant to be haunted. Phenomena people have reported included seeing the ghost of a particular old man seated at table thirteen and in other places around the restaurant.

CENTRAL

Avonlea Bed and Breakfast (Westminster)

This house was owned in Civil War times by a very cruel and abusive man. It is believed to still be haunted by the ghosts of several slaves whom he murdered brutally in his basement.

Cocky's Tavern (Westminster)

This historic building was recently reopened with great fanfare and applause after a lengthy renovation project. One or more ghosts apparently haunt the tavern, at least one of which is thought to be that of a Civil War soldier who tramps up and down the stairs, moves pictures when he is displeased, and even helps himself to drinks at the bar. There have also been reports of sightings of a woman in green colonial dress, pictures jumping off walls, objects falling from the back of shelves, ghostly voices, and more.

Fire House (Ellicott City)

This building is said to be haunted by a few of the old firemen who used to work there. Phenomena include doors slamming on their own, disembodied footsteps, and apparitions.

Hampton Mansion (Towson)

Hampton Mansion was the largest private home in America when it was completed in 1790 and is today considered to be one of the finest examples of Georgian architecture in the country. Reports of ghosts at this palatial manor are common, but some of the eeriest stories are associated with the chandeliers. It is said that when they crashed to the floor, the death of one of its residents was imminent.

Hayden House (Ellicott City)

There are many stories about the Hayden House—or Oak Lawn as it was previously called—and the mysterious events that went on there. They probably peaked in the 1970s, when the house was occupied by the district court and the county office of parole and probation. Clerks and secretaries often reported lights turning on and off by themselves, a coffee pot that would heat up even when it was unplugged, and the sounds of phantom footsteps echoing throughout unoccupied parts of the building.

Heart Beat Bridge (Ellicott City)

Years ago, at a house opposite the bridge, a man cut a woman's heart out and threw it into the stream below. To this day, if people go there and turn off their engines, they can supposedly still hear her heart beat. The bridge is located off Bonnie Branch Road.

Jericho Covered Bridge (Joppatowne/Harford County)

The last remaining covered bridge in the county, this one-hundred-foot-long span was built between 1850 and 1865 and is believed to have been the site of numerous lynchings in the years during and after the Civil War. Victims, sometimes several at a time, are said to have been hanged from the upper rafters.

Phenomena people have reported at the bridge include apparitions, orbs in their photographs, and car engines dying midway while crossing it.

The Lawn (Elkridge)

This historic home is believed to be haunted by a poltergeist that has terrorized everyone who has lived there since the 1950s.

Lilburn (Ellicott City)

Lilburn is one of the most beautiful homes in the town of Ellicott City, and it is also one of the most notorious of the town's haunted residences. The unexplained happenings here have given rise to ghost stories that date back more than a century, and they continue to this day.

Mount Ida (Ellicott City)

Located above the main streets of Ellicott City is an historical mansion called Mount Ida. It is now home to the offices of the Friends of the Patapsco Female Institute, which looms on the hill above it, and has been restored magnificently to become an Ellicott City showcase. It also plays host to the spirit of one of its former owners, a woman who passed away in the 1920s.

Old Opera House (Westminster)

Now a printing facility, this building is said to be haunted by a man who was murdered at the back exit after a performance in which he appeared.

Patapsco Female Institute (Ellicott City)

The well-preserved ruins of the Patapsco Female Institute sit high above Ellicott City on Church Road. The school had the distinction of being one of the first female institutes in the south when it was officially opened in 1839. One of its early students was Annie Van Derlot, the daughter of a rich southern planter, who died of pneumonia during her first winter at the school. Annie's ghost is said to linger there, roaming the ruins where her classrooms and dormitory used to be.

Peddler's Run (Harford County)

For more than eighty years, a ghost was known to haunt a lonely section along the banks of the Susquehanna River. After the skull of a murdered and decapitated peddler was found and then properly buried, however, the ghost was apparently put to rest and has not been seen since.

Perryman Mansion (Harford County)

On the Perryman peninsula in southern Harford County there exists an old and crumbling manor house that was once the estate of the Boyer family. The once-extravagant, multilevel mansion was abandoned by its longtime residents decades ago when Baltimore Gas & Electric Company purchased the home along with 250 acres of land on which to build a regional plant. The legend of the Perryman Mansion has grown over the years thanks to its remote location and imposing demeanor. Common reports include mysterious voices, horrible stenches, and collections of animal bones both in and outside the house.

Rocky Hill Cemetery (Woodsboro)

It is said that there is a tombstone in Rocky Hill Cemetery that bleeds. As the story goes, the woman who is buried there had warned her husband before she died that if he remarried and his new wife was cruel to her children, her tombstone would bleed. The inscription on the tombstone reads: "This stone is at the grave of a mother who died leaving several small children." The husband remarried, and it is said that he and the stepmother were very cruel to the children. The cemetery is located on Coppermine Road in the left hand corner three rows back in the middle of the row.

Seven Hills Road (Ellicott City)

There are seven hills behind historic Ellicott City. It is said that if someone drives to the seventh hill at midnight, they will be chased by a demon car that appears out of nowhere. But be careful, as people have lost their lives in accidents on this road.

U.S. Naval Academy (Annapolis)

The ghost of a cadet beaten to death by his comrades in 1907 has reportedly appeared to other students in the century since his violent and untimely death.

NATIONAL CAPITAL

Black Rock Road (Germantown)

Psychic investigator Ana Bruder of the Maryland TriState Paranormal group saw the ghostly figure of a black man, possibly a Civil War-era slave, standing by the water near this road early one morning.

Game Preserve Road (Germantown)

Numerous phenomena have been reported along this road, especially around a narrow bridge where a woman and her child are said to have been killed by the members of a gang (e.g., people have claimed to hear the spirit of the child crying on especially dark and quiet nights). Psychic investigator Ana Bruder of Maryland TriState Paranormal has detected spiritual presences along this road.

Inn at Buckeystown (Frederick County)

This historic inn is believed to be home to several ghosts, all of which seem to concentrate on their particular areas of the inn and remain unaware of each other.

Montpelier Mansion (Laurel)

Many of America's founding fathers—including George Washington, Thomas Jefferson, and John Adams—visited this historic mansion in the late 1700s and early 1800s, and since then people have reported seeing all of their ghosts there.

Oaklands (Laurel)

A multitude of ghostly phenomena have been reported in this eighteenth-century Georgian mansion, including the sounds of a horse galloping up the driveway at a particular time, the front door opening and closing, and a woman sobbing. Shades of a small boy, a young woman, and a black man and woman have all also been seen in various parts of the house and its grounds.

Old St. Mary's College (Columbia)

Many legends and stories have grown up around this college involving the many spirits people have seen and ghostly noises they have heard over the years. There is also an urban legend about an insane priest who supposedly killed five girls by hanging them, and some say they girls haunted the building where they were murdered.

Paint Branch Home (Adelphi)

This venerable mansion is currently being used as a retirement home. It is said that the spirits of former slaves still haunt the house. They do not appear to be violent, but rather have been known to linger around bedrooms and fill the house with their singing.

EASTERN SHORE

Bleeding Rock of White House Farm (Kent County)

Located on a knoll behind an early eighteenth-century farmhouse off of Route 213 between Kennedyville and Chestertown, this rock was originally located in a nearby field until 1944, when highway workers moved it from what is now a roadway to its present location. It is said by many to periodically bleed, the result of the tragic death of an indentured servant girl, who while fleeing her dreary lot for a new life with her lover fell from the horse on which she was riding, struck her head on the rock, and was killed. The ghost of George Washington, who also visited this farm during the era of the American Revolution, is also sometimes said to itinerantly haunt the site, along with a number of other ghosts and phenomena like disembodied footsteps.

Cecil County Detention Center (Cecil County)

Knowingly built on the site of an Indian village and graveyard dating to at least the fifteenth century, numerous strange phenomena have been reported at this detention center, which was opened in 1984. People have claimed to experience disembodied footsteps, lights turning off and on by themselves, and howling sounds that seem to be moving quickly through hallways. At least one person has also claimed to be attacked by the materialized spirit of an Indian chief or shaman, who he struggled to defend himself against most of one night.

Haunted House Calls
(Easton/Talbot County)

This story involves a country doctor with a drinking problem who, at some indeterminate point in the past, pursued his vocation in the area around Easton. One night, he was summoned to help an acquaintance who had accidentally been injured with a firearm but, being in his cups, he got lost driving his buggy, and by the time he arrived, his friend had already died. The alcoholic physician became despondent and died of some misfortune soon thereafter (e.g., falling drunkenly off his buggy and breaking his neck). Since then, people have periodically claimed to see the spectral form of the doctor, complete with horse and buggy, driving along the darkened roads of the county, forever trying to make it to his injured friend on time and calling out to anyone he passes, "Show me the way!" According to tradition, the doctor is interred at the White Marsh Church burying ground. (See the separate chapter in this book on White Marsh Church.)

Ghostly Horses (Cecil County)

Over the years, many stories have arisen in this horse country area of spectral horses and handlers alike, which have been spotted especially during early morning hours or when the mist lays heavily over the rolling fields. A specific legend involves the Ghost Mare, whose antics include draining full troughs of their water. Horse graveyards are also a characteristic feature of this area, and some of the ghostly sightings have been associated with them.

Hanging Tree (Tunis Mills)

It is believed that slaves were hung from the "hanging tree." If it is quiet, and visitors sit under the tree, they may begin to hear and see the dead. Some have reported hearing bodies of those who had been hanged drop onto their cars from a branch above.

Inn at Mitchell House
(Tolchester/Kent County)

Built in the eighteenth century, this historic inn is believed to be haunted by at least one ghost, that of a British naval officer mortally wounded in the nearby Battle of Caulk's Field in August 1814. He was subsequently taken to the house and died in its kitchen. Phenomena people have reported include rocking chairs moving on their own, disembodied noises, and animals appearing to react to or interact with invisible entities that may be the ghosts of animals.

Oldfield Point Road (Cecil County)

A number of people living in homes along this road, not far from the reputedly haunted Cecil County Detention Center in Elkton, have claimed to witness all sorts of strange phenomena in the area, including circles of fire in the woods and nighttime chanting. Some have postulated that the presence of as-yet-undiscovered Indian burial grounds and villages in the area might account for these incidents.

Screaming Polly (Cecil County)

This screaming ghost that haunts the northern reaches of the Eastern Shore, especially south of the Bohemia River and north of the village of Cecilton, would seem for all practical purposes to conform to the characteristics of the legendary Celtic banshee. She is believed to be the spirit of a serving girl, probably from the Colonial era, who, in many versions of the tale, died in a snowstorm, but possibly also by being run over by a carriage, or some other misfortune. What led to her demise varies from story to story, but in the most common version, she was with child by a prominent landowner and died while wander-

ing through the countryside, seeking aid from slave and free-
man alike but being spurned by all. Screaming Polly is typically
described as being pale and wearing a white dress and, like the
legend of Big Liz—which has its roots a few counties further
south on the Eastern Shore—she is sometimes said to be decapitated and carrying her shrieking head under her arm.

Visions in the Air (Talbot County)

One night in September 1881, numerous people throughout
the county, especially around the village of Royal Oak, reported
seeing great formations of angels and soldiers maneuvering,
dancing, and otherwise moving through the cloudy nighttime
sky. Various explanations were given, the most compelling possibly being that the spectral forms were honoring the late President James A. Garfield, who had been assassinated at about that
time. These phenomena were reported in the *Morning News* of
Wilmington, Delaware, which referred to them as "Visions in
the Air."

SOUTHERN

Cartegena Manor (Drayden)

Located along the banks of a branch of the St. Mary's River,
the Colonial-era manor house is said to have slid into the river
one night, killing all of its occupants. The area is now reputed
to be strongly haunted, and people have witnessed phenomena
that include apparitions and ghost lights. Other ghost stories in
the surrounding area include one about a large, spectral black
dog that has been seen dragging a chain while trotting along
Cherryfield Road.

Church Road Cemetery (Broomes Island)

Located in this small waterfront community on the Patuxent River, the old cemetery on Church Road is reputed to be haunted. One story associated with it claims that if someone circles the cemetery three times, a fog will begin rolling in, and they will hear little girls laughing.

Devil's Ball Yard (St. George Island)

During the War of 1812, the British used the little island of St. George in the Potomac river as a burying grounds for their killed soldiers and sailors, and uncounted numbers of them were buried all around it. One particular spot was used as a mass grave and, for years afterward, it remained smooth, perfectly circular, and devoid of any vegetation, prompting tales to arise that the Devil himself held monthly balls there and that the dead danced around in it.

Patuxent Road (Odenton)

This is yet another variation on the "Cry Baby Bridge" stories popular throughout this region of Maryland. According to the story associated with it, a woman and her baby were killed one night many years ago when trying to cross a narrow old bridge along the road. Late-night visitors to the site have reported seeing the woman—complete with stroller—as well as the car, which is said to vanish suddenly after it is spotted.

WESTERN

Backbone Mountain (Garrett County)

This highest geographical point in the state of Maryland is believed by some to be haunted by the spirits of those who have met their lonely fates upon its slopes.

City of Frederick (Frederick County)

Reputedly haunted sites in this old town include the Barry Hall Frederick Campus, which is reputedly haunted by the evil Mary Walker, and Hood College, which was built on the site of an old saloon from the Civil War and where late at night people can still hear ghostly hooting and hollering.

Hager House (Hagerstown)

A dark figure has been seen on the porch of this eighteenth-century house, along with phenomena like disembodied footsteps, chairs that rock on their own, and a corncob doll that mysteriously appears in various places throughout the house.

Landon House (Urbana)

Built originally in the eighteenth century as a silk mill and used successively as a girls' school and a military academy, this historic hall served as the site of J.E.B. Stuart's famous Sabers and Roses Ball during a brief period of Confederate occupation in 1862. Since then, it has been home to numerous ghosts, some benign and others frightening, including those of a number of dogs believed to have died in it.

"I was with my group, Maryland TriState Paranormal, and we were at the Landon House doing an investigation one night," paranormal investigator Jim Wissert told me. "There's a basement, with long steps that go down, and we were standing downstairs. On the inside of the door you can see scratch marks from, supposedly, some dogs the Confederates had locked up in the basement, and which apparently starved to death, as the story goes. But while we were standing there, we heard a series of scratches on the door—like a dog scratching at the door. I got chills. It was pretty spooky."

Miller's Church (Hagerstown)

Urban legends claim that this church was used for Satanic rites and in the years since people have reported seeing various apparitions—including that of a young woman hanging from an oak tree in front of the church and a phantasmal hearse that chases people!

Mount Saint Mary's College and Seminary (Emmitsburg)

Founded in 1808, this oldest independent Catholic college in the country is believed to be haunted by a number of very active ghosts, including the shade of one of its former presidents and a violent poltergeist that occupies one of the dormitory rooms.

Old Castle (Mount Savage)

Nestled in the mountains of Maryland, this home was designed to look like Craig Castle in the Scottish Highlands. It is believed by some that a previous owner, whose name was Ramsey, has come back to permanently stay at the castle, noted for its intricate library and great hall.

Old Depot (Frostburg)

Inexplicable sounds have been heard coming from this old railway station, including the sound of a steam whistle even when no trains are present and even stranger ones from a tunnel running from it under Main Street.

Rose Hill Cemetery (Hagerstown)

People have claimed to hear screams of help and smell the stench of burning hair coming from the crematorium located on the grounds of this cemetery.

Saint Joseph's College (Emmitsburg)

This former women's college served as a field hospital during the Civil War, and ghosts that have been seen here include a doctor, those of soldiers who died at the site, and the woman who led the college and oversaw the efforts to tend to the wounded who were brought there.

Further Reading/Bibliography

This section lists all the titles used during the research for this book, along with a number of others that are listed for their potential value to ghosthunters in general and those visiting sites in Maryland and the surrounding area in particular.

Alexander, John. *Ghosts: Washington's Most Famous Ghost Stories* (The Washington Book Trading Company, 1988).

Allen, Thomas B. *Possessed: The True Story of an Exorcism* (Doubleday, 1993).

Belanger, Jeff. *Ghosts of War: Restless Spirits of Soldiers, Spies, and Saboteurs* (New Page Books, 2006).

Blackman, W. Haden. *The Field Guide to North American Hauntings* (Three Rivers Press, 1998).

Blatty, William Peter. *The Exorcist* (Harper & Row, 1971).

Downer, Deborah L. (Ed.). *Classic American Ghost Stories: 200 years of Ghost Lore from the Great Plains, New England, the South and the Pacific Northwest* (August House, 1990).

Elizabeth, Norma, and Roberts, Bruce. *Lighthouse Ghosts: 13 bona fide apparitions standing watch over America's shores* (Crane Hill Publishers, 1999).

Guttridge, Leonard F. *Our Country, Right or Wrong: The Life of Stephen Decatur, the U.S. Navy's Most Illustrious Commander* (Tom Doherty Associates LLC, 2006).

Hauck, Dennis William. *National Directory of Haunted Places* (Penguin Books, 1994).

Hladek, L'aura. *Ghosthunting New Jersey* (Clerisy Press, 2008).

Holzer, Hans. *The Ghosts That Walk in Washington* (Ballantine Books, 1971).

Holzer, Hans. *Window to the Past: Exploring History Through ESP* (Pocket Books, 1970).

Kachuba, John. *Ghosthunters: On the Trail of Mediums, Dowsers, Spirit Seekers, and Other Investigators of America's Paranormal World* (New Page Books, 2007).

Kachuba, John. *Ghosthunting Illinois* (Emmis Books, 2005).

Kachuba, John. *Ghosthunting Ohio* (Emmis Books, 2004).

Kaczmarek, Dale. *Field Guide to Spirit Photography: The Essential Guide to Cameras in Paranormal Research* (Ghost Research Society Press, 2002).

Kaczmarek, Dale. *Illuminating the Darkness: The Mystery of Spook Lights* (Ghost Research Society Press, 2003).

Kaczmarek, Dale. *National Register of Haunted Locations* (Ghost Research Society).

Okonowicz, Ed and Kathleen. *Crying in the Kitchen: Stories of Ghosts That Roam the Water* (Myst & Lace Publishers Inc., 1998).

Okonowicz, Ed. *Haunted Maryland: Ghosts and Strange Phenomena of the Old Line State* (Stackpole Books, 2007).

Pugh, Dorothy. *Ghost Stories of Montgomery County* (Montgomery County Historical Society, 1988).

Scharf, J. Thomas. *History of Maryland, From the Earliest Period to the Present Day* (Tradition Press, 1967).

Scott, Joseph. *A Geographical Description of the States of Maryland and Delaware* (Kimber, Conrad, and Company, 1807).

Taylor, Troy. *Spirits of the Civil War* (Whitechapel Productions, 1999).

Varhola, Michael J. *Ghosthunting Virginia* (Clerisy Press, 2008).

Ghostly Resources

HAUNTED LOCATIONS WEB SITES

Following are a number of sites with information useful to anyone interested in ghosthunting in general and in the state of Maryland in particular. It is deliberately short and includes only the best and most relevant sites.

America's Haunted Road Trip

www.americashauntedroadtrip.com
This is the official site of the America's Haunted Road Trip series of books. Check it out for information about haunted sites around the country, discussions on all sorts of paranormal topics, and supplemental information about the sites covered in this book.

Maryland Ghost and Spirit Association

www.marylandghosts.com
This site is run by paranormal investigator Beverly Litsinger, president of the Maryland Ghost and Spirit Association, who has conducted investigations around the state of Maryland, including ones at a number of the sites covered in this book.

Maryland TriState Paranormal

www.marylandtristateparanormal.com
MTSP is an organization dedicated to educating and aiding the community on paranormal phenomena. Its research team is devoted to the study, observation, and documentation of evidence for ghostly phenomena and uses many methods, both conventional and unconventional, to achieve these goals.

Michael J. Varhola's TravelBlogue

http://varhola.blogspot.com
This site contains travel-related information relevant to haunted sites covered in this book and can be a useful guide to ghosthunters traveling around not just the state of Maryland but the United States in general.

Washington D.C. Metro Area Ghost Watchers

www.dchauntings.com
A source of information about paranormal investigation of ghosts, haunting, and entities in Washington, D.C., Virginia, and Maryland.

RADIO SHOW AND PODCAST WEB SITES

Following are a number of sites associated with radio shows and podcasts devoted to ghosthunting, the paranormal, and similar subjects. Most of them have available archived interviews with Michael J. Varhola and other America's Haunted Road Trip authors.

Carolina's Paranormal Society Pee Dee Paranormal Research Society

www.carolinasparanormal.com
This nonprofit paranormal investigation team located in south-central North Carolina performs services throughout the states of North and South Carolina, using scientific methods to collect data.

Explore Your Spirit with Kala

www.exploreyourspirit.com
Hosted by author, metaphysical teacher, intuitive, and speaker Kala Ambrose, this show focuses on the metaphysical, spiritual, and paranormal subjects.

Ghost Mafia

http://theghostmafia.mypodcast.com
Hosts Nathan, Bob, and Blaine take listeners into the realm of the paranormal and beyond, interviewing a wide variety of guests about ghosts, paranormal phenomena, cryptozoology, and other related subjects.

Paranormal Podcast

www.paranormalpodcast.com
Hosted by Jim Harold, this program delves into every aspect of the unexplained and talks about such things as the paranormal, UFOs, psychic phenomena, life after death, ghosts, and more.

Para X Radio

www.para-x.com
Para X Radio broadcasts all paranormal content from all sides of the
paranormal universe. It is unbiased and promotes equality by inviting anyone to
share their opinions during live shows, through the chat room, and call-ins.

X-Zone Radio

www.xzone-radio.com
Hosted by Rob McConnell and produced in Hamilton, Ontario, Canada, this
show brings the world of the paranormal and the science of parapsychology to
its listeners on live radio, satellite, and the Internet.

GHOST TOURS

Baltimore Ghost Tours

(410) 522-7400
P.O. Box 38140
Baltimore, MD 21231
www.baltimoreghosttours.com
info@baltimoreghosttours.com

These tours are well-researched and professionally presented, and this historic
seaport makes for the perfect setting. There are three tours: the original Fells
Point Ghost Walk, which we can wholeheartedly recommend; the Fells Point
Pubwalk; and the Mount Vernon GhostWalk (this Mount Vernon is a historic
Baltimore neighborhood, not the Virginia home of George Washington).

Walking Ghost Tour of Historic Annapolis

(800) 979-3370 or (212) 209-3370
12 Church Circle
Annapolis, MD 21401
www.ghostsofannapolis.com

Take a lantern-led ghost walk through the historic downtown district on a spine-
tingling journey into Annapolis' dark and troubled history. Meet some of the
state capital's more spirited residents and visit the most horrific haunted sites
of this historic seaport. There is also a Haunted Pub Crawl that takes visitors to
some of the city's most haunted taverns. Tours depart from the front porch of
the Maryland Inn, located at the corner of Main Street and Church Circle.

Candlelight Ghost Tours of Frederick

207 Harpers Way
Frederick, MD 21702
(301) 668-8922
www.marylandghosttours.com/index.html

Based upon factual events and actual eyewitness encounters, Frederick's Candlelight Ghost Tour takes visitors to numerous centers of paranormal activity in historic downtown Frederick, including the Barbara Fritchie house. Tours are offered from June through November and begin at 124 North Market Street.

Olde Ellicott City Ghost Tour

(410) 313-1900 or (800) 288-TRIP (8747)
Howard County Tourism Inc.
8267 Main Street
Ellicott City, MD 21043
www.howardcountymd.gov/HCT/HCT_GhostTours.htm
ghosts@visithowardcounty.com

Ellicott City is perhaps the most actively haunted town in America. It is a former mill town on the beautiful Patapsco River with a good selection of restaurants, pubs, and antique shops. Howard County Tourism offers two well-researched ghost tours, which take visitors through the historic town center. Part I is on Friday evenings, and Part II is on Saturdays.

Ghost Walks in Historic Savage Mill

(410) 313-1900 or (800) 288-TRIP (8747)
8600 Foundry Street, #2022
Savage, MD 20763-9513
www.howardcountymd.gov/HCT/HCT_GhostWalksSavageMill.htm
ghosts@visithowardcounty.com

Today, Savage Mill is a lovely hub of restaurants, bakeries, clothes stores, and the high-quality antiques that Howard County is famous for . . . and, of course, ghosts! To chronicle the Mill's history as well as its otherworldly past, a ghost tour has been created with true stories about mill workers and their sometimes violent ends. Tickets are purchased and tours begin in the food court of Historic Savage Mill.

St. Michaels Ghost Tour

(888) 312-7847
Dockside Express Ltd.
P.O. Box 122
Tilghman, MD 21671
www.docksidexpress.com/ghosttours.html
info@docksidexpress.com

Join the costumed guide for a lantern-led stroll through the historic streets of St. Michaels, a quaint waterfront village on Maryland's Eastern Shore. Discover the tales and legends of ghosts, ghouls, and odd occurrences in this otherwise quiet Victorian town. Tours are operated by reservation only and depart from the Mill Street information booth.

Visiting Haunted Sites

Maryland is divided into six regions for purposes of this book: Baltimore City, Central, National Capital, Eastern Shore, Southern, and Western. Nicknamed the "Free State" and the "Old Line State"—for the Mason-Dixon Line, which runs across its northern and eastern edges—Maryland is divided into twenty-three counties and one county-equivalent, Baltimore City. The state capital is Annapolis.

Geographically, Maryland is not a large state, having an area of just 12,407 square miles, with a maximum north-to-south width of 101 miles, and a maximum east-to-west length of 249 miles. It is, however, among the oldest states in the country, and has a rich, varied, and turbulent history that has contributed to an exceptionally high number of haunted sites. It also contains a variety of communities and landscapes, from some of the busiest metropolitan areas in the country to sparsely populated rural locales, and from mountainous terrain in the west to extensive areas of shoreline in the east and south.

Directions to many of the managed sites in the following section are available through their Web sites or by calling the site for more information. The sites' zip codes are included in some cases, even when a site does not have a specific address, as an aid in electronic mapping or with GPS systems. Sites without phone numbers, Web site URLs, or email addresses are typically those without any organized management useful for purposes of visitation.

Every effort has been made to ensure that the following information is accurate—and in most cases is what the authors used while doing the fieldwork for this book—but ghosthunters are advised to confirm as much as possible before heading out themselves. Updates will also be posted as needed to the America's Haunted Road Trip Website (www.americashaunted

roadtrip.com) and readers are encouraged to post their own updates and additional information.

BALTIMORE CITY

Baltimore is the largest city in Maryland and is located along the banks of the lower Patapsco River, a tributary of the Chesapeake Bay. Founded in 1729—twenty-three years after the earlier Port of Baltimore—it has been a major seaport since then, and its Inner Harbor was once the second largest port of entry for immigrants and a major manufacturing center. It is named for the Baron Baltimore, George Calvert, the first hereditary lord of the Maryland colony. Much of the state's maritime and War of 1812 history is associated with this area.

USS *Constellation*

(410) 539-1797
Pier 1
301 East Pratt Street
Baltimore, MD 21202
www.constellation.org
administration@constellation.org

At least three ghosts are believed to dwell upon this famous warship that has long been a subject of paranormal investigation, including one of a sailor executed for dereliction of duty—and another that of the captain who ordered him put to death.

Fells Point (Southeast)

(410) 675-6751
Fells Point Visitor Center
1724 Thames Street
Baltimore, MD 21231
www.fellspoint.us
info@fellspoint.us

Many spirits, including that of Edgar Allan Poe, are believed to haunt the former bars, boarding houses, and bordellos of this once-rowdy seaport area that is now famed for its 120 bars and active nightlife. Parking can be an issue in this neighborhood, especially on weekends, so leave yourself plenty of time to find a spot.

Fort McHenry National Monument and Historic Shrine

(410) 962-4290
2400 E. Fort Avenue
Baltimore, MD 21230-5393
www.nps.gov/fomc

Many incidents of ghostly activity have been told about this brick fort that was the object of the battle immortalized in "The Star-Spangled Banner." Stories have included those of specters walking the ramparts, disembodied voices, and levitating furniture.

Old Baltimore Shot Tower

(410) 605-2964
Carroll Museums Inc.
800 E. Lombard Street
Baltimore, MD 21202
www.carrollmuseums.org
info@carrollmuseums.org

Built in 1828, this 238-foot-tall ammunition manufacturing structure was the tallest building in the United States until the construction of the Washington Monument. Passersby frequently hear strange sounds coming from within it after it has been closed to visitors and it is widely reputed to be haunted. It is maintained and operated as a museum by the nearby Carroll Mansion and can be visited with advance reservations.

Edgar Allan Poe House and Museum

(410) 396-7932
203 Amity Street
Baltimore, MD 21223
www.eapoe.org

Located eight blocks from where Edgar Allan Poe is buried, this is one of the many houses the author lived in during his life. Phenomena people have reported at the site include the sensation of someone tapping them on the shoulders, mysterious muttering voices, lights moving around in the house when no one was in it, inexplicable cold spots, and windows flying open or slamming shut.

Pride of Baltimore II

(410) 539-1151
1801 S. Clinton Street
Suite 250
Baltimore, MD 21224
www.pride2.org

This authentic reproduction of a nineteenth-century clipper topsail schooner is believed by some to be haunted by the spirits of four crew members who died when its predecessor, *Pride of Baltimore,* was sunk in 1986 by a white squall. The address listed above is a mailing address and, when it is in port, *Pride of Baltimore II* is berthed at Baltimore's Inner Harbor near the location of USS *Constellation* on East Pratt Street.

USCGC *Taney*

(410) 396-3453
Pier 3
301 E. Pratt Street
Baltimore, MD 21202
www.baltomaritimemuseum.org
administration@constellation.org

Many staff of the vessel and visitors alike—especially those participating in overnight programs—have reported constantly catching movement out of the corners of their eyes when aboard and seeing spectral forms gliding across its decks and past its open hatchways.

USS *Torsk*

(410) 396-3453
Pier 5
301 E. Pratt Street
Baltimore, MD 21202
www.baltomaritimemuseum.org
administration@constellation.org

This vessel is reportedly haunted by the spirit of a sailor trapped on its upper deck when it had to submerge. It is run as part of the Baltimore Maritime Museum.

Westminster Hall and Burying Ground

(410) 706-2072
c/o Westminster Preservation Inc.

500 W. Baltimore Street
Baltimore, MD 21201-1786
www.westminsterhall.org
westminster@law.umaryland.edu

Edgar Allan Poe is among the one thousand prominent Baltimoreans buried at this site, which dates to the eighteenth century, and his unquiet shade is among those that people have reported seeing walking its grounds on moonlit nights.

CENTRAL

Situated in the middle of the state and sharing boundaries with all of the other regions in the state, this region is made up of Anne Arundel, Baltimore, Carroll, Harford, and Howard Counties and is home to the state capital of Annapolis (the city of Baltimore, which is entirely enclosed within this area, has many unique characteristics and is thus treated as a separate region for purposes of this guidebook). Much of the state history related to the War of 1812 is associated with this region.

Druid Ridge Cemetery

(410) 486-5300
7900 Park Heights Avenue
Pikesville, MD 21208
www.druidridge.com

Visitors have experienced many episodes of unearthly activity at this sprawling, beautifully maintained hilltop necropolis, which houses the remains of about forty thousand people, many of them members of prominent Baltimore families.

Historic Ellicott City

(410) 313-1900
Howard County Tourism Council, Inc.
8267 Main Street, P.O. Box 9
Ellicott City, MD 21041
www.ellicottcity.net
edward@visithowardcounty.com

Charming Ellicott City is perhaps the most actively haunted town in the entire state of Maryland. Reputedly haunted sites in or near it include the Judge's

Bench Saloon where a noisy ghost that tampers with the plumbing is said to be one of many that haunt this old tavern. Another is thought to be that of a young woman named Mary who hanged herself on the third floor in years past and whose spirit lingers there still.

St. Mary's College

Ilchester/Ellicott City, MD 21043

Better known as "Hell House" in the surrounding area, this former Roman Catholic seminary on a hilltop overlooking the Patapsco River is now a strange, mysterious, and overgrown ruin that is widely believed to be haunted. It is located on the heights above the south side of the Patapsco River near where Ilchester Road intersects with the B&O Railroad line.

NATIONAL CAPITAL

This region consists of the two Maryland counties, Montgomery and Prince George's, that are adjacent to the District of Columbia and is overall the most urbanized of the various areas into which the state is divided. Much of its history and culture are closely associated with that of Washington, D.C., and it is home to many people affiliated with the federal government and its various agencies. Many of the sites of interest in it are accessible via the Washington Metrorail system or other forms of public transportation.

Beall-Dawson House (Rockville)

(301) 340-2825
103 W. Montgomery Avenue (MD 28)
Rockville, MD 20850
www.montgomeryhistory.org/museum_beall_dawson
info@montgomeryhistory.org

The Beall-Dawson House was listed on the National Register of Historic Places in 1973. Outbuildings on the property include an original brick dairy house and a mid-nineteenth-century one-room Gothic Revival frame doctor's office which was moved to the site for use as a museum. It is believed to be haunted by, among other spirits, some ancestors of the authors of this book.

Bladensburg Dueling Grounds

3619 Bladensburg Road/MD 450 (approximately)
Colmar Manor, MD 20722

Bladensburg Dueling Grounds lies just across the border of the District of
Columbia and for many years in the early days of American history, men fought
duels of honor here . . . and their deaths left many ghosts behind. Among these
was Stephen Decatur, one of America's greatest heroes in the first decades of
the nineteenth century. It is located at the intersection of Bladensburg Road/MD
450 and 38th Avenue.

University of Maryland

(301) 405-1000
College Park, MD 20742
www.umd.edu

A number of sites on this sprawling campus are reputed to be haunted,
including Easton Hall—from which more than one unfortunate freshman has
plummeted from upper-level windows—the Rossborough Inn, and the Stamp
Student Union. It is bounded by Route 1 on the east and University Boulevard/
MD 193 on the north and west. Email addresses and other specific contact
information for departments and individuals are available through the university
Website.

Exorcist House

3250 Bunker Hill Road (approximately)
Mount Rainier, MD 20712

Located outside of Washington, D.C., this area was the site of the historic
haunting that provided the basis for the book *The Exorcist*. It is located at the
intersection of Bunker Hill Road and 33rd Street.

Surratt House Museum

(301) 868–1121
9118 Brandywine Road
Clinton, MD 20735
www.surratt.org
surratt@surratt.org

Over the years, witnesses have claimed to see the unquiet ghosts of various
members of the conspiracy to assassinate President Abraham Lincoln in this

nineteenth-century inn and tavern owned by Mary Surratt—convicted of treason
and the first woman to have been executed in the United States.

Mount Airy Mansion

(301) 856-9656
8714 Rosaryville Road
Upper Marlboro MD 20772
www.dnr.state.md.us/publiclands/southern/rosaryville.html

This Colonial-era mansion achieved fame as a haunted site when the London-
based Society for Psychical Research conducted an investigation there in the
1930s and identified a number of particular ghosts residing in it.

St. Mary's Cemetery

(301) 424-5550
520 Veirs Mill Road
Rockville, MD 20852
www.stmarysrockville.org
stmaryrockville@yahoo.com

This eighteenth-century cemetery is the final resting place of F. Scott Fitzgerald
and, in addition to being treated almost like a shrine to the great author, is
believed by many to be haunted by his spirit. Contact information provided here
is for the parish, which is custodian of the site, but more information about
the cemetery itself is available through other sources. The site is located at the
intersection of Veirs Mill Road/MD 28 and Rockville Pike/MD 355.

Waters House

(301) 515-2887
12535 Milestone Manor Lane
Germantown, MD 20876
www.montgomeryhistory.org/waters_house
info@montgomeryhistory.org

This historic farmhouse in northern Montgomery County is believed to be
haunted by a number of ghosts—including those of both slaves and horses that
were once kept in the buildings behind it!

EASTERN SHORE

This largest region of Maryland, which shares the DelMarVa Peninsula with Delaware and Virginia, is the most isolated from the rest of the state and the most sparsely populated (being home to just 8 percent of the population). It is made up of nine counties, Caroline, Cecil, Dorchester, Kent, Queen Anne's, Somerset, Talbot, Wicomico, and Worcester. It is a largely agricultural area but also includes large areas of marsh, river, and shoreline—as well as numerous islands—and is a popular vacation destination for people interested in the attractions of the Chesapeake Bay and Atlantic Coast.

Blackwater National Wildlife Refuge

(410) 228-2677
2145 Key Wallace Drive
Cambridge, MD 21613
www.fws.gov/blackwater
fw5rw_bwnwr@fws.gov

The malignant spirit of a mule believed to have been demonically possessed in life has haunted this swampy area since a group of teamsters lured it to its death in a pool of quicksand in the early 1800s.

Chesapeake Bay Maritime Museum

(410) 745-2916
213 N. Talbot Street
St. Michaels, MD 21663
www.cbmm.org

At least one of the buildings at this museum complex is reputed to be haunted by the ghost of a woman believed to have provided various personal services to sailors. It is located in historic St. Michaels, a picturesque little Eastern Shore community founded in the late seventeenth century that is today both a popular tourist attraction and the location of many ghost stories.

Furnace Town Living Heritage Museum

(410) 632-2032
3816 Old Furnace Road

Snow Hill, MD 21863
www.furnacetown.com

This abandoned foundry town is haunted by the ghost of Sampson Hat, a slave who stayed in the town after everyone else left and lived there until the age of 106. Even death could not sever his link to the forsaken community, however, and to this day his shade has been seen guarding the remains of its blast furnace.

Ghost Light Road

Old Railroad Road
Hebron, MD 21830

A number of ghostly phenomena have been reported along this lonely road, to include a yellow ball of light that has been known to chase people and cars alike, poltergeist activity in nearby homes, and an abandoned house believed to be haunted. Its actual current name is Old Railroad Road.

Henry's Crossroads

Three-way intersection of Drawbridge Road, Steele Neck Road, and Griffith Neck Road.
Henry's Crossroads, MD 21869

People have reported seeing the ghosts of a pair of Gypsy lovers riding a white horse along the roads running through the swamps around the area known as Henry's Crossroads (sometimes also called Drawbridge).

Mill Street Inn Bed-and-Breakfast

(410) 901-9144
114 Mill Street
Cambridge, MD 21613
www.millstinn.com
jennis@millstinn.com

Built in 1894, this beautiful Queen Anne home now run as a B&B is located in the heart of Cambridge's historic district, making it an ideal base of operations for anyone interested in visiting local attractions—including a number of reputedly haunted sites.

Patty Cannon's House

Finchville, MD 21632
Few people have been more loathsome than Patty Cannon, who regularly

murdered and robbed people and kidnapped free blacks and sold them to Southern slaveholders, and her evil presence can still be felt in the area where she lived. A historical marker that briefly describes her activities is located at the intersection of MD 392/Finchville Reliance Road and MD 577/Reliance Road, but the house behind it was not really Cannon's. It was instead apparently located a few hundred yards to the east, just north of the intersection of MD 392/Finchville Reliance Road and Line Road, where it would have straddled the Maryland-Delaware state line.

White Marsh Church

Intersection of US 50/Ocean Gateway and Manadier Road
Trappe, MD 21673

For many years, passersby and nighttime visitors have reported seeing spectral forms walking amongst the ancient ruins of White Marsh Church and the weathered stones of its surrounding graveyard. It is located about five miles south of Easton and eleven miles north of Cambridge on US 50/Ocean Gateway.

SOUTHERN

This region is a large peninsula formed by the confluence of the Potomac River and the Chesapeake Bay and is made up of three counties, Calvert, Charles, and St. Mary's. It was once home to many formerly flourishing towns, ports, and plantations that no longer exist, marked today only by historic placards, copses of trees, open meadows, or handfuls of restored structures. It has traditionally been both a staunchly Roman Catholic and pro-Southern region and was noted for its Confederate sympathies during the Civil War.

Charlotte Hall Historic District/St. Mary's County Welcome Center

(301) 884-7059
Corner of MD 5 and Charlotte Hall Road
Charlotte Hall, MD 20622
http://tour.co.saint-marys.md.us/tourismtemplate.asp?content=welcomecenterrcontent.asp

This historic district in the hamlet of Charlotte Hall includes thirteen buildings of historic or architectural interest—one of which houses the Mary's County

Welcome Center—and two natural springs that were once believed to have healing properties. Various ghost stories are associated with the district and its buildings.

Christ Episcopal Church and Cemetery

(301) 884-3451
25390 Maddox Road
Chaptico, MD 20621
www.christepiscopalchaptico.org
office@christepiscopalchaptico.org

Founded in 1683 and once a thriving port, the town of Chaptico in St. Mary's County is now little more than a crossroads, the most prominent feature of which is Christ Episcopal Church, built in 1736. The graveyard of this church is widely considered to be haunted and, when one considers its history, there is little wonder that it would be.

Cry Baby Bridge

Indian Bridge Road
Great Mills, MD 20634
Ghosts of two women and a baby are said to haunt the desolate stretch of road near this bridge. It is located toward the lower end of Indian Bridge Road, which originates around the middle of St. Andrew's Church Road in the north and terminates about five miles later at MD 5 in the south. Parking can be found a few hundred yards south of it at the Cecil's Mill Historic District, which consists of a few stores set up in historic buildings. The walk down the road to the bridge can be a bit hazardous, however, as there is not much shoulder to the road before it drops off into the marshy ground; ghosthunters need to be careful that they don't become one of the spirits haunting the site.

Piney Point Lighthouse, Museum, and Historical Park

(301) 769-2222
44720 Lighthouse Road
Piney Point, MD 20674
www.stmarysmd.com/recreate/museums/ppl.asp

Over the years, this nineteenth-century lighthouse has acquired a reputation for being haunted and, while somewhat off the beaten track, has received some attention from ghosthunters. Workers at the site have reported numerous strange phenomena, including hearing people speak to them when no one else was present.

Point Lookout State Park

(301) 872-5688
11175 Point Lookout Road
Scotland, MD 20687
www.dnr.state.md.us/publiclands/southern/pointlookout.html

This area contains several highly haunted sites, including Point Lookout Lighthouse, where people have reported apparitions, odd smells, and spectral footsteps. Another hotspot in the park is the site of Camp Hoffmann, one of the largest Union prisoner-of-war-camps during the Civil War.

Port Tobacco Village

(301) 934-2474
Chapel Point Road
Port Tobacco, MD 20677
www.mdmunicipal.org/cities/index.cfm?townname=PortTobacco
tomr@mdmunicipal.org

The historic courthouse in this virtual ghost town that was once a thriving Colonial-era port may be the location of a "Peddler's Rock," a boulder near which a peddler and his dog were robbed and murdered around the time of the Revolutionary War. The dog is believed by many to be a ghost, and its forlorn howling can sometimes be heard near the lonely site.

Saint Mary's Historical Society

(301) 475-2467
41680 Tudor Place
Leonardtown, MD 20650
www.stmaryshistory.org
smchs@md.metrocast.net

One winter in the late 1600s, a suspected witch froze to death beside a seaside boulder in this town after her home was burned by townsfolk. The rock was later moved to a spot in front of the Saint Mary's Historical Society building, where visitors claim they can feel the malign presence of the witch—who is still blamed for maladies that occur in the town.

Samuel Mudd House

(301) 274-9358
3725 Dr. Samuel Mudd Road

Waldorf, MD 20601
www.somd.lib.md.us/MUSEUMS/Mudd.htm
fluhartd@verizon.net

Dr. Samuel Mudd was one of the people imprisoned by the government on suspicion of being involved in the conspiracy to assassinate Abraham Lincoln. His embittered ghost is believed by some to still dwell within the farmhouse where he and his family lived during the Civil War, and where he died fourteen years after President Andrew Johnson pardoned him in 1869.

Sotterley Plantation

(301) 373-2280/(800) 681-0850
44300 Sotterley Lane
Hollywood, MD 20636
www.sotterley.com
officemanager@sotterley.org

Sotterley Plantation is an eighteenth-century mansion on ninety-five acres of rolling fields, gardens, and riverfront that is today operated as a historic site, offering tours, activities, and educational programs. Features include an original slave cabin, customs warehouse, smokehouse, necessary, and corn crib, and formal garden.

WESTERN

This wooded, mountainous "upstate" region includes for purposes of this book, from west to east, Garrett, Allegany, Washington, and Frederick Counties, and its largest towns are Frederick, Hagerstown, and Cumberland. Home to many small, isolated communities, this hilly area is much more rural than the heavily developed Maryland regions to its south and east and, from both a geographical and a cultural point of view, feels much more akin to neighboring West Virginia. Both of the major battles fought in Maryland during the Civil War— Antietam and Monocacy—took place in this region.

Antietam National Battlefield

(301) 432-5124
5831 Dunker Church Road

Sharpsburg, MD 21782
www.nps.gov/anti

Site of the single bloodiest day of America's bloodiest conflict, during which more than twenty-two thousand casualties were inflicted, the shades of Civil War soldiers have long been seen marching across the fields where they were violently slain. In 1890, the U.S. government classified Antietam as a National Battlefield, and since 1933 the National Park Service has administered it. The park encompasses 2,725 acres of the estimated 3,255 acres over which the battle was fought, and includes the battlefield itself, a visitor center, a national military cemetery, and a field hospital museum.

Burkittsville

(301) 834-6780
500 E. Main Street/P.O. Box 485
Burkittsville, MD 21718-0485
www.burkittsville-md.gov
mayor@burkittsville-md.gov

Home of "Blair Witch," Elly Kedward, who was banished in 1785 for witchcraft, Burkittsville is located on MD 17, about four miles north of the intersection with US 340. It is actually a very pleasant-looking little town and seems interested in promoting its nonwitch-oriented history.

The Carriage Inn

(304) 728-8003
417 E. Washington Street
Charles Town, WV 25414
www.carriageinn.com
StayAtTheCarriageInn@comcast.net

Located just across the Maryland state line in Charles Town, West Virginia, this beautifully restored, Civil War-era bed-and-breakfast was both the location of a historic meeting during the war and the home of a Southern spy. It is also an ideal location for anyone exploring many of the sites located in Western Maryland, especially Washington County.

Church of Saint Patrick

(301) 777-1750
201 N. Centre Street
Cumberland, MD 21502

www.geocities.com/churchofsaintpatrick
SPcumber@archbalt.org

For more than 140 years, people in the local area have held that this old
Catholic church has been haunted by the shade of a Civil War soldier who was
executed for killing his commanding officer.

City of Frederick

(301) 600-2888/(800) 999-3613
c/o Tourism Council of Frederick County Inc.
19 E. Church Street
Frederick, MD 21701
www.fredericktourism.org

Largely due to its proximity to several of the Civil War's bloodiest battlefields,
many ghosts are believed to haunt the homes and other buildings of one of
Maryland's oldest cities. Possibly the most famous is Civil War patriot Barbara
Fritchie, whose house is open to visitor during the summer month.

Gabriel's Inn (Ijamsville)

(301) 865-5500
4730 Ijamsville Road
Ijamsville, MD 21754
www.gabrielsrestaurant.com
Gabrielinn@aol.com

Once a mental institution, this site is now a charming rural inn that specializes
in fine French cuisine, overseen by the ghost of the restaurant's first owner. It
is believed to be haunted both by former residents and by casualties of the Civil
War Battle of Monocacy, one of whom now resides in the wine cellar.

Gathland State Park

(301) 791-4767
Off MD 17, one mile west of Burkittsville, in Washington and Frederick Counties
www.dnr.state.md.us/publiclands/western/gathland.html

This park is located on the site of the fierce Civil War Battles of South Mountain
and Crampton's Gap, just outside the village of Burkittsville. For many years,
people have claimed to see spirits of soldiers killed in the fray marching
through the surrounding woods in a ghostly repetition of their last actions.
Parts of the site have been maintained by National Park Service since 1904, and
it was made a Maryland state park in 1949.

Monocacy National Battlefield

(301) 662-3515
5201 Urbana Pike
Frederick, MD 21704
www.nps.gov/mono

Spirits of Civil War soldiers slain in this brutal 1864 battle have for many years been witnessed marching across it, unaware perhaps that nearly a century and a half has elapsed since they fell in combat.

Schifferstadt (Frederick)

(301) 668-6088
Frederick County Landmarks Foundation Inc.
1110 Rosemont Avenue
Frederick, MD 21701
www.frederickcountylandmarksfoundation.org
info@fredcolandmarks.org

Built around 1758, what is now known as Schifferstadt Architectural Museum is the one of the oldest and most historic buildings in the City of Frederick, Maryland, and among the best examples of early Colonial German Architecture in the country. It is still believed to be haunted by its builder, Joseph Bruner, as well as his descendents and many others who have lived, visited, or taken refuge there.

Acknowledgments

When I think about ghosthunting and America's Haunted Road Trip, I tend to picture myself alone, either on a dark road en route to some haunted site or singlehandedly exploring it, flashlight in hand. While that really is sometimes the case, however, most of the times someone else is actually with me. And even when I do end up by myself, many others have usually played a role in getting me there.

Foremost are my parents, Michael H. and Merrilea Varhola, without whose help it can truthfully be said this book might never have been finished. They provided support for this project in any number of ways: My father wrote five of the chapters in this book and contributed to a number of the other sections. Moreover, midway in the writing of this book, I moved away from the Washington, D.C., area to Texas. Fortunately, my parents lived in Maryland and generously invited me to stay with them for the better part of two months; and both of them accompanied me on trips to multiple sites (never hesitating to pick up the tab for lunch or dinner on the road).

My wife, Diane, also deserves a good deal of recognition. While she was not able to accompany me to most of the sites covered in this book—which would have been her preference—she provided constant moral support from our new home in Texas, which she moved us into largely by herself. And, to a much greater extent even than my editors, she monitored my progress on *Ghosthunting Maryland* and helped ensure that I kept my nose to the grindstone.

Two other people, my daughter Hayley Waters and friend Bob Waters, also provided invaluable logistical support during the development of this book, including providing me with hospitality and a place to stay on a number of occasions.

My editors and the other staff members at Clerisy Press—including series editor John Kachuba, my friend Jack Heffron, and marketing and publicity managers Howard Cohen and Kara Pelicano—also deserve recognition for their continuous support before, during, and after completion of this book.

One group of people that I would especially like to thank are those who took the time to accompany me out to the sites covered in *Ghosthunting Maryland*, discuss them with me, or otherwise contribute their points of view to the various chapters. These include my friend Chip Cassano, with whom I have investigated sites everywhere, from Providence, Rhode Island, to Paris, France; my friend Dominick Salemi, who was inspired enough by our experiences together to add a paranormal department to his magazine, *Brutarian*; and my friends Brendan Cass and his mother Susan Cass.

I would also like to thank the individuals of the various paranormal groups I interacted with during the development of this book, who provided information, feedback, and encouragement, and, in some cases, also accompanied me on visits to haunted sites. They include Ana Bruder, Chris Wojtaszek, and Jim Wissert of Maryland TriState Paranormal; Carol LaRiviere and Debra Robinson of Gabriel's Paranormal Society; Margaret Ehrlich, Julie Leese, Maria Blume, Wendy Super, Amy Twigg, Renee Cannon, Samantha Silverman, Ed, and Darla of Inspired Ghost Tracking; John Warfield with the Washington D.C. Metro Area Ghost Watchers; Beverly Litsinger of the Maryland Ghosts and Spirits Association; and Beth Brown and Henry of Para X Radio.

Another group of people that deserves recognition are those associated with the sites covered or places visited in this book, who in many cases provided support beyond what might be obvious in these pages. They include Sean and Shirl DeLawder, owners of Gabriel's Inn; Matt at the Carroll Museums; Paul

O'Neil of USS *Constellation*; Amy Lynwander, Missy Rowell, and Leanna Foglia of Baltimore Ghost Tours; Luann Marshall of Westminster Hall and Burying Ground; Terry Trembeth, Marty Schoppert, and W. Edward Lilley of Olde Ellicott City Ghost Tour; Joanna Church and Alison Dineen of the Montgomery County Historical Society; Anne Turkos, Liz McAllister, Jennie Levine, and David Ottalini of University of Maryland College Park; Laurie Verge of the Surratt House Museum; Monsignor John Myslinski and Kevin D. of St. Mary's Church; Skip and Jennie Rideout of the Mill Street Inn; April Havens of Piney Point Lighthouse Museum and Historic Park; Danny Fluhart, Ed Mudd, Henry Mudd, Louise Mudd Arehart, and the other staff members of the Dr. Samuel A. Mudd House; the ladies at the St. Mary's County Visitor's Center; the proprietor and staff of the Café des Artistes restaurant; the proprietors and staff at the Cecil's Mill Historic District; Elvira with the Furnace Town Living Heritage Museum; Janine Jensen, Robin Bell, and their colleagues at Chesapeake & Hudson Inc.; and Greg Glewwe, his wife, Diane, and their son, Gareth, at the Schifferstadt Architectural Museum.

I would also like to both thank anyone I have neglected to mention here who helped me with this book and to beg their forgiveness for my lapse! As I recall or am reminded of their contributions, I will be sure to acknowledge them on the America's Haunted Road Trip Web site.

Finally, I would like to thank all of the many Marylanders who took the time to tell me ghost stories, give me directions to everything from haunted sites to gas stations, and otherwise provide information, support, or encouragement for this project.

ABOUT THE AUTHORS

MICHAEL J. VARHOLA is a freelance author, editor, and lecturer who specializes in nonfiction and travel-related subjects and runs game manufacturing company Skirmisher Publishing LLC. He has a lifelong interest in the paranormal and has conducted investigations worldwide, including sites throughout Europe and the United States. His other books include *Ghosthunting Virginia*, *Everyday Life During the Civil War*, *Shipwrecks and Lost Treasures: Great Lakes*, and *Fire and Ice: The Korean War, 1950–1953*. He stud-

ied in Denver and Paris before earning a degree in journalism from the University of Maryland, College Park. He currently resides in Spring Branch, Texas.

MICHAEL H. VARHOLA is a professional counterintelligence officer and a longtime resident of the state of Maryland. His life-long dream has been to be a professional writer, and he plans to begin writing full-time after retiring in 2010. In the meantime, he has been contributing short pieces to his son's books. These include chapters in *Shipwrecks and Lost Treasures: Great Lakes* and *Ghosthunting Virginia*, as well at this current work. In his spare time, he is also working on a novel, which is set in the Ottawa River Valley in 1634 during the fur wars.

Hop in and head out to other great destinations or
America's Haunted Road Trip.